HUNGRY LISTENING

INDIGENOUS AMERICAS
Robert Warrior, Series Editor

Chadwick Allen, *Trans-Indigenous: Methodologies for Global Native Literary Studies*

Raymond D. Austin, *Navajo Courts and Navajo Common Law: A Tradition of Tribal Self-Governance*

Lisa Brooks, *The Common Pot: The Recovery of Native Space in the Northeast*

Kevin Bruyneel, *The Third Space of Sovereignty: The Postcolonial Politics of U.S.–Indigenous Relations*

Glen Sean Coulthard, *Red Skin, White Masks: Rejecting the Colonial Politics of Recognition*

James H. Cox, *The Red Land to the South: American Indian Writers and Indigenous Mexico*

Daniel Heath Justice, *Our Fire Survives the Storm: A Cherokee Literary History*

Brendan Hokowhitu and Vijay Devadas, *The Fourth Eye: Māori Media in Aotearoa New Zealand*

J. Kēhaulani Kauanui, *Speaking of Indigenous Politics: Conversations with Activists, Scholars, and Tribal Leaders*

Thomas King, *The Truth about Stories: A Native Narrative*

Scott Richard Lyons, *X-Marks: Native Signatures of Assent*

Aileen Moreton-Robinson, *The White Possessive: Property, Power, and Indigenous Sovereignty*

Jean M. O'Brien, *Firsting and Lasting: Writing Indians out of Existence in New England*

Shiri Pasternak, *Grounded Authority: The Algonquins of Barriere Lake against the State*

Dylan Robinson, *Hungry Listening: Resonant Theory for Indigenous Sound Studies*

Steven Salaita, *Inter/Nationalism: Decolonizing Native America and Palestine*

Leanne Betasamosake Simpson, *As We Have Always Done: Indigenous Freedom through Radical Resistance*

Paul Chaat Smith, *Everything You Know about Indians Is Wrong*

Lisa Tatonetti, *The Queerness of Native American Literature*

Gerald Vizenor, *Bear Island: The War at Sugar Point*

Robert Warrior, *The People and the Word: Reading Native Nonfiction*

Robert A. Williams Jr., *Like a Loaded Weapon: The Rehnquist Court, Indian Rights, and the Legal History of Racism in America*

HUNGRY LISTENING
RESONANT THEORY FOR INDIGENOUS SOUND STUDIES

Dylan Robinson

INDIGENOUS AMERICAS

University of Minnesota Press
Minneapolis
London

The University of Minnesota Press gratefully acknowledges funding for this book from the AMS 75 Publication Awards for Younger Scholars of the American Musicological Society, supported in part by the National Endowment for the Humanities and the Andrew W. Mellon Foundation.

An earlier version of "Writing Indigenous Space" was originally published as "Welcoming Sovereignty," in *Performing Indigeneity,* ed. Yvette Nolan and Ric Knowles (Toronto: Playwrights Canada Press, 2016). An earlier version of chapter 2 was published as "Listening to the Politics of Aesthetics: Contemporary Encounters between First Nations/ Inuit and Early Music Traditions," in *Aboriginal Music in Contemporary Canada: Echoes and Exchanges,* ed. Anna Hoefnagels and Beverly Diamond, 222–48 (Montreal: McGill-Queen's University Press, 2012). An earlier version of chapter 5 was published as "Feeling Reconciliation, Remaining Settled," in *Theatres of Affect,* ed. Erin Hurley (Toronto: Playwrights Canada Press, 2014).

Copyright 2020 by the Regents of the University of Minnesota

All rights reserved. No part of this publication may be reproduced, stored in a retrieval system, or transmitted, in any form or by any means, electronic, mechanical, photocopying, recording, or otherwise, without the prior written permission of the publisher.

Published by the University of Minnesota Press
111 Third Avenue South, Suite 290
Minneapolis, MN 55401-2520
http://www.upress.umn.edu

The University of Minnesota is an equal-opportuniRty educator and employer.

Library of Congress Cataloging-in-Publication Data
Names: Robinson, Dylan, author.
Title: Hungry listening : resonant theory for indigenous sound studies / Dylan Robinson.
Description: Minneapolis : University of Minnesota Press, 2020. | Series: Indigenous Americas | Includes bibliographical references and index.
Identifiers: LCCN 2019036824 (print) | ISBN 978-1-5179-0769-3 (pb) | ISBN 978-1-5179-0768-6 (hc)
Subjects: LCSH: Indigenous peoples—Canada—Music—History and criticism. | Music—Canada—History and criticism. | Decolonization—Canada. | Appropriation (Arts)—Canada. | Multiculturalism—Canada.
Classification: LCC ML3563 .R63 2020 (print) | DDC 780.89/97071—dc23
LC record available at https://lccn.loc.gov/2019036824

UMP LSI

For Keren

CONTENTS

Introduction / 1

    Writing Indigenous Space / 27

1. Hungry Listening / 37

    Event Score for Guest Listening I / 75

2. Writing about Musical Intersubjectivity / 77

    xwélalà:m, Raven Chacon's Report / 107

3. Contemporary Encounters between Indigenous and Early Music / 113

    Event Score for those who hold our songs / 147

4. Ethnographic Redress, Compositional Responsibility / 149

    Event Score for Responsibility: "qimmit katajjaq / sqwélqwel tl' sqwmá:y" / 191

5. Feeling Reconciliation / 201

    Event Score to Act / 233

Conclusion / 235

ACKNOWLEDGMENTS / 259

NOTES / 267

BIBLIOGRAPHY / 289

INDEX / 309

INTRODUCTION

> The Eskimos are such an astonishingly unmusical race that the composer really has to wring his material to make it musically presentable. There is a marked similarity between an Eskimo singing and Sir Winston Churchill clearing his throat.
>
> —R. Murray Schafer, "On the Limits of Nationalism in Canadian Music" (1961)

What can we hear through Schafer's description of Inuit throat singing? Does your aural imagination (or audiation) hear such astonishingly unmusical voices, a requiem for Winston Churchill clearing his throat? Do Schafer's words sonify compositional violence—the "wringing" of Inuit voices? Can you hear settler desire for Indigenous "presentablility" or "civility" as Indigenous throat songs (games) are processed through settler colonial musical logic? Or perhaps is it impossible to hear anything beyond Schafer's own voice, with its opinionated rhythm, its racist timbre. *Hungry Listening* focuses on a range of encounters between Indigenous song and Western art music (also called classical music or concert music) such as the one described in Schafer's writing. It examines how we listen to such encounters in the moment of their sounding, and how writing allows certain moments of sonic experience to be heard while foreclosing upon others. Additionally, at various points through this book I will ask you to consider the relationships you have with particular voices—how your positionality guides the way you listen to musical subjectivity.

Hungry Listening is concerned primarily with performances of art music that include Indigenous performers. While non-Indigenous composers throughout the twentieth century largely followed a com-

Introduction

positional model that resourced Indigenous music and often placed it in service of musical nationalism, the late twentieth and early twenty-first century saw composers and classical music organizations begin to explore compositional models where Indigenous artists, musicians, and singers were offered opportunities to perform as ensemble members and soloists in art ensembles and compositions.[1] *Hungry Listening* traces this shift in compositional practice alongside other encounters: aesthetic and structural encounters that take place within music composition and performance; listening encounters that take place between the listening subject and the listened-to subject (music, sound); and the encounter between you, the reader, this book, and the listening positionalities embedded in this textual relationship.

The title of this book, *Hungry Listening,* is also a reflection on sonic encounters between particular perceptual logics, and between particular bodies, within a larger conceptual framework of critical listening positionality. As a form of perception, "hungry listening" is derived from two Halq'eméylem words: shxwelítemelh (the adjective for settler or white person's methods/things) and xwélalà:m (the word for listening). shxwelítemelh comes from the word xwelítem (white settler) and more precisely means "starving person." The word emerges from the historical encounter between xwélmexw (Stó:lō people) and the largest influx of settlers to the territory during the gold rush.[2] In 1858, thousands of xwelítem (largely men) arrived in a bodily state of starvation, and also brought with them a hunger for gold. In the context of this book, I use shxwelítemelh to refer to a form of perception: "a settler's starving orientation." I use shxwelítemelh and xwélalà:m individually and together throughout the book in order to address positionalities of the listening encounter (how we listen as Indigenous, settler, and variously positioned subjects), but also to guide this book's larger questions around the ontological and epistemological stakes of what listening is. In bringing these words together I place them in an admittedly uncomfortable pairing between Indigenous and settler orientations toward the world. They are words that in all likelihood would never be brought together by fluent Halq'eméylem speakers for this very reason; xwélalà:m points toward a xwélmexw-specific sensory orientation, while shxwelítemelh explicitly identifies a non-Indigenous sensory orientation. Placed together, shxwelítemelh xwlala:m / "hungry listening" names settler colonial forms

Introduction 3

of perception. However, their superimposed positionality also seeks to acknowledge the current reality of many if not most Indigenous people at various points of perceptual in-between: of knowing, learning, and using resurgent forms of perception. As a xwélmexw swíyeqe qas te má:l—an Indigenous, cis-gendered man and father—who grew up in the suburbs just outside of what is today known as Vancouver, and at a distance from my mother's family in Skwah, shxwelítemelh xwélalà:m here also refers to my own listening positionality. Like the vast majority of Indigenous people across the lands known as the United States and Canada today, I have also learned normalized and unmarked forms of settler colonial listening. Thus, shxwelítemelh xwélalà:m does not reduce simply to "listening through whiteness;" it is a state of perception irreducible to racial identity. As with any expression of positionality, hungry listening must be understood on a continuum of listening practices that includes subtle and significant gradations of normativity; shxwelítemelh xwélalà:m is not the same practice for an Asian American settler-arrivant as it is for a person who is Cree, two-spirited, or transgender. It is a "civilizing" sensory paradigm that has been imposed on Indigenous people who grew up within residential school, boarding school, and day school systems; who were part of the sixties and seventies scoop; who have been disenfranchised by the Indian Act and forced migration; who grew up on-rez and in urban centers. Practices of hungry listening have been passed on intergenerationally through families, and continue to be defied through culturally immersive learning environments within Indigenous communities across the globe.

Reframing Musical Encounters: Intercultural, Inclusionary, and Nonintegrative

One of the motivating forces that led to the development of this book is the dramatic increase of Indigenous participation in art music since the early 1990s across a variety of forms and artistic media. This includes work by composers Andrew Balfour (Cree), Raven Chacon (Navajo), Barbara Croall (Odawa), Ian Cusson (Métis), and Brent Michael Davids (Moheican); Indigenous musicians and singers including composer-cellist Dawn Avery (Mohawk), composer-cellist Cris Derksen (Cree, Mennonite), composer-violist Melody McIvor (Anishinaabe), composer-singer Jeremy Dutcher (Wəlastəkwewiyik ~ Maliseet), and mezzo-soprano Marion Newman (Kwagiulth, Stó:lō ~ Xwchíyò:m, Irish); artists who have worked with classical musicians and recorded classical music include Peter Morin (Tahltan), Duane Linklater (Omaskêko Cree), Tanya Lukin Linklater (Alutiiq), and Kent Monkman (Cree); and a large number non-Indigenous chamber ensembles, orchestras, and individual musicians and composers who have worked with Indigenous performers including the Spakwus Slolem dancers (Skwx̱wú7mesh), throat singer Sylvia Cloutier (Inuk), the Northern Cree Singers, and experimental singer Tanya Tagaq (Inuk). This range of Indigenous composers, musicians, artists, and ensembles represent only a small portion of those involved in projects where Indigenous song and art music have intersected since the 1990s. In the United States, growth in this area has been propelled by Indigenous youth mentorship initiatives including the Native American Composer Apprentice Project, founded in 2001 and led by composer-mentors including Brent Michael Davids, Raven Chacon, and Jerod Impichchaachaaha' Tate (Chickasaw), as well as Arizona Opera's 2016 initiative *The Stories We Tell*. In Canada, however, this growth has been propelled by arms-length governmental funding bodies seeking to impel classical music and opera companies to demonstrate increased diversity in their programming.[3]

In a more general sense, an increasing intersection between Indigenous music and classical music is not isolated from the larger context that informs collaborations between non-Western musicians and classical music ensembles across North America. "Cross-cultural" or "intercultural" performance has been commonplace between classical music ensembles and performers from non-Western cultural traditions since the 1990s. Examples include the work of the Kronos String Quartet, cellist Yo-Yo Ma's *Silk Road Project*, Ravi Shankar's collaboration with Yehudi Menuhin, in addition to a wide range of collaborations between Asian musicians and Western art music ensembles.[4] In Canada, intercultural collaborations led by ensembles include the Evergreen Club Contemporary Gamelan and the Vancouver Inter-cultural Orchestra, musicians such as sarangi player Aruna Narayan and pipa players Wen Zhao and Liu Fang. These musicians, in addition to art music ensembles across Canada, have been supported by the federally funded Canada Council for the Arts and other regional arts councils' funding mandates, which were in turn shaped by Canada's Multiculturalism Act of 1988,

Figure 1. Tanya Tagaq improvising with Jeffrey Zeigler, formerly of the Kronos Quartet, and Hank Dutt *(background)*, March 25, 2006, Zankel Hall, Carnegie Hall, New York City. Photograph by Richard Termine.

with the emphasis it places on the recognition and accommodation of cultural diversity.[5]

Increasingly, this intercultural work has situated Indigenous and non-Western musicians center stage. In doing so, such inclusion could be understood as seeking to redress a history of compositional "resourcing" and appropriation of non-Western music exemplified by Schafer's compositional "wringing." Yet to include Indigenous and non-Western musicians in such work may just as easily take part in a representational politics that does not necessarily address the structural inequities that underpin inclusion. As many of the works discussed in this book will illustrate, inclusion can just as easily participate in an elision of reciprocal relationships between collaborating partners.

Compelling scholarship on intercultural performance including that of Jason Stanyek (2004), Ric Knowles (2010), and Marcus Tan (2012) has significantly advanced theories of cultural negotiation and encounter within music and theater. Scholars who write about collaboration across cultural difference would likely also refer to the performances examined within the pages of this book as "intercultural." Yet while "intercultural performance" does describe the intersection of classical and Indigenous music that *Hungry Listening* focuses on, the term is not precise enough to capture the particular politics of aesthetics that subtends this music in the period following Canada's official enshrinement of official multiculturalism and subsequent Truth and Reconciliation Commission on the Indian residential schools. This roughly forty-year period of recognition politics has seen policy development by the Canadian government that has centralized inclusion within a framework of good relations, and in doing so has set the agenda for arts councils to distribute federal and provincial funding to projects that similarly prioritize inclusion. *Hungry Listening* thus proposes a terminological shift that recharacterizes a subset of intercultural Indigenous music and performance as "inclusionary." The phrases "inclusionary music" and "inclusionary performance" are used throughout the book to signal how Indigenous performers and artists have been structurally accommodated in ways that "fit" them into classical composition and performance systems. The operational emphasis on "fit" situates Indigenous work and performers as a contribution to—or an enrichment of—art music performance. Such inclusionary efforts bolster an intransigent system of presentation guided by an interest in—and often a fixation upon—Indigenous content, but not Indigenous structure. This apathy toward Indigenous structures of performance and gathering leads to epistemological violence through art music's audiophilic privileging of and adherence to its own values of performance and virtuosity. In this framework, while Indigenous singers, instrumentalists, and other performers are increasingly offered space within a composition or on a stage, they are infrequently offered the opportunity to define what venue for performance might be used, the design of the space and audience–performer relationship, and the parameters and protocol for gathering at the site of performance. Inclusionary music, which on the surface *sounds* like a socially progressive act, performs the very opposite of its enunciation. Drawing on the critical literature of inclusion (Mackey 2002; Ahmed 2012), *Hungry Listening* indicts those displays of equality that are more concerned with importing Indigenous content and increasing representation than with redefining the structures of inclusion.

A key argument this book seeks to make is that inclusionary performance reflects models of recognition and accommodation that are similar to those theorized by Yellowknives Dene scholar Glen Coulthard. In *Red Skin, White Masks,* Coulthard describes a shift in the relationship between First Peoples and the Canadian state post-1969 "from a more-or-less unconcealed and coercive structure of domination to one that is now reproduced through a more conciliatory set of languages and practices that emphasize the recognition and accommodation of Indigenous difference" (Coulthard 2011). Coulthard critiques models of recognition that seek to grant Indigenous peoples rights on the terms of the state, and following the work of Frantz Fanon, notes that "in situations where colonial rule does not depend solely on the exercise of state violence, its reproduction instead rests on the ability to entice Indigenous people to *identify,* either explicitly or implicitly, with profoundly *asymmetrical* and *nonreciprocal* forms of recognition either imposed on or granted to them by the settler state and society" (Coulthard 2014b, 25; italics in original).[6] In tracking the shift toward settler colonial strategies of accommodation and recognition, Coulthard's work is integral to any study that seeks to address how settler state governmentality has become internalized in processes (artistic, perceptual, or otherwise) of both Indigenous and settler subjects. This is not to put forward a deterministic correlation between processes of Indigenous-classical collaboration and state strategies of accommodation and recognition. As several examples in the book will show, musical collaboration may equally result in important instances of incommensurable and irreconcilable difference that maintain sovereign values and resist aesthetic assimilation.

When musical models of inclusion demonstrate "profoundly *asymmetrical* and *nonreciprocal* forms of recognition," they do so through a variety of formats and forms. Inclusionary models of collaboration work to normalize the terms of engagement, producing a set of rules dictated by settler composers, classical music ensembles, and new music groups: of course the performance will take place on a proscenium stage, in a concert hall; of course all musicians in the orchestra will wear black; of course the audience will clap not firstly for the music but for the concertmaster's (the first violinist) entrance onto the stage, and then tune all the instruments to make sure there is no variation between instruments playing the same pitches (or "out of tune–ness"); of course we will then clap again once the conductor enters the stage; of course the orchestra will read notated music scores where every note will be performed exactly as written; of course there will be an intermission; of course there will be applause after every composition (but certainly not between the individual movements of the compositions). The examples of inclusionary performance I consider in chapters 3, 4, and 5 show how these logics of Western art music performance not only set the parameters for collaboration but also reinforce a particular idea of what music is. Western art music concert protocols situate this music as an object of aesthetic contemplation.

Yet what if we were to reverse this equation? What if classical music performance was presented using Indigenous logics? What if we were to consider the potential of concert music to serve one of the many functions that Indigenous songs do: as law, medicine, or primary historical documentation.[7] The idea that concert music might be reassessed as a form that may serve other functions—that is, that it might be used to explore functional ontologies that operate through much Indigenous song—remains unrealized. Indigenous logics, as structures rather than content, are generally not considered in the everyday operations of music performance, compositional practice, and listening. Rather, consistent with what Eva Mackey calls the culture of multicultural "enrichment" in Canada, Indigenous songs and musicians serve as a resource that adds to art music without disrupting the norms of concert music performance or ontologies of music-making. Inuk throat singer and experimental vocalist Tanya Tagaq here notes her experience of "being part of projects where my voice would be used as an ingredient in someone else's stew" (*National Post* 2017), an experience that encapsulates a still too-common experience of Indigenous participation in classical and new music.

Many works examined in *Hungry Listening* exemplify this form of inclusionary music performance. They may demonstrate a sharing of space—a visual and kinetic intermingling of bodies on stage, an acoustic blending of musics, or a mixed use of languages—but this integration often remains premised on finding a way to "fit" Indigenous musicians into Western paradigms of performance. In such performance, the fundamental tenets of Western musical genres and form remain intact, thereby reinforcing settler structural logic: the structure of the aesthetic might be enriched by *other* sights and sounds without unsettling the worldview it supports. In so doing, inclusionary performances often make space for and accommodate Indigenous cultural expression while enervating Indigenous political and cultural impact.

And yet, in naming these examples, it is important not to tell this story of Indigenous participation in classical music as one that is entirely centered on a lack of Indigenous agency, on loss, or on what Eve Tuck identifies as "damage-centered" narratives (Tuck 2009, 409). For this reason, as a counterbalance to my examination of "inclusionary performance," I will also offer examples of what I call "Indigenous+art music." Like the encounters between Indigenous music and Western art music that fall within this category, the term "Indigenous+art music" foregrounds a resistance to integration, and signals the affectively awkward, incompatible, or irreconcilable nature of such meetings. Linguistically, the logogram "+" in "Indigenous+art music" speaks to the point of encounter itself and is employed in order to resist the conflation of difference within the encounter by conjoining (rather than merging) two areas of sound practice. I use the term in order to disrupt "intercultural music's" implications of union, hybridity, syncretism, and reconciliation. The "+" here offers an important distinction, a delimitation of sovereignty based not on style but on contrasting ontologies of what song *is* from Indigenous and Western perspectives. This "+" also marks the space of listening itself, as a mark made by lines connecting and moving outward toward other space; it asks how we as listeners attend to being between these ontologies and sound worlds.

Critical Listening Positionality

In a provocatively titled 2015 blog post, "On Whiteness and Sound Studies," for *Sounding Out!* Gustavus Stadler asks: "What does an evernearer, ever-louder police siren sound like in an urban neighborhood, depending on the listener's racial identity? Rescue or invasion? Impending succor or potential violence?" Stadler's provocative post reveals the relative absence of race in the emerging canon of sound studies, and calls for "scholarship that explicitly confronts, and broadcasts, the underlying whiteness of the field" (Stadler 2015). Following close on the heels of Stadler's critique, another post, this time in *Musicology Now,* the blog of the American Musicological Society (AMS), saw racialized and white scholars engaging in a provocation of a different kind: Pierpaolo

Polzonetti's 2016 blog post, "Don Giovanni Goes to Prison: Teaching Opera behind Bars," while not focused on race explicitly, became the focus of a larger debate on the whiteness of musicological scholarship, and the AMS as an organization, which was soon followed on social media by the hashtag #AMSSOWHITE.[8] As an Indigenous scholar who has experienced racism through both my formative music training within normative and colonizing structures of music programs, and through my continued association with music studies, I argue that examining structures of inclusionary music and performance and finding ways to move beyond settler colonial structures of classical music composition, presentation, and listening are long overdue.

In addition to case studies that examine inclusionary structures of music composition and presentation, *Hungry Listening* contributes to the work of decolonizing music studies by examining normative and unmarked forms of listening privilege within *settler colonial listening positionality* and the larger category of *critical listening positionality*.[9] "Settler colonial listening positionalities" can be generally understood as particular assemblages of unmarked structures of certainty that guide normative perception and may enact epistemic violence. Defining settler colonialism as a state of perception builds upon Patrick Wolfe's foundational principle of settler colonialism as a "structure" rather than an "event" of invasion (Wolfe 1999, 2). *Hungry Listening* here significantly expands Wolfe's work to relocate those structures from an external (and often institutional) point of origin in the outside world to an internal location constituted through subjectivity itself. More particularly, settler colonial positionality here also questions the degree to which states of settler perception—along with Western epistemology more broadly—are subtended by possession (Moreton-Robinson 2015) and extraction (L. Simpson and Klein 2013). Like positionality itself, engaging in critical listening positionality involves a self-reflexive questioning of how race, class, gender, sexuality, ability, and cultural background intersect and influence the way we are able to hear sound, music, and the world around us. Critical listening positionality also engages how perception is acquired over time through ideological state apparatuses at the heart of subjectivation (Althusser 2014). As part of our listening positionality, we each carry listening privilege, listening biases, and listening ability that are never wholly positive or negative; by becoming aware of normative listening habits and abilities, we are better able to listen otherwise. The practice of critical listening positionality also builds upon Mary Louise Pratt's notion of the contact zone that would understand listening as a sonic encounter wherein "disparate cultures [of the listener and listened-to] meet, clash, and grapple with each other, often in highly asymmetrical relations of domination and subordination" (Pratt 2008, 7).[10] Of particular significance for this study is the sensory emphasis Pratt places on the "clash and grapple" of encounter, and how this resituates listening to musical subjectivity and alterity as a visceral process. This characterization asks us to consider how listening takes place as a haptic and proprioceptive encounter with affectively experienced asymmetries of power. Critical listening positionality thus seeks to prompt questions regarding how we might become better attuned to the particular filters of race, class, gender, and ability that actively select and frame the moment of contact between listening body and listened-to sound. Within the innumerable combinatory possibilities of listening positionality, chapter 1 provides a layered analysis oriented toward persistent settler colonial listening regimes, forms of decolonial listening that counter normative listening practices, and resurgent listening practices based in forms of Indigenous sensory engagement and ontologies.

Writing Redress

My reconsideration of how we might write otherwise about listening is one part of a larger historiographic critique regarding the epistemic violence embedded within normative structures of academic disciplines. This critique takes part in a larger disciplinary call for redress that insists upon "demand[s] for accountability, compensatory action, and concrete reparations" (Henerson and Wakeham 2013, 9). My figuration of "disciplinary redress" is a corrective not only to non-Indigenous authority and its discursive control over narrating Indigenous history and cultural practice, but to the epistemic violence that takes place at the level of language and structure of writing itself. Disciplinary redress demands that individual disciplinary mischaracterizations of Indigenous knowledge are made known;[11] that non-Indigenous scholars amend their citational practice to prioritize Indigenous writers, knowledge keepers, and artists; and that Indigenous methodologies and forms of writing and knowledge dissemination are not merely accepted within the areas of publication and peer review but are understood as vital contributions to scholarship.

Central to this process of disciplinary redress is both the examination of colonial inheritances that structure a given discipline as well as reckoning with how certain areas of research are delegitimated within that discipline. One aspect of comprehensive redress in musicology involves assessing the normative epistemic violence of writing about music, which is the primary task of chapter 2. In contrast, more granular reassessments of musicological and music history writing on Indigenous music might start by redressing the depoliticized history of writing about art music in Canada more generally. In particular, this work involves examining how Canadian music history's centralization of multicultural and landscape-based tropes of Canadian musical exceptionalism are not benign choices for surveying characteristic national traits but instead have political implications through their dis-location of Indigenous presence, sovereignty, and histories of land stewardship. While this focus on Canadian music history is not the primary work *Hungry Listening* seeks to undertake, a brief consideration of it is useful for understanding the inclusionary and Indigenous+art case studies examined later in the book. On the whole, Canadian music history texts, though not typically focused on different forms of listening to musics in Canada, have nonetheless guided how students learn to listen by rehearsing narratives of Indigenous music as the resources and foundation for a Canadian musical aesthetic.

Indigenous music receives attention in the earliest surveys on music in Canada by Helmut Kallman (1960) and Willy Amtmann (1975). In each case, the author's focus on the historical beginnings of music in Canada is underpinned by Canada's "Indigenous foundation," permanently situating Indigenous music in the past rather than understanding its continuance. Situating Canadian identity as defined by Indigenous values, culture, or métissage is a common feature in Canadian music histories beginning with those by Amtmann and Kallman, but also in the work of public intellectual John Ralston Saul (as discussed in chapter 3), folklorist Ernest Gagnon, and Canadian composer R. Murray Schafer (as discussed in chapter 4). Central to each of these claims is the appropriation of Indigenous thinking and culture *as* Canadian, an appropriation that reduces Indigenous thought and culture to resources for the project of defining a national aesthetic. Continuing this focus on Indigenous music as a resource for Canadian composers is Elaine Keillor's 1995 essay "Indigenous Music as a Compositional Source: Parallels and Contrasts in Canadian and American Music." In her essay Keillor documents composers' "incongruous" and "disastrous" attempts to incorporate Indigenous music into their compositions, but also what she deems more successful "melded products." Specifically, Keillor argues that aleatoric and atonal music of the mid-twentieth century has provided a more suitable "home" for embedding Indigenous music. The continuum that Keillor constructs—from disastrous incorporation to successful melding—leaves untouched ethical questions regarding how any of these integrations (disastrous or successful) might entail appropriation or breaching Indigenous protocols. In so doing, Keillor perpetuates an evolutionary notion of Canadian and U.S. music's development where the composer needs to simply find new techniques and musical forms to better use the resource that Indigenous music provides. Her title, "Indigenous Music as a Compositional Source," belies an extractivist approach to Indigenous song that is part of the larger hunger and starvation addressed in my earlier discussion of a shxwelítemelh orientation toward the world. Such writing not only situates Indigenous music as the foundation and source for the development of a Canadian musical exceptionalism but affects the ways in which inclusionary music is listened to. To frame Indigenous music as a national resource is to guide the listener toward hearing musical (and nation-to-nation) relationship as one of integration where such integration means Indigenous assimilation within shxwelítemelh form and function. It may further mean hearing Indigenous subjectivity existing within an aural domain of "home," a mis-audition of Indigenous belonging within—or to—the settler state. Worse, it may guide the listener toward not only hearing belonging but toward naturalizing a relationship of ownership. Listening itself may become an act of confirming ownership, rather than an act of hearing the agonism of exclusive and contested sovereignties.

How, then, might we instead hear the resourcing of Indigenous music as the settler colonial resource extraction that it is? The thinking of Anishinaabe writer Leanne Betasamosake Simpson and public intellectual Naomi Klein on "extractivism" here provides one useful way to reframe aesthetic resources. While Simpson and Klein discuss extractivism as a relationship to pipeline and natural resource development in First Nations territories across Canada, Klein notes "extraction isn't just about mining and drilling, it's a mindset—it's an approach to nature, to ideas, to people" (L. Simpson and Klein 2013). Simpson follows, but situates extraction in an Indigenous context:

> Extraction and assimilation go together. Colonialism and capitalism are based on extracting and assimilating. My land is seen as a resource. My relatives in the plant and animal worlds are seen as resources. My culture and knowledge is a resource. My body is a resource and my children are a resource because they are the potential to grow, maintain, and uphold the extraction-assimilation system. The act of extraction removes all of the relationships that give whatever is being extracted meaning. Extracting is taking. Actually, extracting is stealing—it is taking without consent, without thought, care or even knowledge of the impacts that extraction has on the other living things in that environment. That's always been a part of colonialism and conquest. . . . Colonialism has always extracted the indigenous— extraction of indigenous knowledge, indigenous women, indigenous peoples. (L. Simpson and Klein 2013)

I propose that extractivism has relevance for examining those operations of discursive settler colonialism that extract cultural practices and resituate them as contributions to defining exceptionalist narratives that are materialized in Canadian music, visual art, or performance. As I will discuss in chapter 1 on hungry listening, extractivism also characterizes settler colonial forms of perception. While naming this extractivism moves toward the disciplinary redress of discursive settler colonialism, it is only a start. What needs to happen for such naming to result in change at the level of perception in general and listening in particular?

Put most simply, what is required is a basic engagement with the social and political histories and present realities of First Peoples across Canada through the music we perform and through an ever-deepening awareness of different Indigenous musical ontologies and epistemologies. Yet as the following chapters assert, to truly move beyond settler colonial structures of perception requires much more than a nonextractivist approach. It requires more than simply doing the opposite of extraction—the centering of Indigenous knowledge within music curricula, music program notes, and in everyday discussions. To challenge settler colonial perception requires reorienting the form by which we share knowledge, the way we convey the experience of sound, song, and music. In an academic setting, this involves reorienting the normative places, flows, and relationships wherein we share this knowledge. One example of this approach is the subject of chapter 4, where I discuss changing the terms and space for redress in the work of Mike Dangeli and Keane Tait in responding to the appropriation of a Nisga'a song in *Three Songs of the West Coast* by composer Ernest MacMillan. More generally, this approach is enacted through different forms of critical-affective writing that I identify as resonant theory that I engage in throughout the book.

Resonant Theory

Given that listening is guided by discursive framing of the texts we read (not just music history surveys but also program notes, marketing, and reviews), *Hungry Listening* argues that forms of listening otherwise are incited by writing that composes the experience of what and how we hear. In chapter 2, this focus will come to the fore in a discussion of not only how writing engages sensory experience but how, from Indigenous perspectives, the act of listening should attend to the relationship between listener and the listened-to. *Hungry Listening* here conceptualizes the space of sonic encounter as a space of subject–subject relation. Moving away from a conceptualization of the listener as the sole subject in the act of listening, *Hungry Listening* reorients this act toward the life, agency, and subjectivity of sound within Indigenous frameworks of perception. Yet unlike a meeting between people from different cultures where the face-to-face encounter with the other holds the potential for ethical accountability in a Levinasian sense, the meeting that takes place between sound and listener is much less charged by an ethical precondition of responsibility. In other words, the meeting between listener and listened-to is bounded by a Western sense orientation in which we do not feel the need to be responsible to sound as we would another life. Sound's perceived lack of subjectivity here results in an asymmetrical relationship where the listener's response can be one where they

Introduction

dismiss, affirm, or appropriate sound as content. Although sound is not capable of meeting or resisting our listening advances, the subjectivity of sound and the ethics of meeting musical subjectivity have been at the heart of recent debates regarding musical experience (Jankélévitch 2003; Abbate 2004; Kramer 2004b). The focus of chapter 2 addresses music–listener contact as a form of intersubjectivity—or subject (listener) to subject (music) relation—through examples of Indigenous song that have life. The chapter traces these relations alongside forms of performative writing that have similarly attempted to grapple with the intersubjective experiences of artistic and musical alterity.

Drawing on a range of writings, including queer, new materialist, Indigenous, and performative texts, many of the book's case studies consider the life of songs and listening encounters with sonic subjectivity. In writing of these encounters, I examine how writers describe musical experience as giving voice to that which evinces the "something beyond control," as Olivia Bloechl writes, of "subaltern diachrony . . . the distinctive temporalities of mysticism, possession, ecstasy, or other altered states [that contrast] with the secular, disenchanted time that is the basis of historical thought" (Bloechl 2005, 14). "None of this," notes Bloechl,

> sits easily with norms of music history. We are not used to granting ancestors, gods, or spirits agency in our histories . . . The prospect of doing so is perhaps daunting, but well worth attempting in the hope of moving the music disciplines beyond Eurocentrism. Indeed, I submit that we have little choice but to look toward diachronic historiographies of many sorts as we try [to] come to terms with the contested inter-cultural encounters. . . . Rationalist and universalist spatio-temporal schemes can only be of limited use in relation to situations of performance, creation, representation, or exchange in which at least two distinct cosmologies and ideologies of music were in play, each of which differs in turn from those that inform our present-day histories. (15)

Writing disciplinary redress may, at times, also require inviting Indigenous ancestors into the space of writing through different forms of address. At other times, writing redress may also require speaking of listening relationships that entail repulsion, alienation, or require an active refusal of epistemic violence upheld by Western models of "good writing." While writing of repulsion, alienation, resentment, and anger has a long history in feminist, black, and Latinx studies, such affective clarity has not gained similar purchase in music studies. In considering the discursive resonance of writing affect, and the potential of writing as a strategic orchestration of anger, Audre Lorde asserts:

> Women of Color in America have grown up within a symphony of anger, at being silenced, at being unchosen, at knowing that when we survive, it is in spite of a world that takes for granted our lack of humanness, and which hates our very existence outside of its service. And I say *symphony* rather than *cacophony* because we have had to learn to orchestrate those furies so that they do not tear us apart. (Lorde 1981, 129; italics in the original)

Without seeking to appropriate the specific experience Lorde here speaks of, it is important to acknowledge how Indigenous and other racialized musicians, composers, and scholars regularly negotiate unmarked colonial structures in music publication and performance and also that, in speaking out against these structures, the affective timbre of our voices is still often dismissed as strident or bitter (Robinson 2017). As the final chapter of this book illustrates, in the years since former Canadian Prime Minister Stephen Harper's 2008 official apology to residential school survivors, the public capacity to hear resentment and repulsion remains questionable within prevailing affective atmospheres of reconciliation. Specifically, as discussed in chapter 5's examples of the 2010 Vancouver Cultural Olympiad, the growing rhetoric of "consensus through friendship" has increasingly emphasized the necessity for settlers and Indigenous people to come together in dialogue as a form that is understood *in and of itself* as reconciliation. While it may provide an important arena for the education of settlers, this coming together in dialogue relies on awareness raising as its primary form of change. Yet as Eve Tuck compellingly argues, such practices of social change elide the primary and substantive actions of restitution and redress:

> This theory of change assumes that people are unaware of an injustice or issue or illness or social calamity—and that in making them more aware, we ready them to take appropriate action. It is a theory of pre-change. It assumes that people will generally do the right thing with the right information. It anticipates that the reason for inaction thus far is missing information, or lack of depth of understanding of the significance of need. (Tuck 2018, 160)

Tuck further asserts that the tendency for awareness raising is to locate the agency for change primarily within the settler subject. While awareness raising may lead to important change over time, it is not a precondition that it will do so. Indeed, Bruno Cornellier's work on settler and Indigenous dialogue illustrates the unidirectional benefit of such dialogue for settlers, while maintaining that the problem is not actually the issue raised by Indigenous people (in Cornellier's essay, the ethics of representing Inuit people by a Quebecois settler filmmaker), but instead a lack of public dialogue for discussing "both sides" of the story (Cornellier 2016). To fix the problem, simply add dialogue. *Hungry Listening* takes up these questions around public dialogue further in chapter 4, where focus is given to the audience–artist/performer relationship within the framework of Indigenous gathering and visiting, dialogical art, and social art practice. This book emphasizes the particular importance of refusing models of dialogue predicated on the settler unidirectionality of knowledge sharing, emphasizing instead those forums that allow both affective experience (whether repulsion or wonder) to emerge and provide sovereign space for Indigenous people to continue to define and enact the work of resurgence.

In contrast to work in critical race, feminist, and Indigenous studies, within the particular context of music scholarship, intersections of race and affect have seen far less theorization. What critical-affective work has emerged has often been met not just with dismissal but with reactionary response that sometimes verges on hyperbole. Early responses to the growth of feminist and queer musicology in the 1990s, for example (van den Toorn 1991; Barkin 1992; van den Toorn 1995), saw this work as no more than "fashionable political ideology."[12] More recent dismissal of critical race–oriented musicological critique took place as part of the brief but trenchant #AMSSOWHITE debate in 2016, which followed from a specific examination of racialized language in Polzonetti's aforementioned 2016 blog post "Don Giovanni Goes to Prison" on teaching incarcerated men about opera. In this debate, ethnomusicologist Gabriel Solis noted that "to write about an incarcerated population as one that needs analytical approaches to classical music to help them control their emotions, as you do in this essay, suggests that in fact it is a population whose problem is emotions that are out of control" (Solis, February 19, 2016, comment on Polzonetti 2016). Still others critiqued the offensive nature of Polzonetti's racializing language and the characterization of rap music as "blatant lyrics and pounding beats" as "the musicologicial equivalent to the N-word" (Robert Fink, February 17, 2016, comment on Polzonetti 2016). Still others rose to Polzonetti's defense, noting that critics were missing the point of Polzonetti's good work, the intentions behind his public musicology in prisons, and the writing that emerged from his encounters. What became immediately apparent from the range of response across the blogosphere is how white privilege remains deeply entrenched in music disciplines. Scholars writing anonymously on the *brownamsavenger* were particularly transparent about the ways in which "white fragility" continues to derail essential decolonial work and how such flashpoints carry a particular tax for emerging music scholars of color. The author of *brownamsavenger* in particular is here worth quoting at length for the clarity and cogently expressed stakes of musicology's racism:

> those of us who have grown up "raced" in some fashion have at least developed some coping tactics for talking about race. We learn how to: absorb the static, pick our battles, find openings, de-escalate confrontations, assess risks, refuse to be baited or distracted, channel our energies, or simply walk away when it's not worth it anymore. None of these are easy, and they all cost us psychically in many ways, but that sense of familiar dread when a race-based controversy kicks up is a sign that we at least have our bearings.
>
> Many of the white folks who find themselves on the defensive in this debate, however, rarely have to confront race-based stress in their lives. And so, when they're confronted with race-related criticism or forced to examine their own racial privilege, there is a good chance that they'll switch to the rhetorical equivalent of "Code Red," using increasingly aggressive tactics to deflect attention away from the invisible column of white supremacy that supports them in the world. We end up having to soothe them with, "Yes, yes, you're still a good person (we hope)" and "Yes, sure your intentions were good, but . . ." In many cases, they succeed in polarizing the debate to such an extent that they can walk away from the encounter without ever having seriously listened to their interlocutors, convinced that they are "unreasonable" or "overreacting."
>
> We don't really know what to do with white fragility quite yet. It demands a lot of extra emotional and discursive labor, and it

consistently falls on the feet of the junior and brown among us. . . . In some cases, maybe we need to treat them like fragile, easily-startled analysands, providing them with soft-voiced, reassuring hand-holding as we walk them through their complicity in white supremacy. But we're also pretty sure that many of them need a rude awakening. (*brownamsavenger* 2016)

In response to this censorship of affective critique, *Hungry Listening* stands alongside *brownamsavenger's* critical-affective, public interventions to amplify the alarm of "rude awakening."[13] It also stands alongside critical-affective writing by musicologist Ellie Hisama, whose work on repulsion and the music of John Zorn demonstrates the importance of giving voice to affective experiences in order to confront racializing musical representations "that we understand to negate, devalue, and disrespect who we are" (Hisama 2007, 72). Hisama's writing here serves not only as a vital instance of centering repulsion within music analysis, but also opens up to other possibilities for critical-affective forms of music study. Theorizing the resonance of repulsion and other cognate affects including alienation, anger, and resentment through "close listening" and sensory analysis are central to *Hungry Listening's* aim of writing redress. Yet given Tuck's argument against merely "documenting damage" in Indigenous writing, and increasing scholarship that calls for "reparative" writing to galvanize future change, it is equally important to name the full range of affect in our experience of inclusionary and Indigenous+art music. How we analyze affective experiences of boredom, disgust, love, inertia, embarrassment, nostalgia, and hunger—and trace the movement between these—is key in the study of listening positionality. As I write this appeal, I am reminded that for Hisama to even have to write in 2007 about the importance of analysis oriented to repulsion, and for me to propose a scholarly expansion of affective critique, speaks to the strong disciplinary aversion to affect that requires such an argument to be made to begin with. That such affective critique has become expected and even privileged in feminist, queer, critical race, and cultural studies means that at the same time this argument may feel unexceptional and even mundane to the book's readers in these fields, to readers in music studies it may be as polarizing as the debates described earlier in this section. To be clear to my readers across these fields, the contribution *Hungry Listening* seeks to make is both that music study might continue to experiment with forms of analysis for the affective experience of music, and that the linguistic and written forms for such analysis might be redefined in ways that move beyond epistemic violence and discursive racialization of disciplinary norms of writing and analysis. For this reason, a key aspect of the writing that follows is its refusal of normative scholarly form and its subsequent affirmation of Indigenous temporality.

Refusal and Resurgence

Refusal has become a central tenet of critical Indigenous studies, and particularly in the work of Audra Simpson, David Garneau, Leanne Simpson, and Glen Coulthard. As the centering of Indigenous knowledge, practice, and language, we might similarly consider resurgence as refusal that refuses to mention that which is being refused. *Hungry Listening* adds to this work through a distinction between content refusal and structural refusal. In content refusal, Indigenous scholars have resisted the Western imperative for all knowledge to be accessible at all times, acknowledging that Indigenous epistemologies uphold context-specific practices of knowledge sharing. Western premises of knowledge acquisition and dissemination sit in stark contrast with situated and context-specific practices of Indigenous knowledge sharing guided by protocol. Audra Simpson and David Garneau, in particular, bring practices of content refusal into focus. For Mohawk scholar Audra Simpson, refusal is

> a political and ethical stance that stands in stark contrast to the desire to have one's distinctiveness as a culture, as a people, recognized. Refusal comes with the requirement of having one's *political* sovereignty acknowledged and upheld, and raises the question of legitimacy for those who are usually in the position of recognizing. (A. Simpson 2014, 11)

Simpson's work places limits on what knowledge from her ethnographic research with the Mohawks of Kahnawà:ke might be shared publicly. She marks this refusal in her writing in order to alert readers to a different model of community accountability that Indigenous scholars uphold and as a statement of epistemological sovereignty at odds with the

Western demand for complete accessibility. Métis artist and art critic David Garneau has similarly historicized Indigenous refusal in artistic practice, pointing toward Pacific Northwest Nations' "screen objects" that refuse settler desire for their original spiritual purpose:

> Screen objects resemble the sacred things they imitate but do not include their animation. These sculptures, masks, and garments have the patina of the originals but none of the meaning, ritual, or context. They are cultural artifakes—reasonable facsimiles designed for others and to give nothing essential away. The hope is that colonizers might settle for the appearance and leave the essential undisturbed. My favourite example comes from the Haida who carved argillite to look like authentic ceremonial pipes, only the holes in the bowl and stem did not meet. Visitors bought signifiers of Haida culture but could not enjoy full use. (Garneau 2016, 26)

For Glen Coulthard and Leanne Simpson, refusal emerges through "grounded normativity," a multiplicity of Indigenous nation- and community-specific frameworks

> based on deep reciprocity, that are inherently informed by an intimate relationship to place. Grounded normativity teaches us how to live our lives in relation to other people and nonhuman life forms in a profoundly nonauthoritarian, nondominating, nonexploitive manner. Grounded normativity teaches us how to be in respectful diplomatic relationships with other Indigenous and non-Indigenous nations with whom we might share territorial responsibilities or common political or economic interests. (Coulthard and Simpson 2016, 254)

This grounded normativity is not so much about the active refusal of settler colonial logics—which would in fact recenter their power—but instead serves to keep our attention focused on "Indigenous place-based practices and associated forms of knowledge" (Coulthard 2014b, 60). Elsewhere, Simpson states that refusal is located in resurgent thinking that is "not concerned with dismantling the master's house, that is, which set of theories we use to critique colonialism," but instead "with how we (re)build our own house, our own houses" (L. Simpson 2011, 32). For many other Indigenous writers, refusal takes the form of affirming an exclusively or at least predominantly Indigenous citational community through their work. This refusal functions as a corrective to the history of Indigenous knowledge extraction, misrepresentation, and claiming of authority by settler scholars. In doing so, it returns authority to Indigenous people and reemphasizes the importance of language in the construction of knowledge.

Although strategies of refusal are employed by *Hungry Listening*, the book does not exclusively prioritize Indigenous theory and methodology. To adhere solely to the work of Indigenous writers would limit the politics of intersectionality that draws alliances between shared concerns with decolonization. Pursuing such an intersectional politic necessitates that Indigenous writers and scholars draw on, strategically use, and reframe *all* the tools available to us. This is not to say that we exclusively engage these tools outside of their original intent, but it does mean assessing the relevance of scholarship by settlers and variously identifying black, Latinx, Asian, and LGBTQ2 scholars as tools for demolishing colonial infrastructure and then "rebuilding our house." In chapter 2, this results in a charting of performative modes of writing not exclusive to Indigenous writers who have made significant contributions in this practice. To focus exclusively on Indigenous thought here would be to disregard the significant history of performative writing by queer and feminist settler writers and scholars of color, not to mention the wealth of writing and critique on writing about musical experience within music studies.

The refusals offered by Audra Simpson, David Garneau, Leanne Simpson, and Glen Coulthard act primarily as refusals of content. They withhold information, they affirm and center Indigenous perspectives, and they demarcate Indigenous sovereignty upon the page. *Hungry Listening* draws on these forms of refusal, but is more interested in the potential of what I call structural refusal. Actions of structural refusal are formal and aesthetic strategies that impede Indigenous knowledge extraction and instrumentalization. Forms of structural refusal counteract the epistemic violence of normative writing by exercising a range of interventions including forms of Indigenous resurgence (oratory, language, syntactical rhythm) and non-Indigenous aesthetic strategies (Brechtian *verfremdungseffekt*, the *détournements* of the Situationist International). If Indigenous knowledge and culture is mined and extracted, then it would follow that another key intervention for disrupting the flow of extraction and consumption would be the blockade:

24 Introduction

> They [blockades] are a crucial act of negation insofar as they seek to impede or block the flow of resources currently being transported to international markets from oil and gas fields, refineries, lumber mills, mining operations, and hydroelectric facilities located on the dispossessed lands of Indigenous nations. These modes of direct action . . . seek to have a negative impact on the economic infrastructure that is core to the colonial accumulation of capital in settler-political economies like Canada's. (Coulthard 2014a, 50)

Expanding on Coulthard's advocation of the blockade, *Hungry Listening* examines the potential of written, visual, and aural obstructions deployed as forms of sensate sovereignty. As forms of sensate sovereignty these forms act as a limit of knowledge that is felt viscerally, proprioceptively, and affectively beyond the page. I read David Garneau's conceptualization of "irreconcilable spaces of Aboriginality" (Garneau 2016, 26) as one strategy within this framework:

> Irreconcilable spaces of Aboriginality are gatherings, ceremony, nêhiyawak (Cree)–only discussions, kitchen-table conversations, email exchanges, et cetera, in which Blackfootness, Métisness, and so on, are performed without settler attendance. It is not a show for others but a site where people simply are, where they express and celebrate their continuity and figure themselves to, for, and with one another without the sense that they are being witnessed by people who are not equal participants. When Indigenous folks (anyone, really) know they are being surveyed by non-members, the nature of their ways of being and becoming alters. Whether the onlookers are conscious agents of colonization or not, their shaping gaze can trigger a Reserve-response, an inhibition or a conformation to settler expectations. (Garneau 2016, 27)

Building upon Garneau's theorization, the strategies of sensate sovereignty I offer not only seek to convey knowledge and experience otherwise to the normative strictures of the essay form, but also provide a structure of knowledge sharing for Indigenous folks to enter into. My improvisations in structural refusal seek to effect an epistemic shift in where and how we perceive Indigenous sovereignty.

Writing Sovereignty, Reading Sovereignty

sq'eq'íptset íkw'elò, kwexáls sq'eq'ó, xwélmexw qe xwelítem.

Ts'áts'eltsel xwoyíwel tel sqwálewel kw'els me xwe'í sq'ó talhlúwep íkw'elò.

Hungry Listening addresses two specific readerships: xwélmexw/Indigenous readers in the first instance, and non-Indigenous/settler/xwelítem readers in the second. The epigraph above is both for you and also not for you. It is written for a readership yet to come, for future generations of fluent Halq'eméylem readers and speakers, of which there are currently few. It is written from a willful presumption of the future many. While the introduction of any book can be considered a space of welcome, seeking to care for the reader by guiding and preparing them for the writing to come, the Halq'eméylem epigraph at the opening of this section marks the first limit of this welcome. My words gather; together, they are an act of gathering, of gathering strength and acknowledging Indigenous voices and bodies, rather than acting as a container of Indigenous content. They seek to modify the unmarked structures that define the book as a form accessible to all readers at any time. In the coming pages, I ask you to affirm Indigenous sovereignty with the following injunction:

If you are a non-Indigenous, settler, ally, or xwelítem reader, I ask that you stop reading by the end of this page. I hope you will rejoin us for chapter 1, "Hungry Listening," which sets out to understand forms of Indigenous and settler colonial listening. The next section of the book, however, is written exclusively for Indigenous readers.

WRITING INDIGENOUS SPACE

ey swayel el sí:yá:m siyá:ye.
Barbara Holman el ta:l.
tl'elaxw li te Ts'elxweyeqw, yewa:lmels, tem mímele.
Ruth Gardner el sí:silelh.
Barbara Evelyn Garner sts'o:meqw qe Robert Craig Gardner
sts'o:meqw—teli te Skwah.
Qwotaseltil Charlie Gardner el th'ép'ayeqw—te má:ls te Robert
Gardner.
tel'alétsechexw?

éy kws hákw'elestset te s'í:wes te siyolexwálh: it is good to remember the teachings of our ancestors. I open this place of gathering with a phrase I learned from el siyám siyáye, my friend and mentor Lumlamelut Wee Lay Laq. It is a phrase used when we gather together with other upriver folk. These words acknowledge the work of our Elders and sí:yá:m / respected leaders to create a space of creative and intellectual possibility for the current and future generations of Indigenous artists and thinkers. The resurgent work Indigenous artists and scholars offer today has been made possible only because the work of those who have gone before us—our Elders, sí:yá:m, artists, and other ancestors—who, through their work, have brought Indigenous spaces into being both by chipping away at and demolishing the colonial foundations of Western institutions and by building new structures that provide spaces of possibility for younger generations of Indigenous scholars and artists. It feels good to affirm the hard-won existence of these spaces, while at other times it feels as though we are celebrating the minimal—the single seat at the table—as if the hosts and guests for this dinner party were primarily Indigenous. As Canadian institutions struggle with how to implement decolonization in this post–Truth and Reconciliation Commission moment, Indigenous artists and scholars find ourselves in a time of relative opportunity. Yet this opportunity comes with a certain level of precarity—our leadership is requested or demanded—and without it there is the risk of institutions implementing "Indigenous structures" without actual Indigenous engagement. Even when we take on this burden of opportunity, our contributions can also come at the cost of being co-opted within continuing systems of colonial logic. And so, we celebrate as if our kitchen-table conversations now regularly include guests from across our nations, when this is still far from the case. I am more often than not still the only Indigenous person at the majority of academic tables at which I sit; perhaps the same holds true for you in the various institutions and other dialogues you are part of. This is not to dismiss the real opportunities and support that institutions have provided. But what, asks Mohawk curator Ryan Rice, will remain once the "reconciliation celebrations" are over? What will the hangover feel like?[1] For now, the party is in full swing, and while we do karaoke, show off our best dance moves, and fill spaces with our laughter, it is also good to consider who has been invited (or not invited) and for what reasons.

Speaking of party, I want to open this written space for Indigenous gathering with an incongruous representation of Indigenous gathering: a scene from an opera by Mozart that represents a potlatch. Vancouver Opera's 2007 adaptation of Mozart's opera *The Magic Flute* brought a large number of First Nations artistic collaborators as well as the First Peoples' Heritage, Language, and Culture Council (now the First Peoples' Cultural Council) to this particular party. Living in Brighton, England, at the time of its first performance, I did not attend the opera, but learned much about the production through colleagues' stories of their involvement, and in particular from a friend, Marion Newman, a Kwagiulth/Stó:lō mezzo-soprano who had been a part of the production:

> There was a scene during one of the dress rehearsals of the opera, when I wasn't on stage, and I took that opportunity to take a look from the audience at how the set and costumes all looked on stage. This was the moment when the chorus came in wearing different regalia, ranging from the North to the West, as if they were arriving at a potlatch. They all came forward in a half circle as the curtains parted and I was completely taken aback at the emotion I felt come over me. I realized that this was the closest I'd ever come to seeing just how beautiful it

must have been to see the different villages arriving at a special event, back in the day of my great-grandparents and before. An event that I have never had the chance to experience because for a long time the potlatch was outlawed, the masks and regalia confiscated, and people were forced to give up their religious ceremonies, their form of government and their way of keeping a record of the important moments in life. (qtd. in McQueen et al. 2011, 323)

Newman had twice described to me the second act's opening scene—meant to represent a gathering of Northwest coast First Nations—as profoundly moving. Without having attended the performance, I was transported by Marion's description of the experience of witnessing our history—as in a potlatch itself—a history of abundance and fullness of families and communities gathering together. The longing and pride mixed within her telling gave me a glimpse of the powerful affective impact of this performance for her. And so, when Vancouver Opera announced that they would remount the production in 2013, I knew I needed to see it.

The work of so many Indigenous collaborators on *The Magic Flute*—the designs by Kwak'waka'wakw artist John Powell; choreography by Michelle Olson of the Tr'ondëk Hwëch'in First Nation and artistic director of Raven Spirit Dance; and leader of the Skwxwú7mesh dance group Spakwus Slolem, S7aplek Bob Baker, among many others—was stunning and powerful. And yet, emerging from the audience at the end of the performance, I keenly felt that this important work of individual Indigenous artists was still unable to penetrate the colonial logic of the opera. In a postshow interview I organized with Indigenous audience members, Deanna Reder, a Cree/Métis scholar noted: "I attended the Opera hoping to see an Indigenized *Magic Flute* that was infused with Coast Salish logic and referenced stories in the hən̓q̓əmin̓əm̓ language; instead I saw *The Magic Flute* all dressed up." Continuing, Reder conveyed how she was

> elated by the beauty of the Coast Salish design. It's grand and it's impressive and it's really striking and beautiful. For those who live here, and who are familiar with local ceremonies, there are points of recognition when you recognize the setting, when you recognize the ceremonial display. That being said, despite these moments of recognition, my overall reaction to the opera was that of alienation. It seemed

30 Writing Indigenous Space

> to me to be *The Magic Flute* in Coast Salish drag. (*The Magic Flute,*
> audience member Deanna Reder)[2]

This fact of "dressing up" the opera in "Coast Salish drag" conveys the sense of playing with identity effected in drag, yet occurring not in the intentional way in which drag operates.[3]

In the space of inter-national gathering represented in the long-house scene, what most fascinated me was what could be called a kind of "gestural drag" or "wannabe affectation" where non-Indigenous opera singers embodied a gesture used by Northwest coast First Nations of raising up both arms in thanks and recognition. In gatherings held by Stó:lō, xʷməθkʷəy̓əm, Skwxwú7mesh, Səlilwət, and other Northwest coast communities, the gesture affirms the message of a speaker whose words have been particularly powerful. The same gesture when it is embodied by carved welcome figures is meant to signify welcome. In the *Magic Flute*'s operatic adaptation of this gesture, however, as chorus members raised their arms to each other the gesture was reduced to a casual handshake. In "costume regalia," singers walked toward one an-other and quickly raised their arms up as if to say, "Hey, how are ya?" and repeated the gesture as they milled about the stage in front of the longhouse. I remember laughing out loud, and then quickly realizing that other audience members were looking at me. Made into an every-day greeting, the adaptation of this gesture speaks to its gradual pro-liferation within a settler Canadian public sphere as a "new" form of thanks decoupled from its power to demonstrate deep respect. Used in this way, it also spoke to those of us who were part of the opera's Indige-nous audience able to recognize its infelicity, as the "trying on" of Indig-enous drag. It signaled an epistemological limit and the important fact that this gesture cannot simply be "picked up" and deployed. Its failed deployment undergirds its importance as a lived gesture, as a felt gesture that speaks in sovereign recognition of those important words spoken by sí:yá:m when Stó:lō, xʷməθkʷəy̓əm, Skwxwú7mesh, and Səlilwət communities gather together. It exists as a limit of "indigenization" for non-Indigenous folks.

Marion, my friend, I do not know what to do with the divergent fact of how we felt this gathering in such different ways. I want to honor your experience—much more than that, I want to see it, hear it. Each time I heard you describe your experience I could hear its vitality come alive through your voice; I can hear your heart listening; I can hear you hear its power through your words' care-ful attention to our history. To other friends now reading, and those whom I do not yet know: I do not know what to do with our strongly felt difference, our perception of social efficacy at odds, responses to our material propositions for change reduced to fractious scenarios of mutual exclusion. These years have been full of celebratory institutional recognition—Giller, Polaris, Polaris, Sobey after Sobey, institutional invitation and demand—we're having a great party, yet the hangover has already begun. Particularly in relation to Indigenous visual arts, our discursive practice as Indigenous people— our behavior discussing strongly felt difference—at this party has been less than convivial and generous, and in many instances continues to dismiss, belittle, and at times bully. We find challenge in expressing such difference without perpetuating shaming's lateral violence. And yet I am reminded of the fact that for Northwest coast people, our "shaming" songs and "shaming" poles have assumed this colonial affect "shame" for practices that are much more about accountability to and within our communities. And who does not find challenge in hearing challenge expressed? Humility in listening to each other's calls for that which is not enough, for that which we find overly simplified, for accountability to our ancestors and coming generations, is a practice of resurgent listening. I hope you, Marion, and other Indigenous friends and colleagues who read this now might hear my words within this book, and other Indigenous calls for increased aesthetic, political, and kinship accountability as a desire for a new discursive resurgence that embraces the expression of strongly felt difference and moves against the drive for reductive consensus.

The critique I and other Indigenous spectators offer here and throughout this book does not negate the beauty of the Indigenous work that takes place within the intransigent settler structure of inclusionary performance and Indigenous+art music. They coexist in a way that does not consign Indigenous participation therein to victimry. Nor do such Indigenous participations within settler colonial forms necessarily conscribe Indigenous artistry therein to the same vacuity that motivates normative, settler colonial, and heteropatriarchal systems of composition and presentation. In this way, Indigenous resurgent perception and listening also necessitate the kind of palimpsestic (multi-

32 **Writing Indigenous Space**

layered) sensory engagement I detail in the next chapter. Such layered forms of seeing and listening allow the "not enough" to exist alongside the fullness of Indigenous creative vitality. Such layered and elastic perception undermines the settler colonial desire for the fixity and stability of knowledge, instead replacing it with a necessarily shifting understanding of response and responsibility to one another.

Other-Than Welcome

The brief, one-minute scene in *The Magic Flute* where settler opera singers raise their hands to each other as if they are giving handshakes exists as both a representation of cultural vitality *and* a failed application of Indigenous gesture within the bodies of settler opera singers. It exists as both a failed marker of welcome that is evacuated of its significance as a gesture of respect, *alongside* its importance, as Marion Newman describes, of Northwest coast First Peoples' intercommunity kinship in gathering together.[4] In similar ways the gesture resists the global migration of Indigenous welcome that has come to exist in post-contact carved figures now commonly known as "welcome figures" and "welcome poles." Such figures work to extend atmospheres of welcome to settler and tourist publics and, I would argue, are mostly unrecognizable to settler Canadian and tourist publics alike as figures that are created in order demarcate the sovereignty of the people whose territory they are guests in. While these figures might be understood as a kind of "immigration checkpoint" for Pacific Northwest First Peoples, the settler gaze consumes them as cultural display.[5] Like immigration officials, they ask me to remember my responsibility as a guest and visitor. Their living presence asks me to remember the larger kinship bonds we share between our communities in Coast Salish territories. And yet, because of the way that such figures are put to work in legitimizing the agendas of the state and the neocolonial force of the crown and its corporations, although I can understand the sovereign impetus of these welcome figures, I often do not feel their sovereignty extend across the spaces they are located in. I do not feel their incursion upon the logics of the state. Despite the masterful work of the carvers and artists who bring these figures to life, for me the figures' placement often tends to act conversely as an Indigenous stamp of approval for the development, corporation, or organization they raise their arms up to. Such is the case for the 2010 Olympic and Paralympic Games, the entryway of the BC Hydro building in downtown Vancouver (taking part in a willful amnesia of BC Hydro's extensive land expropriations), and as tourist spectacle in photo-op encounters with the welcome figures at the Vancouver airport. As with the case of the longhouse scene in *The Magic Flute,* as these welcome figures express sovereignty that exceeds their placement within settler architectures, so to do the spaces in which these figures are placed seek to neutralize their political intervention through architectural and institutional frames of political recognition. As airports, opening ceremonies, and crown corporation building foyers make claims of inclusion and accountability through these figures' incorporation, so the figures themselves question this incorporation. And yet, even though we as Indigenous people are able to see and hear the sovereignty of these figures—against the way they are made to perform a politics that supports the very structures of the state that they are created to challenge—it is important not simply to allow ourselves to support settler colonial logics that are invested in perpetual inclusion. To move beyond the recognition politics of inclusion means insisting on the necessity of shifting other (infra)structures of support that frame, display, hold, and contextualize our work.

To resist the claiming done by these colonial frames necessitates refusing inclusion and taking actions that bring new spaces of sovereignty into being. To do this here, in this gathering upon the page or screen (depending upon your current reading situation), I've asked non-Indigenous, settler readers not to join us. Perhaps this makes you feel uncomfortable. It has made me feel uncomfortable at various times I have done it in the classroom and for gatherings I have organized. At certain times I have been subjected to non-Indigenous colleagues' indignation arising out of a sense of entitlement that their prior work with Indigenous people should gain them access to a space I requested they not enter. Reconciliation's rhetoric tells me I must work hard to form new relationships with the state, to seek alliances with settler organizations and individuals, and to make spaces open to anyone who might hold the desire to learn of any and all things Indigenous. Such is reconciliation's daily demand upon Indigenous people. Reconciliation is celebrated across Canada these days with increased conviction, as is the celebration of indigenizations and decolonizations within academic and other government-funded institutions. Yet with this prefigurative celebration that comes prior to substantive structural transformation, we also celebrate forms of our mere recognition and inclusion. To frame this within a critical context is not to ignore the substantial "reparative" (Sedgewick) utopian (Dolan, Muñoz), and affirmative (Braidotti) work that continues to give energy to the daily and extraordinary actions of sovereignty we practice. Yet celebration of such structural transformation is premature for reasons I do not need to name to Indigenous readers gathered here, reading together this page or screen.

I have called for this space as a way to continue working through the potential in forms of Indigenous sovereign gathering, or what Métis artist and scholar David Garneau calls "irreconcilable spaces of Aboriginality," as spaces that provide "moments where Indigenous people take space and time to work things out among themselves," moments that exist outside of the colonial attitude "characterized not only by scopophilia, a drive to look, but also by an urge to penetrate, to traverse, to know, to translate, to own and exploit" (2016, 23). Through inventing and constructing different forms of sovereign space we provide each other with a means to work things out with each other, finding ways to work outside of the gaze of settler colonial knowledge production, and refusing forms of indigenization that do not serve the needs of the Indigenous artistic, scholarly, and home and "non-home" communities we belong to. Our words, like Northwest coastal Nations' welcome figures, are still too often used to legitimize other non-Indigenous actions and institutions. At the very least, I hope that this space of gathering will prompt discussion of how we might develop other models for creating Indigenous spaces that refuse to feed the hungry gaze, and hungry listening, of xwelítem. Many of these have already been developed, including Rebecca Belmore's touring of *Ayum-ee-aawach Oomama-mowan: Speaking to Their Mother* to Indigenous communities; David Garneau's call for sovereign display territories (2016); Ogimaa Mikana's work installed on a large billboard (Barrie, Ontario, 2014) with black text on white background that reads in untranslated Anishinaabemowin, "Gego ghazaagwenmichken pii wii Anishinaabemiyin"; and by the exhibition *cəsnaʔəm, the city before the city* at the Museum of Anthropology at University of British Columbia curated by Musqueam curator Jordan

Wilson and Museum of Anthropology curator Sue Rowley (discussed in chapter 1). Enacting sovereignty may feel like a precarious undertaking for the force by which non-Indigenous readers, spectators, and listeners experience their exclusion. However, as some of these projects demonstrate, not all irreconcilable spaces of Aboriginality require the exclusion of settler presence. Some of these spaces are defined by a refusal to take up the logic of settler systems, whether that be the refusal of translation (Ogiima Mikana), or the refusal for Indigenous belongings and life to be displayed for the desire of museum spectators' hungry gaze (čəsnaʔəm).[6] For those spaces that do require xwelítem, O'serón:ni, k̲'amksiiwaa, Zhaagnaash, and other settler subject exclusion—exclusions of the settler gaze, listening, presence, and occupation of space—as in the gathering you have joined here—the point is not so much that exclusion is felt (though this can itself be an important experience), but that the space is structured and guests determined according to what we deem necessary for our work to commence.

Musicologist Suzanne Cusick opens her essay "On a Lesbian Relationship with Music: A Serious Effort Not to Think Straight" with a statement that remains untranslated. Cusick's essay seeks to inscribe space for speaking differently, "to try to speak both truly and helpfully," despite her great fear of what she might be able to say—and perhaps what she can convey—in attempting to do so. Yet I also read Cusick's opening paragraph as her resistance to translating being, as a queer sovereign act, and in many ways as containing a knowledge that was intended to lie beyond many readers' (or at least my own) accessibility. It is a choice to intentionally speak to a specific community of something personal. Writing here, my choice to define a sovereign space for your reading—but equally as important as a sovereign space for thinking and writing—I feel a similar pressure to try to speak both truly and helpfully, to convey something of use, perhaps a teaching that has been shared with me that expresses some core xwélmexw value or epistemology. This pressure is not merely internalized. I have previously been in situations where colleagues have insisted that I rationalize the creation of such space; they have demanded that I demonstrate how this form of work will achieve specific goals and serve reconciliation's supposed necessity of intersectional knowledge inclusion. To capitulate to these demands is to undercut the usefulness and potential of such spaces for thinking and speaking without the capitalist certainty of knowledge production and dissemination. Such spaces do not need to be content driven; neither are they constructed to say essentially "Indian things" in essentially "Indian ways."[7] Nothing that I write here is a secret or confession. I offer nothing confidential or sacred.[8] By creating care-ful spaces of partial, limited inclusion we offer the possibility to say things differently, for different ways of speaking to emerge in spaces designed to deter the feeling of being watched and listened to; such spaces seek to dispel what we might call "settler atmospheres." This is the point. For even when settler readers have worked hard to decolonize the desire for knowledge and the extractivist drive to accumulate that is embedded within settler modes of listening, looking, and gathering, the *feeling* of the settler gaze remains; we hear the colonizing ears of hungry listening mine our words. This gaze, this listening is felt regardless of the decolonizing self-work an ally may have undertaken. We may feel this gaze and sense hungry listening from the walls that surround us and from the very configuration of non-Indigenous spaces we occupy. We may similarly feel this gaze and sense hungry listening through the normative Western forms we employ to share knowledge (the essay, the conference panel, the class). These structures necessitate sharper anti-colonial interventions than reconciliatory inclusion is able to provide us with. To deflect this gaze and divert hungry listening, spaces must be filled with Indigenous voices, bodies, laughter; we must fill our spaces with our songs, our karaoke, our generous difference.

th'ítolétsel el sí:yá:m sí:yáye. I thank you for joining me here, and my hope is that we will continue to have opportunities for conversation and to work together in other spaces. In the next chapter we will rejoin non-Indigenous, settler readers.

For any non-Indigenous, settler readers who chose to read within this space of Indigenous sovereignty against my explicit request, I ask:

What are the reasons you continued to read?

For what reasons do you continue to read?

ONE
HUNGRY LISTENING

> When lawyer Peter Grant asked Chief Mary Johnson to sing a
> Gitksan song as an essential part of her evidence on the "Ayook," the
> ancient but still effective Gitksan law, Judge McEachern objected. He
> said he did not want any "performance" in his court of law. "I can't
> hear your Indian song, Mrs. Johnson, I've got a tin ear."
>
> Most of us non-Aboriginal Canadians also wear a tin ear. It
> seems natural because we have worn it all our lives. We are not even
> aware of the significant sound we cannot hear.
>
> —Walt Taylor, *The Three Rivers Report,* July 15, 1987

Taylor's description of Justice McEachern's "tin ear"—his inability or
willful refusal to hear Gitksan song as an Indigenous legal order that
Gitksan people understand it to be—provides just one example of the
many ways in which listening is guided by positionality as an intersection of perceptual habit, ability, and bias. In particular, this chapter examines formations of listening guided by settler and Indigenous positionality, and outlines strategies for resurgent and decolonial listening
practices. It addresses the relative absence of scholarship on listening
from Indigenous, settler colonial, and critical race studies perspectives
in relation to the "whiteness of sound studies"[1] (Stadler 2015). It pursues this objective by proposing a number of non-totalizing conceptions for what different listening positionalities might encompass, and
in doing so calls for further work on racialized and anti-colonial listening formations. I limit my focus here to a handful of Indigenous and
settler listening practices including those shaped through processes of
state subjectivation (official multiculturalism) and "educational reform"
(missionization, residential schools, university music programs), and

those guided by Indigenous and Western ontologies of music through attunement to settler/xwelítem and Indigenous/xwélmexw auditory logics. Detailing these listening positionalities allows us to trace the unmarked normativity of listening but also reveals the ways in which the listening continuum has historically been consigned to a framework wherein one is listening well if one is able to capture the content of what is spoken, or the "fact" of musical form and structure. As this chapter will demonstrate, hungry listening prioritizes the capture and certainty of information over the affective feel, timbre, touch, and texture of sound. Attending to affect alongside normative listening habits and biases allows us to imagine (or audiate) otherwise—to develop strategies for different transformative politics of listening that are resurgent in their exploration of Indigenous epistemologies, foundations, languages, and sensory logics; or, ones that are decolonial in their ability to move us beyond settler listening fixations. The coming pages survey an array of Indigenous and settler listening formations: listening that emerges in relation with Indigenous ontologies of song, listening that is the result of settler colonial attempts to civilize attention and perception, and listening that is strategically flexible, agile, and responsive to the intersectional layering of positionality.

The "Tin Ear" of Settler Colonialism

Any attempt to define what "settler listening positionality" entails must begin by unpacking the unwieldy and reifying term "settler." Historically, the term describes those who first came to the United States and Canada with the intention to stay and make new lives, while more recently the term has become a statement of positionality that seeks to make visible the ways by which non-Indigenous people have benefitted from colonial policy such as Canada's Indian Act and genocidal policies of Indian residential schools. More and more frequently used by non-Indigenous Canadians since the Truth and Reconciliation Commission on the Indian Residential Schools, the term "settler" has become a form of self-identification for those who were not, historically, the first settlers of the already occupied Indigenous lands now known as Canada but nevertheless understand their complicity in ongoing colonial policies that continue to constrain Indigenous rights and resurgence.

As an everyday form of political activism, then, identifying as a settler subject marks oneself as possessing a certain awareness of ongoing inequities faced by Indigenous peoples. Understood as a fixed identity category, however, the term "settler" risks reifying a cohesive and essentialist form of subjectivity that does not take into account subtle gradations of relationship, history, and experience—for example queer settler subjects (Morgenson 2011), immigrants, refugees, and diasporic subjects. Expanding the terms available to speak more precisely about multiple orientations of subjectivity allows increased potential to acknowledge one's *particular* relationships, responsibilities, and complicity in the continued occupation of Indigenous territories. And yet, when offered as mere caveats, acknowledgments of positionality are what Sara Ahmed would call "non-performative" utterances (Ahmed 2004). In contrast to Austin's performative utterance, non-performative utterances don't accomplish what they say they accomplish; they perform a certain righteousness in one's support for the project of decolonization or reconciliation without actualizing individual responsibility that moves beyond mere commitment to change. Eve Tuck and Wayne Yang's oft-quoted assertion that "decolonization is not a metaphor" holds us accountable not to forms of consciousness raising (Tuck and Yang 2012; Tuck 2018) but to examining what substantive action must be taken in the return of Indigenous lands, waterways, as well as the remediation of other "grounds" and the demolition of settler foundations.[2] Within this frame, what does gaining a nuanced understanding of our positionality accomplish? Positionality's importance derives not from its prevalent use as confession or admission of guilt. Instead, its usefulness is predicated upon a step beyond the simple recognition of individual intersectional identity. That step involves understanding positionality not as a static construct, but as a process or state that fundamentally guides our actions and perception. Specifically, to shift from the reified construct of "settler" and toward forms of action that effect more than merely "unsettling" structures requires understanding how the "settling" of settler positionality functions. *Hungry Listening* asserts not only the need to consider the alignment of settler positionality with substantive action but to consider it as a stratified and intersectional *process*. One such way that settler positionality guides perception is by generating normative narratocracies (Panagia 2009) of experience, feeling, and the sensible. In

40   Hungry Listening

The Political Life of Sensation, Davide Panagia describes narratocracy as the privileging of narrative in rendering sensation readable:

> Narratocracy refers both to the governance of narrative as a standard for the expression of ideas and to the rules that parse the perceptual field according to what is and is not valuable action, speech, or thought. . . . by insisting on their narrative qualities, we condition appearances within a system of visibility and sayability that insists on their capacity to make sense. (Panagia 2009, 12)

Narratocracy here guides everything from the inability to hear Indigenous song as a form of legal evidence in land claims to historical attempts at civilizing savage attention. It is to these forms of settler colonial narratocracy that we will turn to first in this chapter's larger discussion of listening positionality.

The overview of settler and Indigenous listening positionalities offered here provides a small cross-section of the ways in which such listening takes place,[3] beginning with a discussion of the ontological differences between Western and Indigenous conceptions of song, and then moving to a historical overview of listening as itself a form of "settlement." The latter focus on the intersection between listening and historical settlement does not begin, as one might expect, with the ways that early settlers listened to the new world and its inhabitants upon their arrival to Canada,[4] but instead with the ways in which a particular group of settlers—missionaries, residential school staff, music teachers—set about to reform the Indigenous engagements with listening, through the action of "settling" perception itself. The act of settling Indigenous listening here does not refer firstly to an occupation of the sound world audibly available to Indigenous people (though this certainly did take place in residential schools through the wholesale replacement of listening to voices and song of beloved siblings and kin with hymnody, English language, and bells). Instead, the colonial imposition of settling listening seeks to compel sensory engagement through practices of focusing attention that are "settled"—in the sense of coming to rest or becoming calm—and in doing so effect perceptual reform sought through the "civilizing mission" of missionaries and the Canadian state. Listening regimes imposed and implemented "fixed listening" strategies that are part of a larger reorientation toward Western categorizations of single-sense engagement, as well as toward Western ontologies of music located in aesthetic appreciation. Such regimes often continue today in an entirely different way through structural listening practices taught to students in university programs, a discussion of which I will return to later in this chapter. Unifying these listening practices is the "civilizing" drive for selective attention that renders listening as a process of the ear rather than of the body.

As many of this book's case studies demonstrate, foundational differences between Indigenous and settler modes of listening are guided by their respective ontologies of song and music. Western music is largely though not exclusively oriented toward aesthetic contemplation and for the affordances it provides: getting through our work days, setting and focusing moods, and creating a sense of home (DeNora 2000). Indigenous song, in contrast, serves strikingly different functions, including that of law and primary historical documentation. A striking example of this clash between Western aesthetic and Indigenous "functional" ontologies of song is apparent in *Delgamuukw v. the Queen* (1985), a land claim trial in which Gitxsan and Wet'suwet'en sought jurisdiction over their territories in northern British Columbia, Canada.

Several scholars have examined the complex history of this trial in detailed and nuanced ways (Mills 1994; Napoleon 2001; 2005), and to fully outline the case is beyond the aim of this chapter. Much oral history was recounted during the court case, and this aspect of the case has been of particular importance to writing on Indigenous legal traditions and customary law. For our purposes here, I will restrict my discussion to the contested inclusion of song[5] in the court proceedings, and in particular the moment when counsel for the plaintiffs directed Mary Johnson, Gitxsan hereditary chief Antgulilibix, to perform a limx oo'y (dirge song)[6] associated with her adaawk (formal, ancient, collectively owned oral history).[7] I quote the full exchange between Justice McEachern and the plaintiff's council, Mr. Grant, for its clear demonstration of the differences between Indigenous and Western ontologies of song:

> **Mr. Grant (Plaintiff's Counsel):** The song is part of the history, and I am asking the witness to sing the song as part of the history, because I think in the song itself, invokes the history of the—of the particular adaawk to which she is referring.
>
> **Justice McEachern:** How long is it?
>
> **Grant:** It's not very long, it's very short.

McEachern: Could it not be written out and asked if this is the wording? Really, we are on the verge of getting way off track here, Mr. Grant. Again, I don't want to be sceptical, but to have to witness singing songs in court is in my respectful view not the proper way to approach this problem.

Grant: My Lord, Mr. Jackson will make a submission to you with respect—

McEachern: No, no, that isn't necessary. If this has to be done, if you say as counsel this has to be done, I'm going to listen to it. I just say, with respect, I've never heard it happen before, I never thought it necessary, and I don't think it necessary now. But I'll be glad to hear what the witness says if you say this is what she has to do. It doesn't seem to me she has to sing it.

Figure 2. "The Law vs. Ayook / Written vs. Oral History" (1987) from *Colonialism on Trial* by Niis Biins (Don Monet) and Skanu'u (Ardythe Wilson) (New Society Publishers, 1992). Artwork by Don Monet.

Figure 3. "A Cultural Hearing Aid," reprinted from the Three Rivers Report, Wednesday, July 15, 1987, in *Colonialism on Trial* by Niis Biins (Don Monet) and Skanu'u (Ardythe Wilson) (New Society Publishers, 1992). Artwork by Don Monet.

> **Grant:** Well, My Lord, with respect, the song is—is what one may refer to as a death song. It's a song which itself invokes the history and the depth of the history of what she is telling. And as counsel, it is—it is my submission that it is necessary for you to appreciate—
> **McEachern:** I have a tin ear, Mr. Grant, so it's not going to do any good to sing it to me. (British Columbia Supreme Court 1985, 670–71)

Following Mary Johnson's singing of the limx oo'y, McEachern continued to demand explanation and justification of it:

> **McEachern:** All right Mr. Grant, would you explain to me, because this may happen again, why you think it was necessary to sing the song? This is a trial, not a performance . . . It is not necessary in a

matter of this kind for that song to have been sung, and I think that
I must say now that I ought not to have been exposed to it. I don't
think it should happen again. I think I'm being imposed upon and I
don't think that should happen in a trial like this . . .

Throughout the trial, Justice McEachern refused to acknowledge the legitimacy of the limx oo'y as evidence, let alone as the equivalent documentation of law as upheld by the Gitxsan people. He conflates the song with "a performance" that can have no effect on pleasing his "tin ear." McEachern treats Johnson's singing as an attempt to win him over, either through the song's aesthetic beauty or the affective appeal of her voice. McEachern cannot hear what Mary Johnson shares as anything other than a song in the Western context of what songs are; or rather, he asserts willful ignorance that it can function as anything other than a song that might penetrate the armor of his "tin ear."

In contrast, it is useful to consider from a Gitxsan perspective what this song is, and the function it holds as an Indigenous legal order. As described by James Morrison (Txaaxwok) during the same trial, the limx oo'y has far more than an aesthetic function; it is far more than a song with the aesthetic powers to please the ear:

Well when, while they ever singing that song, that's memorial, that's
today, when they are singing it and rattle, when they are singing it in
a quiet way, while they are singing that song, I can feel it today that
you can feel something in your life, it memories back to the past what's
happened in the territory. This is why this song, this memorial song.
While the chief is sitting there I can still feel it today while I am sitting
here, I can hear the brook, I can hear the river runs. This is what the
song is all about. You can feel the air of the mountain. This is what the
memorial song is. To bring your memory back into that territory. This
is why the song is sung, the song. And it goes on for many thousands
of years ago. And that's why we are still doing it today. I can feel it.
That's how they know the law of Indian people, as this goes on for
many years. (Napoleon 2001, 169)

"I can feel it," says Morrison, "I can hear the brook, I can hear the river runs . . . the air of the mountain." Songs at their best serve this function of memory, they capture a time in our lives, they produce nostalgia. I want to refrain from categorizing Morrison's word here as a kind of nostalgia, however, given the way that songs, again, *as* law have a function, and are more than representational. In this more-than-representational frame, the limx oo'y is not simply representing the place, speaking about a place, or making those who hear it remember this place; it acts *as* the "law of Indian people." It functions as a primary legal and living document with importance for conveying the embodied feeling of history "to the past [thousands of years of] what's happened in the territory." This embodiment, the literal emplacement of the listener back among sensual experience of place is thus a legal order that functions through embodiment. We must here distinguish between the Western form of law represented in the "The Law vs. Ayook" image (Figure 2) and the Gitxsan construction of law through the singing voice that brings listeners back into relationship with place not just through its hearing but through its feeling. In contrast with Western law, this Indigenous legal order is "felicitous" (Austin) or legitimate *only* because Morrison "can feel it," and by feeling it "that's how they know the law of Indian people."

In the second drawing by Monet we see Chief Mary Johnson attempting to open McEachern's tin ear with a can opener (Figure 3). In a newspaper article by Walt Taylor, a resident of Smithers, British Columbia—and written in response to Monet's drawing—Taylor notes, "the cartoon shows Chief Johnson using her can opener to overcome the cross-cultural deafness caused by the judicial tin ear. *Most of us non-Aboriginal Canadians also wear a tin ear. It seems natural because we have worn it all our lives. We are not even aware of the significant sounds we cannot hear*" (Taylor qtd. in Monet and Skanu'u 1992, 46). The title of this article, "A Cultural Hearing Aid," asks how might we need to reorient our practices of listening, first by recognizing that all of us have adopted settler colonial forms of perception, or "tin ears," that disallow us from understanding Indigenous song as both an aesthetic thing and as more-than-song.

Indigenous ontologies of song ask us to reorient what we think we are listening to and how we go about our practices of listening with responsibilities to listen differently, while also requiring us to examine how we have become fixated—how listening has in effect been "fixed"—in practices of aesthetic contemplation, as a pastime or entertainment, and through its various affordances. In reorienting our listening practices from normative settler and multicultural forms[8] to the agonistic and irreducibly sovereign forms of listening, we must also reconsider what we think we are listening to. This is particularly the case for Indigenous song. Ontologically, many of our songs have their primary significance as law, history, teachings, or function as forms of doing. This is to say they are history, teaching, law that take the form of song, just as Western forms of law and history take the form of writing. Yet they cannot also be reduced to merely an alternative form of Western documentation—the exact equivalent to a book, or to written title of land. I have repeatedly been asked to account for the ways in which our songs serve as law, or how songs have life. At the heart of these questions has been a demand to explain how our songs fulfill the necessary and sufficient *Western* criteria that constitute a thing. To measure the "fit" of Indigenous processes by Western standards subjects them (and the Indigenous person who explains them) to epistemic violence, and reentrenches colonial principles and values.

The song presented by Mary Johnson as a Gitksan legal order is what some might refer to as a "traditional" song, as a song that has existed for many generations. Some may be inclined to draw a line between the capacity of "traditional" Indigenous songs to function as law, medicine, teachings, and primary historical documentation, while understanding more recently created Indigenous songs in contemporary popular genres as not holding such functions. I am hesitant, however, to draw such a sharp line between these categories. For this assertion would imply that Indigenous music composed today, and in contemporary genres, carries less of the teachings, histories, and laws that our older music does. While it may be the case that Indigenous contemporary music does not explicitly claim to enact law, provide healing, or convey knowledge (locations and practices for hunting, for example), my belief is that this knowledge is still present to varying degrees even when not made explicit.

Keeping this context of Indigenous ontology at the forefront of my examination of inclusionary performance and Indigenous+classical music is key for understanding the relationship between Indigenous and non-Indigenous musical and performance encounters. Within the context of Indigenous resurgence, this context holds even greater importance for Indigenous composers and artists as a provocation to reclaim the actions that our songs take part in. Yet to re-claim song as holding a function beyond the aesthetic aspect is little more than a leap of imagination unless we define ways in which we, as listeners, also consider the ways in which listening affirms and legitimates these actions. How does listening serve as an affirmation or legitimation of law? What is listening as a responsibility in documenting our histories (to the extent and level of detail that a book does so)? Reorienting our ears toward Indigenous ontologies of song requires us to return to the place that musicologist Susan McClary found herself nearly thirty years ago. In 1991 McClary, advancing new models for feminist music analysis, noted that in considering the intersections of gender, sexuality, and music, we might reach a point of production un-knowing, where we are "no longer sure of what MUSIC is" (McClary 1991, 19). Decolonizing musical practice involves becoming no longer sure what LISTENING is.

Hungry Listening

As xwélmexw, as a Stó:lō cis-gendered man whose family was displaced from their home community through the legacy of the Indian residential schools, I understand the word "settler" as imprecise in its ability to name both historical relationships between xwélmexw and newcomers to S'olh temexw (Stó:lō territory), and current settler subjectivities.[9] Indigenous languages here go well beyond providing an equivalent term or translation for "settler." Cherokee scholar Jeff Corntassel provides just a few instances of the specific knowledge that comes from Indigenous terms for newcomers: "Yonega is a Tsalagi (Cherokee) term for white settlers, which connotes 'foam of the water; moved by wind and without its own direction; clings to everything that's solid.' Wasicu is a Dakota term for settlers, which means 'taker of fat'" (Snelgrove, Dhamoon, and Corntassel 2014, 16). These terms do not only provide names for newcomers to Indigenous territories but also contain historical relationships and descriptions of settler states of being. Working from these states of being, we can learn much about forms of perception, and paths toward perceptual decolonization. Such is the case with the Halq'eméylem term for settler.

From a xwélmexw perspective, settler subjectivity emerges out of a state of consumption, as discussed in the Introduction. This is not simply a generalization regarding colonization but instead is derived from the historical and contemporary relationships Stó:lō people have had

Figure 4. Ho! For Frazer River. *Harper's Monthly Magazine,* December 1860.

with non-Indigenous people in our territories, experience that is embedded in the Halq'eméylem word Stó:lō people use for non-Indigenous settlers: "xwelítem" ("xwunítum" in Hulq'umínum̓). These words are much more than equivalent terms for "settler"; more accurately they mean "starving person." As I understand it, the words came into use with the first significant influx of settlers to our territories who arrived in two states of starvation. The first of these was bodily—starving very literally for basic sustenance; the second was a starvation for gold. As Keith Carlson has documented:

> In the summer of 1857 less than a hundred non-native men (almost all of whom were associated with the Hudson's Bay Company) lived along the lower Fraser River. Then, between April and July 1858, no less than

30,000 "Starving Ones" arrived in Stó:lō territory seeking the new "El Dorado." (Carlson 2010, 161)

It is an understatement to say that this hunger for resources has not abated with time. xwelítem hunger may have begun with gold, but it quickly extended to forests, the water, and of course the land itself. In the twentieth century the hunger has grown for Indigenous artistic practice. Much has been written since the first uses of the word "appropriation" to define one form of this hunger for Indigenous art and culture, most notably in the foundational work of Indigenous scholars Marcia Crosby (1991) and Loretta Todd (1990). Much has been written on the extraction of Indigenous culture by modernist painters from Emily Carr (Moray 2001) to Jack Shadbolt (Halpin 1986).[10] Yet the extraction of Indigenous song, story, and culture is not merely a product of the past; artists and authors continue to mine Indigenous experience and, as with the previous discussion of Keillor, at times blatantly describe Indigenous culture as a resource that is there to be mined. Such is the case with Joseph Boyden, a writer whose questionable Indigenous descent has been further mirrored in the ways he has described his relationship to an Indigenous community through the language of extraction:

> Boyden left Moosonee with a book in his head; he felt that it might make him successful. Much later, he would tell an interviewer: "I've felt like I discovered a gold mine, and I realized quickly, 'Oh my gosh, no one has written about the Cree of Mushkegowuk before,' and how lucky am I as a writer to have this incredibly rich territory to mine creatively." (Andrew-Gee 2017)

In comparison to debates on appropriation in the visual arts, literature, and film, however, music scholarship has largely refrained from any substantive examination of Canadian composers' appropriation of Indigenous song, a context we will turn to in chapters 4 and 5.

Settler hunger does not merely extend to appropriation of Indigenous song, however. In the realm of inclusionary music between Western art music and Indigenous cultural practices, and particularly in the post–Truth and Reconciliation context, there has been increasing hunger for particular, and we could also say "more easily digestible," forms of Indigenous culture and narratives. The Canadian media continues to offer a steady diet of damage-centered narratives, stories of trauma, and the resultant accounts of healing and transformation. This progression from trauma to healing initiates a circular pattern of consumption that has sustained the public's appetite for a norm (or supposed fact) of "Indigenous lack" and a paternalistically narrated overcoming of such lack. In classical and new music performance, by contrast, palatable cultural expression has been privileged over explicitly political work; friendly forms of coming together have been privileged over agonistic forms of dialogue; and that which is recognizably Indigenous has been privileged over the everyday or urban; and the aesthetic beauty of Indigenous songs has been privileged over recognizing their ontological difference—as forms of law, medicine, and history—to Western music.

In general, hungry listening privileges a recognition of palatable narratives of difference, while in a more specific Western art music context, hungry listening takes part in content-locating practices that orient the ear toward identifying standardized features and types. This is primarily, though not exclusively, the case for audiences encountering tonal repertoire from the Western art music canon that comprises a significant part of the orchestral, operatic, choral, and chamber music ensemble. Audiences with formal music training are taught to identify musical conventions for genre and harmonic progression, or a work's innovative departure from such conventions just enough not to destabilize the generic fit entirely. For those with the opportunity to be disciplined through formal education in Western art music, the ear is thus "civilized" into "higher listening" forms of recognition and identification. Within contexts of informal music education (in preconcert talks and program notes, for example), this identification tends to take place on a programmatic and representational level, as listeners are told to "listen for the x," where "x" may be an animal, or story, or an emotion. Although those without formal music training are often not taught to follow harmonic progressions, this function still occurs at the basic level of recognizing harmonic tension and resolution. Yet in both cases—with and one without formal musical training—the listener orients teleologically toward progression and resolution, just as hunger drives toward satiation. Similarly, for both categories of listener, listening is oriented toward recognition, whether that be the recognition of formal structures, generic features, or particular musical representations and characterization.[11] For both, this "listening for" satiates through familiarity (to feel pleasure from the satisfaction of identification and recognition) but also through certainty (to feel pleasure from finding the "fit" of content within a predetermined framework). Hungry listening is hungry for the felt confirmations of square pegs in square holes, for the satisfactory fit as sound knowledge slides into its appropriate place.

For my music colleagues reading this now, I want to make clear that this is not an argument to eliminate formal analysis or understanding generic conventions. To name the ways in which hungry listening atomizes parts from the whole in service of recognizing their fit within conventional musical structures and forms is not an argument against close reading. Rather, it is a call to understand the ways in which, following from the previous section's recontextualization of song as more-than-aesthetic, an ethics of listening to Indigenous song and Indigenous+art music is premised upon a more holistic form of "feeling the history," as James Morrison said. I turn here to Stó:lō siyám Jo-ann Archibald, who notes how Elders emphasize the importance of listening with "three ears: two on the sides of our head and the one that is in our heart" (Archibald 2008, 8). How, then, does this listening as a form of "feeling the history" from heart and ears together take place? I have returned to this question repeatedly over the past years as a visitor on Haudenosaunee and Anishinaabe lands on which I now live, to ask myself how I might listen as a respectful guest, and in ways that do not seek to extract and apply a particular Haudenosaunee or Anishinaabe listening practice, but nonetheless listen in relation with their knowledge systems. To define new forms of listening-in-relation does not entail simply applying an alternative configuration of listening at will. Unlike iPhone photo filters, one cannot simply select and add noncolonial, feminist, queer, or black listening filters in order to listen otherwise. This reductive approach essentializes critical listening positionality as something that might simply be applied by choice, and fails to recognize that to apply a form of Indigenous listening would also constitute appropriation.

What I want to emphasize in the coming example is how critical listening positionality emerges through an intersection of sqwálewel (thinking-feeling)[12] between two Indigenous forms of attentiveness, one that is brought from "home" (in my case Sólh temexw, and xwélméx experience), the other from the lands on which I am a guest. At Indigenous events held at Queen's University, Mohawk Elders enact protocol for welcoming guests to their territory through the "Thanksgiving Address" or "the words that come before all else." In this practice of welcome, the speaker addresses the different realms of our other-than-human relations, reminding us that humans are one life among many, noting the original instructions the Creator gave to all beings. Thanks is given to the waters, from the largest bodies like oceans and lakes to the small creeks and streams and aquifers. Thanks is given to all the plant life and the grasses that grow, to all the medicine plants, to all the berries, and to the trees growing all around us, who, as we breathe out, breathe back in. Regardless of what time of year this is spoken in, the address takes into account how the life is changing and transforming from awakening in the spring or sleeping in the winter. Thanks is given to the four-legged creatures and to the winged creatures that fly around. If it is the summer, thanks is given to the thunder beings that bring the rains and the replenishing of the water. Thanks is given to the winds that blow over our earth, to the sun, the moon, the stars. Thanks is given to the spiritual people that guide us and help us, for the stories that they bring, and the insight that they bring. Thanks is given to the Creator. And finally, thanks is given to all that has been forgotten or left unsaid.

This process of listening to "the words that come before all else" sustains a moment of heightened presence derived not only from the content that compels me to consider my relations, but from the time, rhythm, and repetition of the words themselves that connect me to a sense of place that is not my own, and slows down the pace of listening to that which comes next. Critical listening positionality is here an intersection between xwélalà:m—the Halq'eméylem word used for listening but better understood as "witness attentiveness" that is called for in longhouse work—and the address of "the words that come before all else" that itself demands another form of attention. In xwélalà:m, witnesses are asked to document the knowledge and history being shared in the equivalent amount of detail to a book, and through the detail of feeling beyond fact. As with Morrison's description of the limx oo'y, this form of longhouse perception involves a holistic documentation of history that includes the feeling of that history's telling. The words that come before all else, whether they are given in Kanien'kehá:ka, English, or a mix of both, intersect with xwélalà:m to effect the temporality of my listening. Indeed, the pace of listening is in direct correlation with the starving attitude of settler colonial perception. To be starving is to be overcome with hunger in such a way that one loses the sense of relationality and reflexivity in the drive to satisfy that hunger. Hungry listening consumes without awareness of how the consumption acts in relationship with those people, the lands, the waters who provide sustenance. Moving beyond hungry listening toward anticolonial listening practices requires that the "fevered" pace of consumption for knowledge resources be placed aside in favor of new temporalities of wonder disoriented from antirelational and nonsituated settler colonial positions of certainty.

The critical listening positionality described above might further be described as a practice of guest listening, which treats the act of listening as entering into a *sound territory*. Here, as with James Morrison's understanding of the limx oo'y, listeners enter Indigenous territory through listening that allows them to "hear the brook . . . hear the river runs . . . feel the air of the mountain." Or not. For non-Gitxsan, and indeed for Justice McEachern himself, this listening positionality entails an inability to hear and sense the land through song. In effect, McEachern's inability to hear Gitxsan legal orders is an important statement of the incommensurability of Western and Gitxsan sovereignty. To ask the question "how do we (anyone) hear Gitxsan legal orders in song?" is to subject it to the same hungry listening determined to render all knowledge accessible to the ear. Critical listening positionality thus understands that in entering Indigenous sound territories as guests, those who are not members of the Indigenous community from which these legal orders derive may always be unable to hear these specific assertions of Indigenous sovereignty, which is not to be understood as lack that needs to be remedied but merely an incommensurability that needs to be recognized. It is also important to note that such felt history encoded in the limx oo'y for Gitxsan people, the words that come before all else for Kanien'kehá:ka, and practicing xwélalà:m for xwélmexw, are forms of connecting back to our lands. Listening is perhaps always a listening through, or in relation with land. Sound territory is not constituted through static boundaries of settlement—a stasis Indigenous people are asked to replicate through the state exclusivity of the treaty process and exclusive borders. Instead, it is constituted through lived experience of movement across our lands that came with hunting, travel to winter

54 Hungry Listening

and summer village sites, intercommunity trade, winter dances, and potlatch. It is not only that land-based knowledge from this movement is encoded within songs including the limx oo'y, but that Indigenous sovereignties of sqwálewel, of knowing-feeling place are reconstituted through the actions of singing and listening. In the next section we will consider how Indigenous mobility hindered settlers' attempts to civilize Indigenous perception into a temporality of productivity. Indigenous mobility was often equated with unproductive use of land and an inability to sustain attention, a perceived lack of focus that missionaries and residential schools alike sought to reform.

Fixing Attention, Fixed Listening

In 1837 Anna Jameson, in her travel narrative *Sketches in Canada, and Rambles among the Red Men,* recounts the words of Ojibway missionary Charlotte Johnston: "She says all the Indians are passionately fond of music and that it is a very effective means of interesting and fixing their attention" (Jameson 1852, 255). "Fixing Indians' attention" is in fact an accurate way to characterize the sensory paradigm shift that early missionaries across Canada sought to effect. "Fixing," of course in the sense Jameson uses it, refers to keeping Indigenous peoples' focus on the word of God rather than on their own cultural practices. As Jameson notes of Charlotte Johnston, wife of William McMurray, an Anglican missionary and Indian agent based in Sault Ste. Marie from 1830 to 1838, Johnston was able to convert the Indians by leading them in hymns with "her good voice and correct ear" (255). In comparison with Charlotte Johnston's missionized ears, it is the Indians' "*in*correct ears" and lack of focused attention that keeps them from their civilization:

> The difficulty is to keep them together for any time sufficient to make a permanent impression: their wild, restless habits prevail; and even their necessities interfere against the efforts of their teachers; they go off to their winter hunting-rounds for weeks together, and when they return, the task of instruction has to begin again. (256)

This settler colonial reading of an Indigenous lack of attention in missionary accounts understands Indigenous forms of attention to the world as "the wild, restless habits" rather than a purposeful agility in attention through Indigenous mobility and proprioception. To missionaries, these wild restless habits are a detriment to the new temporality of learning and living civilized lives. Missionaries thus recognized that new ways of focusing attention were needed. Hymn singing became one of these, with hymns translated into Indigenous languages, where the homophonic ideal of voices moving together was a corrective to the unruly voices of Indigenous people. Yet in order to implement a full sensory paradigm shift toward civilized attention more substantive change was necessary. And so new regimes for the surveillance and limitations of movement would shortly be introduced through government, the principle of these being the Indian agent charged with implementing government restrictions on Indigenous communities, the Indian Act's "potlatch ban" (1884–1951) that curtailed Indigenous legal orders and historical documentation, the pass system that confined Indigenous peoples to reserves, and of course residential schools that tore Indigenous children away from their families, culture, and ways of life. All of these forms of control over the movement of Indigenous bodies did not just limit mobility, but fundamentally restricted the range, flexibility, and time of attention more generally, by restricting Indigenous proprioceptive agency within (and in relation to) our lands.

On the Northwest coast in particular, prior to these policies, Indigenous families and communities traveled widely to summer and winter locations for seasonal harvesting, hunting, and fishing, and traveled significant distances between different villages across the Northwest coast for potlatches and winter dances—gatherings at which important history was orally documented and sovereignty was affirmed. As historian Paige Raibmon has documented, "Potlatches, or rather the mobility they required, also impeded the implementation of colonial policies. Potlatch gatherings frequently foiled agents' attempts to inspect their Aboriginal 'charges.' Agents made arduous canoe trips to villages only to find the site deserted and the population dispersed" (Raibmon 2005, 25). In part because of such "wild restless habits" and their hindrance of the state's ongoing civilization project, the potlatch ban not only censored Northwest coast First Nations from our most important form of oral history transfer—conveyed through singing and dancing that also conveyed our histories—but also worked to reorient sensory knowledge of connection to mobility across First Peoples' lands and waterways.

This is not to say that the ban was wholly successful at curtailing the potlatch and mobility—as the subversive incorporation of potlatch with Christmas celebrations demonstrates—but the enforcement of this sensory regime had a particular felt impact and worked to further delimit and confine sensory experience that is concomitant with the "fixing" of attention. Not only did the potlatch ban seek to eradicate potlatch and winter dances as an important form of oral history and knowledge transfer, it also curtailed the forms of attention we use in such gatherings. For xwélmexw/Stó:lō people, xwélalà:m legitimates oral history through heightened perception that the closest English words would translate as "listening" and "witnessing." In all the longhouse work Stó:lō people do—from law-making to historical documentation—being called as an honored witness means that you have been chosen to be the equivalent to the Western forms that hold law and history; you are called to be "the living book" for this knowledge. When Canada's Indian Act prohibited the potlatch and winter dances from taking place for sixty-seven years, it was essentially the equivalent to banning books that document law and history, and also lessened opportunities to exercise xwélalà:m, a heightened form of perception resulting in richly detailed memory.

The Indian Act's increased and sustained limitation on Indigenous mobility was further extended with the residential schools' enforcement of mandatory attendance for Indigenous children between the ages of seven and fifteen. In many instances children were sent to schools located great distances away from their home communities, making it impossible for them to return to their families and for family members to visit them during the summertime. This decision to locate the residential schools at a distance from students' home communities was made with the intent not just to sever students from their cultural traditions viewed as "savage" by the church and state, but in effect to erode First Peoples' connection to their worldviews and to sever the bonds between students and their families. The deprivation of kinship effected by the schools was part of a new quotidian presence of absence, a systematic subtraction of those everyday moments of singing, speaking, and touch between parents (and grandparents) and their children, and between siblings. Students were most often segregated by gender and age, a form of prohibiting interaction with their brothers and sisters who were attending the same school. The removal of these daily acts of kinship and love were replaced with those of control, separation, and censorship. So successful was this separation from culture and kin that a significant number of survivors testify to returning from residential school to feel like foreigners in their own communities, unable to communicate with family in their languages, and feeling as though they did not belong in the very home they had waited so long to return to.

Survivor accounts often narrate a dual culture shock both on their arrival at residential school and on their return home. As Isabelle Knockwood recounts, on entering the Shubenacadie residential school, "My worldview or paradigm shifted violently, suddenly, permanently," and the sensory shift that accompanied her return from Shubenacadie was equally as profound: "Everything now looks different than it did before Indian residential schooling. The air smells different, the food tastes different, the sounds are different. And my outlook, my perspective on the world has changed in *every* area of my life" (Truth and Reconciliation Committee public testimony, October 27, 2011). Aurally, the disciplining of Indigenous bodies in Canadian Indian residential schools and U.S. Indian boarding schools—"to tattoo authority on colonized bodies via the ears," as Mark M. Smith has written—often took place through "the sound of clock-defined time" (M. Smith 2007, 56). Historian Sara Keyes has documented how, in U.S. Indian boarding schools, "Bells ordered students' lives, dictating when to sleep, rise, learn, pray, and eat. On their way to the dining hall, students marched in time to the sound of a bell. Upon their arrival, two bells rang; one to direct students to pull out their chairs and the other to indicate that they could sit down" (Keyes 2009, 36). Similarly, the regimentation of activity at residential schools was instituted through the use of bells to organize daily activity. In the memory of one residential school survivor from Shingwauk residential school in Sault Ste. Marie, Ontario, this regimentation is remembered as an unremitting demand that Indigenous childrens' bodies conform with clock-defined time:

> On week days the rising bell rings at six o'clock; at six-thirty another bell calls bigger girls to help with the work in the kitchen and dining-room, and the bigger boys to help with the work at the barn; at seven o'clock the bell is rung again to call all to breakfast, and at seven-thirty prayers are conducted. . . . At eight forty-five the warning bell for

classroom work is rung, and at nine o'clock all who have not been assigned to some special duties enter their respective classrooms. Bells are rung again at recess, at noon, and at various times in the afternoon, each ring having a definite meaning, well understood by all, until the final bells of the day are rung for evening study, choir practice, lights out, and go-to-bed. (Truth and Reconciliation Commission of Canada 2015, 518–19)

We will return to this demand to conform to the settler temporality of Western clock-defined time in chapters 4 and 5, both of which examine inclusionary music that requires Indigenous performers to master "being completely on and totally reliable and perfect every time" (Jean Lamon, quoted in Cloutier et al. 2005). For the remainder of this chapter, however, we will shift our focus toward forms of repair and redress that might reenable flexible practices of hetero-audition.

Toward Listening in Redress

Redressing forms of hungry listening—both the "fixing" of listening and listening that fixates upon the resources provided by musical content—requires some ontological reorientation of what we believe we are listening to when we listen to Indigenous music and Indigenous+Western art music. But resisting forms of hungry listening also entails dislocating the fixity and goal-oriented teleology of listening with more flexible listening practices that—like the intersection of attentiveness described between xwélalà:m and the process of "the words that come before all else"—situate listening as a relational action that occurs not merely between listener and listened-to, but between the layers of our individual positionalities.

Martin Daughtry, in his article "Acoustic Palimpsests and the Politics of Listening," sets out to understand what such a layered listening would entail through the metaphor of the palimpsest. The palimpsest is a manuscript written on papyrus or vellum in the Middle Ages that was washed off and then rewritten over, but where faint traces of the previous writing remain. Daughtry uses the palimpsest as a metaphor to envision listening to layered histories and agencies in soundscapes, including faint sound-traces that may be less discernable, or not audibly present at all. Drawing on the structure of the palimpsest, Daughtry asks that we engage with the "scriptio inferior" of music that can be considered a haunting of the manuscript by its earlier layers:

> Over the centuries, as the result of oxidation and other natural processes, the original texts often began to reappear beneath the newer writing. This fact made it possible for scholars of the palimpsest to engage in a kind of textual archaeology: ignoring the most recent layer, they peered back into the past, straining to read the words that had been effectively buried. In Latin these faint textual ghosts were called the *scriptio inferior* (underwriting) or *scriptio anterior* (former writing). (Daughtry 2013, 5)

In Daughtry's politics of listening, listening to the scriptio inferior would "[consist] of the multiple contexts and complicated networks that precede, surround, and are brought into being by a song's performance. It would . . . allow us to listen to history itself. It would enable a panacoustic politics of listening, with all the granularity and dynamism that term implies" (22). This panacoustic politics, like the process of intersection between xwélalà:m and the temporality of the words that come before all else, involves listening within the strata of sound and historical context, which I am extending here to include the additional stratified context of positionality.

In Daughtry's use, the palimpsest metaphor prompts an ethics of listening that somewhat paradoxically seeks to hear the indiscernible and the absent. To illustrate this, late in the essay Daughtry offers a "patently impossible" thought experiment where he imagines what an infinitely layered recording of war might sound like, as an acoustic palimpsest—one similar to Jorge Luis Borges's impossible one-to-one map of an ancient empire—that would capture the war

> in all of its troubling acoustic richness. . . . [T]his impossible recording would capture every breath of wind and every whistled melody within the Afghan theater of operations. We would hear all of the sounds of vehicles and weapons, mountains and cities, the sounds of soldiers and civilians, perpetrators and victims, and bystanders. We would hear the sounds of the displaced, of the dying, and of the dead. (Daughtry 2013, 22)

While Daughtry focuses on the infinite layers of sounds themselves, I would add that such an ethics of listening must also allow positionality to enter into this picture so that this panacoustic politics of listening includes listening *as* soldiers and civilians, perpetrators and victims, settlers and migrants, displaced people, and across these positionalites that we occupy.

Ultimately, Daughtry's essay is invested in an ethics of listening that certain ideologies of the finished product of recording and music making occlude: "we might say that the task of the palimpsestuous listener is to discern both the things that a recording encourages us to remember and the things it urges us to forget, the things that are insistently audible and the things that have long been silenced" (22). Daughtry's work prompts further consideration of what it might mean for listening subjects to recognize our listening privilege and habits, and the responsibility of listening self-reflexively for our various—settler colonial, heteronormative, patriarchal—tin ears. The foundation of critical listening positionality requires becoming aware of normative listening orientations across a range of gendered and racial formations, and developing self-reflexivity around how these are guided by their own specific forms of hunger, starvation, and drive toward knowledge fixity. Developing an awareness of listening positionality here holds potential for listening otherwise, yet the question remains of how—or the extent to which—we might orchestrate such stratified positional listening toward intersectional antiracist, decolonial, queer, and femininist listening practices.

Indeed, an awareness or relationship between such positional strata might lead counterproductively to potential incapacitation through perceptual overload. Focusing on such layers may result in an overvigilance that threatens to elide our relationship with the very song, Indigenous+art music, or inclusionary performance that we seek to hear. Consequently, what Daughtry proposes as a heightened listening mobility through what he calls contrapuntal perception (hearing simultaneous contextual layers), I would reorient as a practice of oscillation (moving between layers of positionality) that seeks not to apply other critical listening positionalites but instead to find greater levels of relationship between the strata of positionality. How this greater relationship of listening oscillation comes into practice will vary from individual to individual, but might begin through detailing specific aspects of one's positionality and then identifying the ways in which those aspects allow or foreclose upon certain ways of looking, kinds of touch, or listening hunger/fixity. This is challenging and detailed self-work to undertake, though the process itself might advance from the simple creation of a list of positionality aspects linked to listening ability, privilege, and habit.

Finding processes for oscillating between layers of listening positionality is not limited to the listener. Strategies for listening otherwise might also be activated by interventions in the unmarked rituals of music performance and forms of composition themselves. The program note, the darkened auditorium with singular focus on the stage, the pre-concert talk—all of these concert rituals can effectively be challenged in ways that open up new layers of listening, as will be illustrated in the event score "*qimmit katajjaq / sqwélqwel tl' sqwmá:y*" that follows chapter 4. Intervening in the space of the concert hall also means intervening in the particular kind of normative focus that such spaces assert. Whether the white cube of the gallery, the proscenium stage–concert hall, the outdoor festival stage, or the black box, each site urges us to think and listen to music in particular ways that may not be conducive to the kinds of listening otherwise we might hope to advance. What happens when we change these sites of listening to include intimate spaces of one-on-one listening, spaces in relation with the land, spaces where audience members are not bound by the particular kinds of attention these spaces assert?[13] New formats allow for a politics of listening that encourages listeners to hear inclusionary music through a critical engagement with the histories, epistemologies, and cosmologies often elided in the inclusionary music examples this book covers. Strategies for de- and re-formatting concert norms afford the potential to question how venues for performance structure hungry listening.

Daughtry concludes his speculation into the politics of listening with an appositely layered auto-critique of the weaknesses of the palimpsest metaphor, including the fact that the palimpsest

> *presumes a privileged vantage point from which all sounds can be heard.*
> To imagine an acoustic palimpsest is to adopt something akin to an omniscient stance. While this stance is relatively common in music scholarship, it obscures the radical situatedness of sounds and of listening. "Listening to the palimpsest" is an imagined activity, and thus is not representative of any individual's actual listening experience. (Daughtry 2013, 29; italics in the original)

Keeping in mind the materiality of the palimpsest is of great importance in order that we not colonize one ontology in service of decolonizing another. Yet, in weighing Daughtry's critique through the palimpsest's historical and material specificity as a document in layers, in which previous layers are only faintly visible, we see that no such visual omniscience exists. To look at a palimpsest is never to see all the layers as equally readable but instead to sense faint traces, some words and symbols more present than others, sometimes below the threshold of recognition as words and symbols, that allow only the knowledge that something beneath lingers. As such, an omniscient view of layers does not exist, just as an omni-audible listening practice is both infeasible and undesirable. To take the metaphor of the palimpsest at its most material means understanding a palimpsestous listening to be similarly oriented toward aural traces of history: echoes, whispers, and voices that become audible momentarily, ones that may productively haunt our listening as significantly as ghosts that linger. Like Daughtry's conception of the palimpsest's layers as ghosts of the manuscript, a decolonial practice of critical listening positionality actively seeks out (or allows itself) to become haunted. Thinking materially from the situation of concert practice, we might even use such haunting as a very literal strategy for whispered interventions to take place during inclusionary works, or between their movements. With advances in directional speaker technology that allow sound to be heard only by individuals within a narrow "beam," decolonial intervention within inclusionary music might then mean composing a counterorchestra of whispers that enacts acoustic haunting. As the aural equivalent of a spotlight, directional speakers make possible individual address within audiences and a potentially insurgent form of aural redress.

Resurgent and Sovereign Listening

So far we have considered forms of listening bias and habit that constitute settler colonialism's tin ear, how settler listeners might learn to identify aspects of—and then improvise with—their listening positionality, and how listeners might be impelled to listen otherwise through interventions in concert ritual, site, and format. But what about Indigenous listeners? What politics of listening might we Indigenous listeners reorient ourselves toward to affirm our political aims and center our epistemological and cosmological frameworks? How might Indigenous people effect resurgent listening? In many instances, scholarly focus has been directed toward resurgent work (performance, artwork, text) that acts as an *index* of sovereignty. It is easier to point, gesture, and listen toward such sovereign "things" that have a certain amount of stability in their objecthood and that paradoxically allow for forms of examination and analysis that are atomizing and extractive. Perception, in contrast, remains much more ephemeral, and though there are various ways to study forms of perception, no sustained engagement with resurgent perception has yet to be offered. What does it mean to engage in resurgent forms of reading, looking, and listening from our various Indigenous perspectives? In this next section we will address forms of listening resurgence and its relation to Indigenous sovereignty.

An increasing amount of writing by Indigenous artists, curators, and scholars over the past twenty years has addressed how Indigenous art and cultural practices do the work of sovereignty by asserting and affirming Indigenous legal orders and protocol visually, aurally, kinetically, materially, and rhetorically, or a combination of these. Here we can include Jolene Rickard's foundational writing on visual sovereignty and Michelle Raheja's examination of visual sovereignty in film, Robert Warrior's examination of intellectual sovereignty, Beverly Singer's description of cultural sovereignty, and Mique'l Dangeli's scholarship on dancing sovereignty.[14] While much of this writing has located sovereignty within specific "works" (artwork, film, writing, dance), each writer to a certain extent emphasizes the processual and relational aspects of creation and production over a static sense of objecthood. And yet, while this list demonstrates a movement away from measuring sovereignty against Western legal definitions, Rickard's 2011 critique that "many Native scholars caught in a system of Western validation have not embraced a more fluid and diverse interpretation of sovereignty" remains important (Rickard 2011, 470). This is not to say that we should be unconcerned with juridical and legal frameworks of sovereignty but instead note that Indigenous practices of sovereignty operate through Indigenous legal logics embedded within song and cultural practice. To date, scholarship on Indigenous artistic sovereignty has tended to treat Indigenous artworks as representations of sovereignty rather than to assess how such works express legal orders that hold equivalence to Western markers of sovereignty. Along similar lines, Indigenous artworks that represent sovereignty are understood as if the sovereignty represented therein is affectively perceived as such by all who experience them. To mark a distinction between how Indigenous sovereignty is expressed and felt is not to say that such works do not assert sovereignty through their form, content, and structure but instead to resist the overgeneralization that indices of sovereignty (wampum belts, coppers, contemporary Indigenous artworks, oration, songs) are necessarily perceived as such by Indigenous and settler viewers alike. To do so is to understand that "visual sovereignty" as a thing or object taking visual-material form is different than the action of sovereign sight or seeing. Sovereign speech does not necessarily provoke specific forms of sovereign listening. And sovereign writing does not guarantee that the reader will engage in an act of sovereign reading. By decoupling the deterministic relationship between sovereign object and reception, we can gain a more nuanced understanding of Indigenous and settler forms of sensory experience that extend beyond the overly reifying subject positions of "Indigenous" and "settler." Doing so allows us to question the difference between listening to an object's expression of sovereignty and listening through sovereignty.

In Canada, listening through sovereignty might further entail disambiguating the physical act of hearing guided by the official multicultural politics of recognition (Taylor 1992) and a listening practice that does not—seeks not to—know what it hears. In the former, hearing serves as an act of recognition, where the listener identifies more than one cultural practice at play and where the content of this cultural difference is heard as multicultural enrichment to Canadian national identity (Mackey 2002). Such content neither disrupts what it means to listen nor unsettles the logics of listening. To contrast this with sovereign listening, we must paradoxically engage a listening that does not reduce what is heard to the knowable, that resists a multicultural categorization of one cultural sound among many, that understands sound in its irreducible alterity, and that moves beyond our recognition of normative musical or performance protocols. Such listening would understand that not all sound can be translated to equivalent analogies, in the way that Richard Rath has described resisting wampum's analogization:

Much of the academic understanding of wampum comes from the use of visual analogies: wampum is "like money," "like writing," "like a gift," or "like a book," to name a few. This is a useful approach, rendering the unfamiliar in terms familiar to the assumed readers. Analogies, however, take us only part of the way and in the process constrain the historical imaginary. Once a certain threshold is passed, the discussion becomes more and more about the thing wampum is like—money, gifts, writing, or book—than about wampum. Analogy tends to make the indigenous practices appear to be never more than a subset of the thing they are compared to, a pale shadow regardless of the capaciousness of the containing ideas. (Rath 2014, 295)

To listen from a sovereign position might be understood both as a Canadian state sovereignty enacted through the previously described forms of official multicultural listening and enrichment-based listening or, alternatively, through frameworks of Indigenous resurgence that refuse the presupposition of settler logic by not beginning in refusal but instead through Indigenous logics. In order to further detail one instance of this form, albeit not in the genre of classical music but in performance action, I turn to my involvement with Tahltan artist Peter Morin in a performance art work in London, England, and Morin's subsequent writing about the collective action he initiated there.

In October 2013, Morin arrived in London (UK), where he was to stage an action inside and outside of Saint Olave's Church, where the first captured Indigenous infant from the new world was buried. In 1577 Martin Frobisher took captive an Inuit man, woman, and infant from Baffin Island. Whereas the man and woman died shortly after arriving in Bristol, the infant was taken to London, where Queen Elizabeth I was keen to claim him as a royal subject. In considering this history, Morin saw connections with the much longer history of First Nations children being taken from their families to Indian residential schools and decided to create a participatory work that would make this history present through a public intervention at Saint Olave's in London. Morin began by approaching the church to discuss the work. After we had much conversation and attempted negotiation with an increasingly anxious Anglican minister who denied that there was proof that the infant was actually buried there, Morin asked the minister, "what *would* you allow us to do in the church in order to honor this child?"

To this, the minister responded, "you are welcome to have a ceremony in your head."

Rather than considering this a defeat, Morin responded to the minister's steadfast refusal of all "pagan" as well as all artistic proposals to honor the child by creating a silent ceremony. For this intervention, Morin gathered together a small group of people to honor the captured infant by holding a procession toward Saint Olave's Church. Morin led the way, silently drumming, allowing each beat of his drumstick to stop just before it hit the drum. Yet as we walked, these visual beats carried just as much resonance, if not more, than if they were aurally present, perhaps because of their sonic censorship. Morin asked us to follow behind him and take turns singing or speaking messages for the infant into a jar of devil's club tea—again nearly silencing our songs and messages, yet having an even more palpable resonance individually as we individually felt the resonance of our voices filling the jar. Before we entered the church individually, Morin asked that we each take some of the devil's club tea into the church, take a moment to remember this child, or "have a silent ceremony in our heads," and then leave the tea somewhere in the church. To conclude the performance, Morin took the remaining tea and washed the exterior wall of the church with it. Immediately following the performance, Morin wrote about the experience of the work:

> today. singing. singing to this baby. remembering this inuit baby. remembering and respecting all of our stolen babies. sitting in silence in the church. holding the medicine of our land. an important collaborator. seeing the baby. holding the baby. reminding the baby we have not forgotten. we do not forget. we love you. we are holding you. crying. laughing. dancing. heart singing. heart drum beats. holding medicine. we are working together. thank you to all of our collaborators. here in london. and there on the land. thank you medicine. you are a powerful force. and then. washing the church with our medicine tea. the words. even a buried heart is still a beating heart. thank you all for helping to remember this still a beating heart.

We could describe Morin's action as sovereign because it asserts a form of responsibility—as a contemporary performance action—that draws on Indigenous logics of honoring our ancestors, and of performance as "doing work"[15] that operates within but outside of the sovereign strictures of the church. We could also identify Morin's subsequent writing as sovereign in its Tahltan emphasis of a rhythm at odds with standardized art-critical modes of writing, and its disruption of syntax and Western structures of argument and ordering of thought. This disruption prompts readers to reorient their mode of knowledge acquisition by slowing down the act of reading and hungry consumption of content. Most importantly, however, both Morin's action and writing enact a mode of sovereignty through their oratorical and performative claim to documenting Indigenous history. Morin's work does so as an oral/aural practice that is legitimated through the presence of honored witnesses (both those Morin invited to join in the action and the larger community he shared the action with via Facebook) who were given thanks for participating in that role following the work. Morin's contemporary form of oral documentation, arising from a Tahltan-specific epistemology of oral documentation—one also shared by other Northwest coast First Nations people through potlatch and winter dances—marks injustice and enacts the collective action of healing. Through its action and form, Morin's work is defined by a logic not explicitly oriented toward, defensive against, or responsive to the work of settler colonial sovereignty. Morin's action is doing sovereignty. Of course no action can live completely outside of some relationship with the state. Morin's work does not begin from this place; it does not do the work of confronting or resisting—and in doing so *centering*—settler colonialism and state institutional structures. Instead, Morin's work is offered primarily for the Inuit infant, for ancestors, and for the different Indigenous artistic, scholarly, and home communities he is part of. To return to the context of sovereign perception, Indigenous participants in the event and online readers—particularly, but not exclusively those from nations within the Northwest coast and northern British Columbia regions—sense the structures (or what I have been calling the "logics") of oral documentation and of honoring through song, through the viscerally silent strike of drum and through the calling for honored witnesses. Through these structures, we participate in *sensate sovereignty*.

Yet while Morin's action on the streets of London and his post-action writing are indifferent to being recognized by settler listeners/readers, this is not to say they are not also seen, heard, and reflected upon by non-Indigenous or settler audiences. It is important to note that some of the participants in the action and honored witnesses were settler colleagues and friends. Morin's work may equally have had some impact on any readers/viewers as a disorientation or redistribution of the sensible (Rancière 2010, 139) as much as it may have engendered a consumptive mode of reading, or be subsumed within the reader's own system of understanding (perhaps as "bad writing" or a "weird artist-thing"). Settler forms of everyday, normative sensory perception are also sovereign, in as much as they operate from an unmarked positionality settlers have come to be interpellated into by national curricula, government policy, and media.

Disambiguating sovereign structures of a performance (or object) and the sovereign reception of the listener or viewer allows us to imagine the many ways in which perception, as a sovereign force, comes into relationship with works that express different sovereignties. This is to say, a sovereign listening may hear differently the soundscape of the territory we are from as a soundscape of subsistence (hunting) rather than one of leisure (with pleasant birdsong and quiet nature), while a sovereign sense of touch for Indigenous material culture (for instance a raven rattle) might be understood as intercorporeal (that is, between human and other-than-human relations) and interrelational rather than as a singular touch upon a nonacting object. To name everyday sensory perception as sovereign marks it as bearing some relation to both the values of settler colonialism and Indigenous nationhood.

xwlálàm, síwél

Understanding practices of Indigenous listening resurgence necessitates more than gaining a mere awareness of the diverse cultural contexts and cultural protocol of Indigenous communities. To gain even partial understanding of these practices requires developing relationships with Indigenous artists, singers, and knowledge keepers. Modes of Indigenous listening resurgence do not find Indigenous song familiar; they do not feed xwelítem hunger. They are indigestible. We might consider their indigestibility similar to the indigestibility of seeds that create new life once the berries have fed us. The desire for the familiarity of Indigenous songs, music, or the recognizability of other elements such as rhythm and instrumentation, is the demand that difference present itself in a form that accommodates settler recognition. It is the desire for frameworks of display that serve the colonial palate and satiate hunger for content.

Such a desire operates equally within the logic of the gallery and museum, where objects are served up for the eye upon white walls, displayed with clear vitrines distinctly illuminated under lighting that removes all shadow. Like the voracious hunger of xwelítem, museum display of Indigenous belongings is similarly oriented to accumulation—the cornucopia of ethnographic salvage. Such display culture removes the other senses from engagement with the belonging—a removal so that the eye can consume uninterrupted. No touch is permitted by the vitrine and glass, as the being and ancestor—for example, a raven rattle—and its life are kept "supported" by this display, removed from touch, removed from sound, removed from land, and positioned for settler gaze. In exhibitions including those such as *c̓əsnaʔəm, the city before the city* at the Museum of Anthropology, curated by Jordan Wilson (Musqueam/xʷməθkʷəy̓əm) and Sue Rowley, the hunger of museum display culture is upended by the decision to de-privilege objects on display and fill rooms with xʷməθkʷəy̓əm voices and hənq̓əmin̓əm̓ language. In Wilson and Rowley's exhibition about the xʷməθkʷəy̓əm city that formerly occupied the place now called Vancouver, no actual historical objects were used in the museum exhibition. Instead, media-rich stories of xʷməθkʷəy̓əm history—and in particular a room devoted to an audio conversation between members of the xʷməθkʷəy̓əm nation—dominated the space habitually occupied by objects. Conceived of by Wilson, this surround-sound audio installation called "Sq̓əq̓ip—gathered together," consisted of a darkened room featuring a single table covered by an oilcloth tablecloth with several photos, surrounded by eight chairs, and filled with conversation, laughter, and sharing of memories amongst si:y̓ém: respected leaders of the xʷməθkʷəy̓əm community. "They conversed for two and a half hours, of their childhood, of shrinking reserve boundaries, of their grandparents and great aunts and uncles, and of their concerns regarding the future of our community," noted Wilson, which was then condensed to twenty-five minutes for the audio installation (Wilson 2016, 485).

Returning to the single-sense privileging of the typical museum display, where belongings are removed from touch, sound, and full sensory engagement, I suggest that "sq̓əq̓ip—gathered together" effects a xwélmexw counterpoint to normative museum experience. That is, although intended for listening, "sq̓əq̓ip" sets what it means to listen in a space that attempts to convey the humor, as well as the "quality of warmth and comfort, [that are] qualities challenging to describe" and are "seldom found in public representations, likely because they are challenging to convey well—they are not easily captured in text format" (Wilson 2016, 484). This warmth and comfort should not merely be understood as an aspect of making the space inviting and comfortable, but instead as an aspect of connection and relationship through the touch of the table and oilcloth, through the darkness of the room, through the presence of the voices situated around the listener and filling the space, through the look of the teapots and cups, the way the voices of these si:ẏém move, share conversation, and listen to one other. This situation of listening in this particular environment cannot be separated into a purely aural experience of listening. Indeed, such a situation shares much in common with larger principles of witnessing in the work of Morin, the work our communities do in the longhouse, and as we gather around various tables in our communities. Wilson cogently describes the role of witnessing in community events and its connection to listening:

> Witnesses can be called upon at any point in the future to provide an account of what they observed at a particular gathering. Witnessing is one example in demonstrating how in our community (and in our neighbouring communities), knowledge, history, life narratives are dispersed amongst many. Thus gathering together as individuals is akin to bringing together components of a history. Spending time with this group underscored the importance of listening, not simply by virtue of us listening to them, but in how they listened to each other. When one person was speaking, the rest of the group listened respectfully—as opposed to waiting for their turn to talk. When the next person shared their thoughts with the group, they would respond in-depth, speaking not only to their own experiences and perspectives, but also to those they just heard. This aspect of the conversation demonstrated how well these individuals listened to one another, retaining what they'd heard and incorporating it into how they perceived the topic at hand. As they made clear about their own learning experiences, active listening was a formative aspect to their growing up in the Musqueam community. This mode of learning, of listening

Hungry Listening

Figure 5. *sq̓əq̓ip—gathered together*, installation view at the Museum of Anthropology, University of British Columbia, 2015. Curated by Jordan Wilson and Sue Rowley. Photograph by Reese Muntean.

> to knowledgeable adults in conversation with one another was echoed throughout our interviews with community members. . . . Howard E. Grant remembers, "Dinner table talk is how I learned who I was. I listened to my grandparents, my grand-uncles, aunts and uncles, and mother. They would gather, have a sit down dinner, and you'd hear them talk. You'd hear them reminisce. You'd hear them talk about what it was, and how it was." . . . In these contexts, listening is as critical as speaking. (Wilson 2015, 22–23)

This understanding of witnessing is not grounded in the visual, as it is in Western conceptions of the eyewitness, but in the aural. It is also evidenced in Salishan languages.[16] As previously mentioned, the Halq'eméylem word "xwlálám" means to witness and to listen. "xwlálám-chexw" means "you are called to witness" and is used in a formal context of longhouse work. "xwlálámaltha," less formally, means "let's listen." xwélalà:m (listening), as a shxwelméxwelh form of attention, is a practice decidedly opposed to hungry listening, which gathers and instrumentalizes content that is heard. Instead, xwélalà:m might better be understood as a practice of gathering that takes place in non-goal-oriented ways. This, however, does not mean that we listen without intention, but rather that the work of listening is not predicated on use-value or the drive to accumulate knowledge. These shxwelméxwelh xwélalà:m, or Indigenous forms of listening, are just one form of many diverse resurgent practices that exist for Indigenous peoples. In a similar way to how James Morrison describes Gitxsan listening to the limx oo'y, xwélmexw listening moves beyond the single sense of listening and involves a practice of síwél, "to become attentive to something, or to prick one's ears." This listening does not isolate the ear as we sense shxwelí resounding land. xwélalà:m is a form of attention in which we are attentive not just to sound but to the fullest range of sensory experience that connects us to place.

Conclusion

To decolonize perception in general, and listening in particular, requires different strategies for settler and Indigenous listeners. While it is important for Indigenous listeners to understand and practice forms of resurgent perception based in our individual nations and communities' cultural logics, for settler listeners decolonial strategies may at times be necessarily agonistic, as encounters between nation-to-nation sound sources and perception predicated upon the rough edges of a conception of democracy based in dissensus. They may, moreover, require new frames for listening that do not treat listening as a single-sense activity, while resisting the hunger to consume alterity and Indigenous content. At the very least, returning to Susan McClary, it requires us to suspend our belief in the certainty of knowing what the act of listening is (McClary 1991, 19). To effect a decolonial crisis in the act of listening— to ask listeners to become "no longer sure of what listening is"—cannot simply entail a willful approach to kick colonial listening habits. Instead, it means shifting the places, models, and structures of how we listen. At times, it may also mean an approach led by artists, composers, curators, and musicians to impose new listening impasses through their work. Such forms of impasse may in fact seem contrary to an idea of decolonial listening based in listening better or removing settler colonial perceptual filters. One example of such an impasse has already been given in written, aesthetic, or sensory blockades discussed at the end of the

Introduction and effected in the previous section for Indigenous readers only. Further examples will be presented in the event score that concludes chapter 4, and in the perceptual impasse of allied artists like visual artist Jin-Me Yoon discussed in the Conclusion. As these examples will demonstrate, unlike the "tin ear" as a willful refusal against listening otherwise, the aesthetic impasse acts to block listening's voracious accumulation of content. Like Brechtian *Verfremdungseffekt,* the listening impasse sends perception off in other directions and slows hungry listening's ravenous appetite in service of increased self-reflection toward one's listening habits, privilege, and biases.

EVENT SCORE FOR GUEST LISTENING I

I am sitting in a room
Limestone walls surround
Limestone lines
inside and outside of the structure I sit within
This building, this house, this room,
is one of many in which I am living

I am living in a city—"often called the Limestone City"—says the City
   of Kingston
I am spending my days in limestone buildings
I sit inside many "of the many charming limestone buildings"—
says the City,
"many of which help tell the story of Canada"

These charming limestone walls—this charming city—built from
   quarries
Quarried from the lands of Haudenosaunee and Anishinaabek
Built from the lands of the Haudenosaunee, the Anishinaabek
Structured by colonial design
to allay anxieties of impermanence

I am sitting in a limestone room that hums
with the subfrequency of colonial quarry and cut
This audible-inaudible sound
resonates my body
My body—xwélmexw body, swíyeqe & yes xwelítem starving person's
   body—
in this room, these buildings, that resonate the story of Canada

Event Score for Guest Listening I

I am listening in a limestone building,
trying not to feel the story of Canada
resonate through my body
shiver through

I am trying to hear the seepage of water through stone
I am trying to hear the labor of quarry, cut and chisel
I am trying to hear these walls as still the land
I am trying not to hear these walls declare their immovability,
declare their charming structure, their necessary structure
I am trying to hear their structure burn down
while dwelling and shelter remain

TWO
WRITING ABOUT MUSICAL INTERSUBJECTIVITY

> I wonder about language with its raw frayed fringes
> delicately trying to express spirit
> as each word drips from lips to rest in blank spaces
> between us
> — Lee Maracle (Stó:lō), *Talking to the Diaspora*

Roland Barthes begins his essay "The Grain of the Voice" with a pointed question: "how . . . does language manage when it has to interpret music?" (Barthes 1977, 179). His answer: "very badly. If one looks at the normal practice of music criticism . . . it can readily be seen that a work (or its performance) is only ever translated into the poorest of linguistic categories: the adjective" (179). To address music performance, or what he elsewhere prefers to call "the body in a state of music" (Barthes 1985, 312) requires something other than mere description. To counteract adjectival overreliance, Barthes argues, involves neither "diverting the adjective you find on the tip of the tongue towards some substantive or verbal periphrasis" (1977, 180), nor developing different structural and formalist models of analysis for understanding music's internal coherence. Instead, Barthes proposes a sonorous, sensate form of writing aimed at articulating music's subjectivity through the materiality of writing itself, what he calls "writing aloud":

> writing aloud is not phonological but phonetic; its aim is not the clarity of messages, the theater of emotions; what it searches for (in a perspective of bliss) are the pulsional incidents, the language lined with flesh, a text where we can hear the grain of the throat, the patina of consonants, the voluptuousness of vowels, a whole carnal stereophony: the articulation of the body, of the tongue, not that of meaning, of language. (Barthes 1975, 66–67)

According to Barthes, writing aloud involves no less than articulating the body through sensorially charged prose: transcribing the proprioception of musical experience through kinaesthetic syntax, or recirculating the grain of the voice through the texture of the text. Scholars have drawn upon Barthes's "The Grain of the Voice"—and his discussion of opera singers therein—to discuss vocality (Dunsby 2009), opera (Halliwell 2014), and the concepts associated with the text including "pulsion" and "grain" (Szekely 2006). What has received less attention in Barthes's writing is the intersection between musical voice in performance and authorial voice in scholarship/writing, that is, how the space between singer/performer and listener-writer is rendered through writing. As Michael Szekely notes, Barthes was largely concerned with the interstices between gesture, writing, and sound. These spaces are encoded in the very separations between terms—*image music text*—given by Stephen Heath as the title of his translated collection of Barthes's essays. We may conceptualize these spaces as the grain between forms of visual, sonic, and tactile perception (as is the case in Laura Marks's concept of haptic visuality addressed later in this chapter), or the trace of body in the media of music, text, and performance: "The 'grain' is the body in the voice as it sings, the hand as it writes, the limb as it performs" (Barthes 1977, 188).

In proposing a form of writing that seeks to articulate this materiality through the "pulsional incidents" of song, Barthes suggests writing itself should move as an active agent, tracing and tracking that which moves music and listener. This movement, he continues, "is carried not by dramatic inflections, subtle stresses, sympathetic accents, but by the grain of the voice, which is an erotic mixture of timbre and language . . . the art of guiding one's body" (Barthes 1975, 66). Moving beyond the adjective, Barthes's writing aloud models a form of what I call *sensory-formalist analysis* where writers' and readers' bodies move alongside music's body. Sensory-formalist analysis is a strategy of apposition where the particulate matter of musical experience is materially engaged through the atmosphere of the page, screen, or other medium. It is a revision of what Susan Sontag, in "Against Interpretation," called an "erotics of art" (Sontag 1966, 10) that turns away from making content out of art, avoiding analysis that "excavates, and as it excavates, destroys; it digs 'behind' the text, to find a sub-text which is the true one." "What is needed," in this turning away from instrumentalizing art, notes Sontag, "is a vocabulary—a descriptive, rather than prescriptive, vocabulary—for forms" (8).[1]

Following Barthes's and Sontag's calls for different orientations toward and relationships of art writing, this chapter surveys a number of sensate and apposite forms for writing about musical experience often referred to as "performative writing."[2] Language, syntax, and grammar operate upon sensorial and affectively rich terms in performative writing, and often foreground intersubjectivity between viewer and artwork, spectator and performance, listener and music, and writer and reader. More specifically, *Hungry Listening* focuses on the intersubjective experience between human and nonhuman actors in music performance by considering object agency in non-representational and new materialist theory alongside Indigenous knowledge regarding nonhuman relations. While Phillip Vannini describes non-representational research as "privilig[ing] the study of relations" emerging from a belief "that life arises from the entanglement of actors—human and non-human animals, organic matter, and material objects" (Vannini 2015, 8), other more critical voices like those of Zoe Todd (2016) and Jessica Horton and Janet Berlo (2013) remind us that the "more-than-human" agency described in new materialism and non-representational theory has long been a quotidian fact of Indigenous lives and epistemologies. There is nothing new, as Zoe Todd asserts, in the way Indigenous kinship extends toward our nonhuman relations, and a large majority of the theoretical work in this area has elided these Indigenous epistemological frameworks. While some of the critical engagement that identifies this elision has been oppositional, I see no reason not to consider these two streams of thinking as mutually exclusive. Considering non-representational theory and Indigenous epistemologies alongside each other can here provide a more nuanced understanding of nonhuman relations, and can help move beyond the anthropocentrism that reinforces the subject's mastery over an object. For the aims of this chapter, and book more generally, I bring these discourses together to consider how performative and other writing forms affirm relations between human and nonhuman subjects, and how the content and aesthetics of this writing challenges the dichotomy between music's limited agency as passive "object," and the listener as the active partner.[3] I also challenge the critique that the author of performative writing acts as an overbearing partner in this dyad, drowning out the musical subject by increasing the volume of the writer/scholar's own voice. Such criticism operates both on an explicit level, as I will later illustrate in the work of musicologist David Levin, and more implicitly in professional guides to writing about music.

Professional guides for writing about music are primarily geared toward postsecondary and graduate students, and thus are mostly concerned with establishing basic writing principles. Among these principles an equation is sometimes made between creative, poetic, and performative forms of writing and "stylistic excess." "Stylistic excess," notes musicologist Jonathan Bellman, "consists of attempts to fortify an argument (in the same way that breakfast cereals of dubious nutritional value are fortified with added vitamins and nutrients) with superlatives, overly colourful adjectives, or exaggerated wording . . . [and] dulls the reader's senses with its procession of highly charged, multisyllabic words" (Bellman 2000, 76). Bellman later describes such writing as mere "authorial musing" and "authorial whim."[4] While we might note a similar resistance to Barthes's critique of adjectives, we should question what criteria are used to determine the efficacy of language in conveying musical experience. At what point does a language composed from "the patina of consonants, the voluptuousness of vowels, a whole carnal stereophony" (Barthes 1975) become "overly colourful" or "exaggerated"? When, in other words, is such writing read as a marker of authorial excessiveness, and when is it read as a marker of the exact excessiveness of our experiences listening to music or other experience of art? By addressing musical experience as an encounter between subjectivities of listener, music, writer, and reader, this chapter unravels the hierarchies of subjectivity that assert the primary importance of the musical subject. The chapter concludes by introducing a third partner in the play of subjectivities: space. Whereas space is often considered as the context within which an encounter takes place, I consider it here as an active subject in itself. I approach this in two ways: first, by considering the space of performance or other sites at which music is listened to, and second, by considering the space of the medium that conveys the experience of listening: the space of the written page or screen, or, in the case of practice-based research, an artistic medium. By considering space as a third subject, I extend my engagement with sensate, apposite forms of writing toward how other arts-based formats for music scholarship might be developed.

To experiment with different forms of writing resonant theory that consider intersubjectivity between listener, music, and space and reach beyond adjectival reliance, I engage in what I call *apposite methodology*. Apposite methodologies are processes for conveying experience alongside subjectivity and alterity; they are forms of what is sometimes referred to as "writing with" a subject in contrast to "writing about." They also envision possibilities for how writing might not just take the form of words inscribed on the page but also forms that share space alongside or move in relationship with another subjectivity. "Writing" in this sense might be considered either a textual *or* material form: song writing, sculptural writing, and film writing. At the heart of these experiments in resonant theory are anticolonial epistemes for sharing experience, that emerge out of the history of performative writing.

Performative Writing, Apposite Methodology

Performative writing, according to Peggy Phelan "enact[s] the affective force of the performance event again" (Phelan 1997, 12). In the realm of music, the affective force of the event is intertwined with the relationship between the listening subject and musical and spatial subjectivity. While performative writing encompasses a wide range of work across the arts and humanities, I begin with examples by writers who explicitly center this relationship between listener and musical subjectivity, and in particular, writing by Wayne Koestenbaum, Kevin Kopelson, and Suzanne Cusick that articulates the positionality of the listener and musical subjectivity.[5] In doing so, the performative writing by these writers names the unmarked normativity of listening through explicitly marking listening positionality. Part of what *Hungry Listening* seeks to expand in musical scholarship is this action of marking the normative discourses of listening positionality (primarily though not exclusively in relation to Western art music) as white, heterosexual, able-bodied, and middle class, through writing that explicitly illustrates and materializes other listening values in/and/from musical subjectivities. In emphasizing the writer-subject's identification (or dis-identification) with the musical subject, a partial aim of performative writing is to expose normative listening practices. Giving voice to identification and dis-identification, the writer-subject destabilizes and unsettles scriptural economies that demand compliance with standardized, "plain English" (Strunk and White 1999). Performative modes of writing by feminist (Cixous 1976, Gallop 2002, Minh-ha 1989), queer (Koestenbaum 1993, Kopelson 1996), Indigenous (King 2003, Sarris 1993, Morin 2016), crip (Eales 2016, Forfa 2016), and black writers (hooks 1992, Lorde 1981) have long worked to disrupt writing's colonizing imperatives, racializing and ableist legitimacies, and phallogocentric norms. The opening that *Hungry Listening* seeks to create in music studies for decolonial writing otherwise draws on this long tradition of performative writing.

In the tripartite context of subject–subject(–subject) relations I outline above, the proximity between listener, music, and space give rise to the methodologies of "apposition" proposed in this chapter.[6] As with its root "to appose," meaning to place side by side or in proximal relationship, an apposite methodology involves a proximal relationship between the method of writing and experience of the writer. While this might lead to the assumption that apposite musicology is an essentially mimetic form (a copy or transcription), I would instead emphasize that the nature of proximity between subjects (listener/music; musical experience and writing) is treated as relational. Apposite forms of writing, through their form, grammar, and language, convey how the writer/listener moves alongside musical or artistic subjectivity. This movement alongside music is not exclusively aimed at conveying intimacies of music's presence; it may equally result in a variety of apposite relationships including keeping music at a distance, oscillations between intimacy and distance, or a kind of "marking time" similar to the experience of traveling alongside other vehicles moving at varying speeds or when gridlocked in traffic.

The vast majority of scholars choose their methodologies for their apposite (that is, in the other sense of the word, "appropriate") capacity to examine the particular objects, phenomena, or experiences we seek to understand. Yet while "methodological framework" implies an appropriate application of theoretical context to the object of study, writing itself (the medium by which we give our ideas form) is largely considered a mere by-product of scholarship. Yet if the method we use to measure phenomena in large part actually determines the result of this measurement, should we not actively pursue writing that is aware of how its form constitutes knowledge and experience? Often referred to simply as writing "style," the choices made in the structure, language, and even typography of writing are usually not considered constitutive of the research itself. No language or writing form is value free. Forms of structural music analysis, for example, enact epistemic violence against Indigenous music, blunting the life it carries. Given this context, apposite methodologies seek a more proximal relationship between writing's form (its materiality, its flow, rhythm, or pace, and the way it structures time) and the form we sense in musical subjectivity. They seek to engage the materiality of writing, in order not to enact violence against musical subjectivity.

The study of music's presence has received sustained attention in the work of musicologists Suzanne Cusick (1994), Christopher Small (1998), Carolyn Abbate (2004), Lawrence Kramer (2004b), Nicholas Cook (2014), and Georgina Born (2019), and philosophers including Vladimir Jankélévitch (2003) and Jean-Luc Nancy (2007), among others. Yet within this work there has been a lack of attention toward how listeners come to understand musical intersubjectivity; musicology and music aesthetics' "tin ears" have largely continued to disregard non-Western perspectives that emphasize music's life and subjectivity. It is these same tin ears that have responded with heteronormative disdain toward queer performative writing. Queer performative writing in particular has been cast as excessively oriented to the writer rather than the object under examination, where the excessiveness of authorial tone, poetics, and reflexivity has been accused of narcissism. To address these critiques of performative writing's narcissism, I turn now to examples where listening and viewing are treated by queer writing as intimate and intersubjective experiences.

Queer Vocal Narcissism and Linguistic Excess

Performative writing's *indisciplinarity*—its violation of disciplinary norms—is the subject of David Levin's essay "Is There a Text in This Libido? *Diva* and the Rhetoric of Contemporary Opera Criticism." Levin's text is to a certain extent representative of the general mistrust by musicologists of performative writing's excess. In particular, Levin expresses concern with the "Neo-Lyrical" queer performative writing of Wayne Koestenbaum's *The Queen's Throat* that "aims for an adequation with operatic form: it emulates the object of its affections; and, perhaps more important, it seeks to render (but not necessarily analyze) the intense affect that can suffuse the experience of opera" (Levin 2012, 122). Such writing loses sight of the musical experience it seeks to engage, according to Levin, and replaces a close reading of music with "a world of emotive stratospherics" (123). Koestenbaum's writing represents an academic crooning "that aspires to *be* a bravura performance as much as a *record* of bravura performances" (124; emphasis in original). In short, Levin argues that Koestenbaum's writing replaces an engagement with musical phenomena with an engagement with the writer's own voice. Koestenbaum is found guilty of logophilic narcissism, expressing (or professing) his love for the sound of his own text over that of the opera. And yet Levin also clarifies that he has nothing against excess itself. Rather, his main concern is that such writing legitimates enthusiasm "at the cost of nuanced textual analysis" (129). Yet can writing that is in an apposite relationship to the subject of analysis not serve as an analysis of the subject? Might the qualities of that apposition (the grain of the text, the rustle of language, the patina of consonants) together actually constitute a non-representational form of analysis in itself?[7]

Levin's language choice of "crooning" and "stratospherics" additionally speaks to performative writing's linguistic excess. This is writing that "gushes" and is seen to constitute a relapse to earlier models of music criticism: the excessive description and verbose effluence of nineteenth-century musical description such as that of E. T. A. Hoffmann, the overuse of metaphor, or worse, what is colloquially known as "purple prose." As Mark Evan Bonds notes:

> Until the 1920s, debates about expression tended to centre on *what* music expressed, not *whether* it could express anything. In the years after World War I, however, a variety of "hard" formalism arose in part as a backlash against what many perceived to be the overwrought expressivity of works from the pre-War decades. (Bonds 2014, 250)

The important distinction between such early forms of music criticism and performative writing is the intention of the author in the latter to use language and structure as a way to comment on their relationship with the subject. While the end goal of music criticism was to a significant extent the embellishment of a poetic writing style, performative writing uses this embellishment (or sparseness, or roughness) to convey something about the subject in question: it attempts to elucidate the non-representational aspects of the subject through forms of sensuous, material textuality. Levin's critique of Koestenbaum is here more applicable to nineteenth-century music criticism's silencing of the particularity of the music it treats by ignoring language as a vector of analysis. In contrast, performative writing might adopt a manic verbosity as an explicit strategy to examine particularly anthemic music (for instance in the postminimalist music of John Adams) or a language of campy excess to speak to music of similar expression (for example the theme song for the 1980s TV show *Dynasty*) and the effect of this music on the listener. In such linguistic miming we should not assume that the writing represents the unrestrained extravagance of the author's voice; just as we are able to pose different (and perhaps at times contradictory) arguments across our scholarship, so too may we expound those arguments through different sensory and affective writing structures and linguistic timbres. The materiality of musicological discourse has an indissoluble relationship with the music it seeks to describe. Moreover, in most instances, this discourse imposes a time and structure upon our understanding of musical meaning that at times runs contrary to the music it considers. Although not focused on music, Svetlana Alpers notes the incongruity between writing and the experience of viewing a visual work:

> the repertory of concepts it [writing] offers for describing a plane surface bearing an array of subtly differentiated and ordered shapes and colours is rather crude and remote. Again, there is an awkwardness, at least, about dealing with a simultaneously available field—which is what a picture is in a medium as temporally linear as language: for instance, it is difficult to avoid tendentious reordering of the picture simply by mentioning one thing before another . . . [The] lack of fit here is formally obvious in an incompatibility between the gait of scanning a picture—in a series of rapid, and rapidly shifting, eye movements— and the gait of ordered words and concepts. (Alpers 1983, 3)

Alpers draws our attention to the disjunction between the experience of viewing an artwork and the reader's experience in reading about an artwork. Musical experience, unlike visual experience, takes place as an aural palimpsest of simultaneously unfolding sound events, and thus is even more remote from the hierarchy of syntax used to convey meaning in writing. By acknowledging that writing is not an empty vessel for knowledge transfer, it becomes imperative to understand how this medium, whether explicitly concerned with its own aesthetic (style) or not, constructs knowledge through its form, structure, language use, tone, and voice. Given this fact of writing's aesthetic signification, we might pay increased attention to writing's craft in practicing what Kevin Kopelson calls "critical virtuosity" (2002). Or perhaps writing is *not* always the best medium for understanding the presence and time of certain musical experiences. Other than its supposed efficiency and efficacy in communication, what makes writing better, for instance, than live dialogue as a mode of working out (thinking) these aspects of musical meaning? By acknowledging the limits of writing as more than argument, we become responsible not just for the arguments we put forward but the form through which we express them. Rather than discounting performative modes of writing as self-indulgent or needlessly opaque, we might instead reconsider how they enable us to engage more precisely with musical performance, or the sensory and affective qualities of artistic experience more generally. We might consider how the structure, form, and language of writing allows us to convey those particular moments of music's sensory presence that draw us toward (or repel us from) music in the first instance. They also provide us with an aesthetic means toward writing intersubjectivity.

Intersubjective Relationships with Ancestors

Intersubjective relationships are not at all extraordinary in Indigenous life and artistic practice. In museums across the globe, glass vitrines display cultural belongings of Northwest coast First Peoples—masks in particular—to the public. Often these displays are filled with a particular kind of mask, depicting its many variations across a region or across time. Such displays offer a cornucopia whose abundance is intended to show artistic and cultural variance. While such displays are offered to members of the general public primarily for their aesthetic contemplation, for Indigenous people the experience of such displays can often be traumatic and triggering. This experience occurs not only because of the histories of cultural prohibition, including the seizure of cultural belongings and the separation of such belongings from our communities, but also because the very "objects" that are held behind glass are not objects at all. Instead, what exists behind the glass goes by other names; they have life, they are living beings, or they are ancestors. Indigenous people have intimate kinship with these beings. As such, the fact that they are "held" behind glass, in drawers, in storage might be understood in terms of the containment and confinement of life. Encountering "loved ones" behind glass, in drawers, and in storage puts into question the ways in which museological standards of "preservation" and "conservation" might instead be understood as containment or even incarceration. In many Pacific Northwest communities, we understand that such beings must be cared for as loved ones; the work that they do is treated as precious and sacred. They are not expected to be in continuous use, but are allowed to rest once they have completed their work. They also have a life cycle, and are not expected to live on forever. In this context, Git Hayetsk Dance Group leaders Mike Dangeli (Nisga'a) and Mique'l Dangeli (Tsimshian) have called museum display a form of "life support" that extends the life of these loved ones beyond their natural life span (Dangeli and Dangeli 2015). Moreover, such beings have specific roles and work to do. The energy these beings expend is respected—for example when drums and masks are used in performance—by "putting them to sleep" after their work is done. Under the continuous gaze of museum display, however, they are forced to perform—to labor—without rest (Hopkins, n.p.).

Increasingly, Indigenous artists have sought to address this context of the museum as carceral space that disconnects ancestors and beings from our communities. The work of Peter Morin (Tahltan) and Tanya Lukin Linklater (Alutiiq) in particular engages in forms of reconnection through music and song. Their use of music and song in these instances bring life, hold life, and serve as intimate acts of reconnecting kinship. For her work *Accompaniment* (2015) at EFA Project Space in New York, Tanya Lukin Linklater invited Laura Ortman (White Mountain Apache) to perform on electric violin. Ortman was asked to perform as one part a larger work that included a bowl Lukin Linklater had commissioned from Alutiiq artist Doug Inga and four small Yup'ik dance fans she purchased at Cama'i Dance Festival in Bethel, Alaska. These fans and bowl were placed unassumingly on top of and beneath a wooden bench, without the typical protection (and disconnection) imposed by a vitrine. Given the title of the work (which was also the title of the exhibition), Ortman's performance might be misconstrued as an "accompaniment" that provides background music for viewing the dance fans and bowl. To understand these belongings as holding life, however, is to recognize that Ortman's work was instead providing company, a form of speaking toward and with the life of these belongings. Ortman subverted the hierarchy of the classical musician as soloist and the attendant value of this system where attention is expected to be directed solely toward the performer. From Ortman's movement toward and around the dance fans and bowl, she established a relationship of performing toward and with shxwelí that takes the form of "bowl" and "dance fans." I speak here of shxwelí as a xwélmexw audience member who felt this connection between the life of sound, materiality, and space. Her movement and sound challenged the inflexibility of hungry listening as a teleological and fixated form of attention. Ortman's performance made visceral relations of intersubjectivity and vitalized life through sound, just as the location of these subjects, with bowl positioned upside down upon the bench with dance fans resting casually on top of and underneath it, refused the normative system of object display. Such intersubjective reconnection is characteristic of much of Lukin Linklater's work that brings Indigenous voices and bodily presence back into relationship with ancestors and the life of Indigenous belongings that have been kept from our communities by museums. This work of reconnecting kinship is also a central feature of work by Tahltan artist Peter Morin.

Morin's work frequently uses song as an intimate form of reconnection with ancestors that have been given nonhuman material form, and in doing so refuses to uphold the museum's imposition of objecthood upon the lives of these ancestors. Examples of this include Morin's work at the Museum of Anthropology in Vancouver in 2013 (see Figure 6) and at the Royal BC Museum in 2012 where he gave a comedy routine for the poles, and my previous discussion in chapter 1 of Morin's performance at Saint Olave's in London in honor of the Inuit infant buried there. We will turn again to Morin's work in chapter 5, where I discuss his Cultural Graffiti series, also performed in London, England. The commonality between all of Morin's work discussed with-

Figure 6. Peter Morin singing to an ancestor at the Museum of Anthropology. Photograph by Kate Hennessy, 2013.

in this book is its focus on intimacies of reconnection. Below, I offer an extended transcription of one of Morin's performances in order to give weight to his words as sovereign expression. The transcription is excerpted from a presentation Morin gave at the Isabel Bader Centre for the Performing Arts in Kingston, Ontario, where he explained his work as a performance artist to a nonhuman ancestor: an amhalaayt (Chief's Headdress). Morin's presentation that evening of February 3, 2016, was part of a series I have organized since 2015 called Conversations in Indigenous Arts, intended to bring together primarily Indigenous artists, scholars, and community members to discuss a common theme. The focus of this particular event was how Indigenous people carry our history in the body and how historical documentation (the archive) takes place through dance, song, and oration. In addition to Peter Morin, it featured leaders of the Git Hayetsk dance group Mike Dangeli (Nisga'a) and Mique'l Dangeli (Tsimshian), and settler historian Coll Thrush. In the lead-up to the event, Mike and Mique'l Dangeli had visited the Agnes Etherington Arts Centre to see cultural belongings from Northwest coast First Nations that had found their way into the collection. Out of

Writing about Musical Intersubjectivity

this visit, the Dangelis had asked whether it was possible to dance one of the belongings—an ancestor in the form of amhalaayt. The excerpts below are transcribed from this evening of performance and oration, beginning with Morin and followed by Mike and Mique'l Dangeli discussing the life of the amhalaayt ancestor:

Peter Morin [*addressing the amhalaayt*]: I want to say that there's been a lot of violence that's happened . . . and we wear it on our bodies.[8] We all wear it on our bodies. I have dreams about making things which refer to Tahltan Nation ways of being . . . but there's a lot of distance between me and the land. Also, there is a lot of distance between me and the original makers as a result of things like the residential schools and governmental policies which were designed to limit our freedom. Also it's so beautiful to see you here, it's so very, very beautiful . . . And your removal also is a part of that loss that we feel.

I do something called performance art that moves inside of the body, and tells partly the history, and the present and future ancestors, as well as provides the chance for moments like this. And so I make things which come from dream spaces . . . because I believe it is people like you who talk to us, and through those places that you are in right now . . . to the places we are in, right now.

I have been trying to sing, as a part of the practice of being alive, and being alive also means making things, and those things fit within what I think of as Tahltan Nation art history. And your history and my history walk side by side, and I want to thank you for that. . . . I know four songs. The first song was composed by a guy named Beal Carlick. The second song is . . . I'm not sure who wrote it . . . it's called 'this little light of mine.' The third song was composed by William Wallaceton. I'm not going to sing all the verses of these songs. The fourth song was composed by Johnny S. Carlick. I want you to know that I . . . I love you.

[*Morin sings these songs into the surface of the drums, for the amhalaayt*]

Mike Dangeli: I really want to thank the staff for giving us this space [*pointing at black curtain*]. The reason we came from behind the curtain wasn't for theatrics [*light laugh from audience*]. It's actually because we don't normally keep our ceremonial beings on display, especially when they have so much power. Because they share that symbiotic relationship like my wife was saying, they see what we see, they breathe the same air that we breathe. And so for us, we treat

Writing about Musical Intersubjectivity

Figure 7. Peter Morin speaking to an amhalaayt ancestor as part of Conversations in Indigenous Arts, at the Isabel Bader Centre for the Performing Arts.

them like our young ones. We keep them in the back . . . you wouldn't change your young ones in front of people, you wouldn't feed them . . . you wouldn't have those intimate times with them in front of an audience . . .

Mique'l Dangeli: It's a restorative practice is what we're saying. Our masks have expended so much of their nox nox—their energy—tonight. So when we are not dancing them, we wrap them in blankets and we put them away, to allow them to have that time to regenerate and to restore their energy so that when they come out again, they can have their full strength. And that's why when we walk through museums and we see our nox nox everywhere . . . we want to visit them . . . but at the same time it's so hard to see them there. We would never do that, to just keep them out everywhere!

Of unique importance for this event was the way in which the staff at Agnes and the Art Conservation program enabled not only the use of the ancestor in the performance but its relocation to a performance space that was not within the white walls of the gallery. As Mique'l Dangeli later noted about the performance,

> The amhalaayt was collected from our people (Tsimshian) in the late 1800s and was more than likely received through trade with the Heiltsuk or Kwakwaka'wakw. Since the frontlet is without the rest of

the headdress, we couldn't dance it. Instead we asked the staff of the museum if they could make a temporary mount that would hold it upright so this powerful ceremonial being could be an honored guest and witness to our work in Haudenosaunee and Anishinaabe territory. At the beginning of our performance, we sang the amhalaayt into the room and placed behind it eagle down in the same manner that we do when we dance. As Mike sang, I blew the down so it would spread into the air from the amhalaayt itself as it was meant to do. We addressed this ceremonial being (I prefer not to use the term object or artifact) in our language as we would our Sm'gigyet (Chiefs) and gave it a prominent place among the other witnesses facing us as we shared our oratory, songs, and dances. (Mique'l Dangeli, Instagram note, February 5, 2016)

Dangeli notes that their treatment of this ancestor is no different than how they would treat their chiefs and matriarchs, giving them a place of honor from which they might receive the song-sustenance offered. Indeed, in the middle of their performance Mique'l Dangeli noted, "I wish we had the opportunity to be fed by and to feed our ancestors—our ceremonial beings—outside of plexiglass . . . like this, more often. It's one of the reasons why we sing and dance in museums, regardless of that history, because it's important that they know we acknowledge them, and that we still love them . . . it's just that we're separated." Song in the work done by Morin and the Dangelis is a form of sustenance used to feed ancestors that take material form. It is life-giving and itself has life. It is part of a system of sustenance that represents "being fed by and feeding ancestors" and as such is part of a relationship of mutual well-being. In relation to the queer and Indigenous intersubjective relationships with songs I have discussed, how do we write about the experience of intersubjective encounter, in ethical ways that do not enact violence against such life? To address this question, I turn to writing that seeks to transmit the intimacy and erotics of nonhuman intersubjectivity.

Song's Intimate Touch

> When I go to the opera house, the performance is a physical sex act between my body and the singer's voice-body. When I listen to an opera recording, the erotic experience becomes a private masturbation fantasy.
>
> —Sam Abel, *Opera in the Flesh: Sexuality in Operatic Performance*

Our relationships with nonhuman environmental, musical, and visual subjects (or what Bruno Latour calls "actants") has been the subject of wide-ranging discussion across disciplines, and across the theoretical discourses of posthumanism, new materialism, and nonrepresentational theory. The very titles of Julie Cruikshank's *Do Glaciers Listen?* (2005) and W. J. T. Mitchell's *What Do Pictures Want?* (2005) evidence this focus on nonhuman agency. Less central in these discussions are questions of how writing engages the tactility and affective sensibility of intersubjective encounters, and reconsiders our ethical responsibility to how we treat nonhuman subjects in the forms of description and analysis we use. While there are numerous trajectories we might follow to begin addressing these questions, two writings in particular on the intimate encounter with artistic subjectivity provide a useful starting point for theorizing what I call *sensory-formalist analysis*.

Laura Marks and Suzanne Cusick are two authors who position the intimacy of artistic encounter as central to their work on film and music, respectively, and through their writing enact what Kevin Kopelson calls *critical virtuosity*. As if responding to David Levin's critique, Kopelson notes that virtuosic criticism, is a form of writing that "should give pleasure—to the reader, not the writer" (92–93). Following Kopelson's focus elsewhere on pianism (Kopelson 1996), critical virtuosity is a sensory domain that includes the haptic and kinetic aspects of dexterity, agility, and the potential for suffusion/drenching of space. Marks's and Cusick's writings are critically virtuosic to the extent that they transduce the intersubjective pleasure of touch in writing, seeking "to make the dry words [of writing] retain a trace of the wetness of the encounter" (Marks 2002, x).

Marks's *Touch: Sensuous Theory, Multisensory Media* (2002) differentiates between three kinds of haptic relationships, each of which may be perceived or enacted independently from the other: haptic visuality, haptic images/cinema, and haptic criticism. Marks begins by noting that haptic visuality is a mode of perception where "the eyes themselves function like an organ of touch" (Marks 2002, 2). This mode of looking "tends to rest on the surface of its object rather than to plunge into depth . . . it is a labile, plastic sort of look, more inclined to move, [to linger, or caress as Marks later states] than to focus" (8–9). Moreover, she continues,

> the term haptic *visuality* emphasizes the viewer's inclination to perceive haptically . . . [alternatively,] a work itself may offer haptic *images* that do not invite identification with a figure so much as they encourage a bodily relationship between the viewer and the image. Thus it is less appropriate to speak of the object of a haptic look than to speak of a dynamic subjectivity between looker and image. (3)

Marks's differentiation between haptic *visuality* and haptic *images* allows the two to function independent of one another: we may perceive artistic works haptically that are not intentionally textured as such by their author. Completing Marks's triad of haptic concepts, haptic *criticism* speaks of perception and objects through writing that itself models "touching, not mastering" (xii). Marks contrasts this model of haptic writing with the project of hermeneutic mastery. Haptic writing has "no need to interpret," Marks notes, "only to unfold, to increase the surface area of experience. By staying close to the surface of an event, I hope to trace a connection between the event's material history, the event itself, me, and you" (Marks 2002, xi). Elsewhere, she describes her aim "to move along the surface of the object rather than attempting to penetrate or 'interpret' it, as criticism is usually supposed to do" (xiii). While such distinctions are important for Marks to distinguish haptic writing as distinct from more traditional hermeneutic criticism, to say this writing operates *outside* of interpretation would be inaccurate. The forms of proximity and connection Marks seeks to effect through her writing bring forward another kind of interpretation, one that I would call *sensory-formalist analysis.* In sensory-formalist analysis the writer seeks to extend the form and structure of the listener/viewer/reader's sensory engagement through their writing. It is an analysis of sensory perception intended to chart the effects of the work's "pulsional incidents" upon the body of the listener/viewer/reader to the same level of detail we would find in any other close reading. To be clear, sensory-formalist analysis is not in and of itself intersubjective. Instead, in foregrounding haptic relationships among film, writing, and visuality through an "uncool, nose-against-the-glass-enthusiasm" for film and media works "as tangible and beloved bodies" (Marks 2002, xi), the sensory-formalist analysis that Marks's work takes part in attunes us to touch as a fundamental component of the intersubjective encounter.

Suzanne Cusick's essay "On a Lesbian Relationship with Music: A

Serious Effort Not to Think Straight" joins Marks in giving attention to the intersubjective intimacy with beloved bodies. Cusick describes her experiences of pleasure and power in these relationships as akin to a relationship with an intimate partner:

> If music might be for some of us, or for all of us sometimes, in the position sometimes called "significant other," then one might look for scrambling and shifting roles with it, for funny power relationships with it, moments when it is the lover—that is the active, pleasure-giving partner—and moments when it is the beloved—the partner who somehow receives pleasure or empowerment. And one might find oneself to be acting out all sorts of, well, positions and "sexual" behaviours with this "lover"/ "beloved." (Cusick 1994, 74)

For those of us who feel that our relationships with music and song—and our experiences *within* them—are central to an analysis of the music itself (and admittedly not all of us do), how should we write in a way that responds to these works as friends, lovers, and kin? How do we get at the sense of touch in writing, or convey being touched by sound, following Marks's lead? Cusick's answer to this question is that, because she identifies the music she loves as another woman, "I try to treat her analytically as I would be treated: as a subject who may have things to say that may be totally different than what listeners expect to hear" (Cusick 1994, 76). Cusick's relationship to music as a significant other bears resemblance to Ingrid Monson's (2008) statement that, like individuals, music has many things to say and may not always act consistently. Perhaps most importantly, because Cusick loves the music she discusses as a significant other, she is compelled by a methodological ethics to describe and understand this music through nonessentializing and nonviolent methods:

> By what feels like instinct, the strongest of instincts, I pass quickly over what feel like essentializing strategies (e.g. describing a work as an example of such and such a form, or Schenkerian analysis). I pass almost as quickly over discursively valued strategies (analysis of harmony, tonal structure) to less-valued "sensual" features like texture and timbre. I feel a deep reluctance to engage in what feels like the dismemberment of music's body into the categories of "form," "melody," "rhythm," "harmony." Because, I think, both the essentializing and the dismembering categories feel akin to those violences as they are

committed on the bodies and souls of real women, and because I am being serious when I say I love music, I cannot bear to do those things to a beloved. (Cusick 1994, 77)

I have quoted Cusick at length to demonstrate how, although she disavows the analytic strategies (formal or harmonic analysis) that she feels dismember music, she does not abandon close engagement with elements of music's materiality such as texture and timbre. To this list of sensory-formalist description we might add other material qualities we are put into relationship with including mass, temporality, movement, and proprioception. Although Cusick describes her partnership with music as one of intimacy, the power relationships that we have with music and sound are undeniably diverse and not exclusively positive. Articulating how power and pleasure circulate in the subject–subject relationship between listener and music here necessitates taking into account the varieties of relationships enacted between a specific listener and a specific piece of music.

Spatial Intersubjectivity

Thus far I have considered performative writing by scholars who acknowledge and affirm intersubjective relationships between listener and music. Yet there is a third subject whose presence plays a significant role in reorienting listeners and music in reception and performance: space. Andrew Eisenberg notes that "it is difficult to identify any work of sound studies that does not deal in some way with space, if only by implicitly incorporating epistemological and ontological commitments with respect to the spatiality of sound" (Eisenberg 2015, 195). Materialist analyses have also sought to engage with the influence of space upon performance (Small 1998; LaBelle 2010; Clarke 2005; Eisenberg 2015). Yet approaches to subjectivity that have been extended toward music, pictures, and film have not found similar currency in the theorization of the subjectivity of space in musical experience.[9]

In relation to this book's focus on listening from Indigenous and settler colonial perspectives, Julie Cruikshank's *Do Glaciers Listen?* (2005) is of critical importance as a text that describes the ways that land listens to human subjects. Cruikshank here describes Tlingit peoples' experiences of glaciers' sentience:

glaciers take action and respond to their surroundings. They are sensitive to smells and they listen. They make moral judgments and they punish infractions. Some elders who know them well describe them as both animate (endowed with life) and as animating (giving life to) landscapes they inhabit. (Cruikshank 2005, 3)

Perhaps because of my work in Indigenous arts and positionality as xwélmexw, such understandings of the subjectivity of place (or "animacy" as it is often referred to in anthropological discourse) seem uncontroversial. sxwôxwiyám, or the oral history of Stó:lō people, includes stories of how Xá:ls the Transformer turned people into stone formations across S'ólh Temexw (Stó:lō lands). Our ancestors are the land.

One way to understand the absence of work on spatial subjectivity in musical experience might be to note the ways in which musical performance and atmosphere seem to combine so as to lessen our perception of spatial subjectivity itself. I am here reminded of classical music performance and the darkened concert hall as being nearly synonymous. Despite this perceived integration of music performance with space, countless examples exist where spatial subjectivity imposes upon that of the music, or vice versa. As with the subjectivities we have already considered, I do not take it for granted that individuals naturally apprehend spatial subjectivity, and not all spaces assert subjectivity consistently. A space with "strong character" might still not necessarily be experienced as nonhuman subjectivity. To acknowledge spatial subjectivity means addressing the ways by which space exerts agency, affect, and character beyond the realm of striking aesthetic impact. In certain cases, it may mean experiencing it as a partner, interlocutor, or kin. For the focus of this chapter, it means rising to the occasion of full participation within interactions between other subjectivities including musical and human actors (listeners/performers). In other chapters, the music I will address, though responding to strong affective experience, will not focus on particular encounters with musical and spatial intersubjectivity. This is not because I do not have such experiences but rather because I have not had these particular experiences with the specific music I analyze. Analysis of intersubjective encounter does not proceed from imposing an intersubjective reading upon experience where subject encounter is not felt. While intersubjective encounters may not be frequent for some, they may not occur at all for others, and this may occur for many reasons including the self-censoring listening of settler colonialism that avoids certain kinds of listening experience, and especially ones that would affirm human–nonhuman relationships.

At its core, my discussion of relationships that occur between human and nonhuman musical and spatial subjects seeks to unseat the anthropocentrism of listening. To wrest listening away from its standard conception as a largely human- and animal-centered activity allows us to understand listening as an ecology in which we are not only listening but listened to. The particular importance of this reorientation toward nonhuman vitality, as philosopher Jane Bennett asserts, lies in its potential to "enhance receptivity to the impersonal life that surrounds and infuses us, [and] generate a more subtle awareness of the complicated web of dissonant connections between bodies, and will enable wiser interventions into that ecology" (4). Bennett's book, *Vibrant Matter: A Political Ecology of Things,* provides multiple examples of the vitality and subjectivity of things and through these examples asks that we look again at how we recognize agency and life. For all its richly detailed examinations of the vibrancy of things, Bennett's work falls short of considering the means by which we come to' apprehend vibrancy across sensory domains, and for listening in particular. Bennett's project, to "inspire a greater sense of the extent to which all bodies are kin in the sense of inextricably enmeshed in a dense network of relations," understands that "to harm one section of the web may very well be to harm oneself" (13). Her aim to inspire a greater sense of kinship between human and nonhuman bodies is of course already quite unexceptional within Indigenous communities. The central fact behind much Indigenous environmental activism is premised on this sense of intersubjectivity that recognizes trees, rivers, mountains, and other places, as kin.

As with *Delgamuukw v. the Queen,* part of this activism has unfolded upon the legal stage of the courtroom. Here, Indigenous people have increasingly pushed the Western legal boundaries of nonhuman rights. The Te Urewara region of Aotearoa/New Zealand, a region understood to be an ancestor by the Māori Tūhoe people, was granted personhood status in 2014 and given "all the rights, powers, duties, and liabilities of a legal person" (Government of New Zealand 2017). On March 20, 2017, the New Zealand government enacted legislation recognizing the Whanganui River as a legal person. Māori noted that "To the Whanganui people, the River is their ancestor, and they the river's descendants" (Cheater 2018). Similarly, in 2017 the Ganges and Yamuna Rivers in India were also granted personhood, meaning that "polluting or damaging the rivers is equivalent to harming a person." In these instances and others of what is sometimes referred to as "environmental personhood" (Gordon 2018), Indigenous people have defended the rights of their rivers as ancestors in the Western court system. This has subsequently allowed them to curtail pollution through forcing the recognition of Indigenous ontologies that understand nonhuman entities as being alive and having life.

This work of challenging Western ontologies that delimit the subjectivity of place does not need to happen exclusively within the courts. It is also important for the general public to encounter such challenges that have the potential to reorient how the public might listen to kinships of place, and through this foster a reduction of environmental harm. The event score prior to this chapter, "Event Score for Guest Listening 1," is one such example that also exists as part of a series of site-specific banners installed in outdoor public settings as part of the *Soundings* exhibition (2019-) I have curated with Candice Hopkins (Tlingit). For the inaugural location, at the Agnes Etherington Arts Centre in Kingston, Ontario, this ten-by-fifteen-foot event score was placed on a cement wall in close proximity to many of Queen's University's limestone buildings:

> Limestone hums
>   with audible-inaudible sound of quarry, cut and chisel
> The subfrequency of colonial labour
>   resonates your body
>
> As these walls declare their immovability,
> Listen instead to the seepage of water through stone
>
> As these walls declare their necessary structure
> Listen instead to the singe and sear of their structures burn down
>
> As these structures declare themselves walls
> Hear these stones, as still the land

In each location that the exhibition travels to, this score is reworked to engage with the built environment and Indigenous territory of the location it is situated in. In Kingston, the first capital of Canada, with its colonial limestone architecture, the score asks viewers quite literally to consider their relationship to the foundations of colonization. The score calls viewers to reassess how they listen to place, but also to the subjectivity of the nonhuman entity called limestone that is understood by Haudenosaunee and Anishinaabe people as having life and existence as an ancestor. This particular instance of reconsidering spatial subjectivity is situated in the location (and ideally upon the very walls) that it addresses. Other spatializations about our experience of musical and nonhuman subjectivity might alternatively begin from the question of what it would mean to "write" using physical and material forms of spaces themselves. This approach bears some relation to David Levin's theorization of dramaturgy and operatic staging as an interpretive "reading" of opera. In *Unsettling Opera,* Levin argues that operatic stagings, and operatic adaptations that are sometimes referred to as *regietheatre,* or "director's theatre," should more properly be understood as "readings" of opera. And yet, to characterize these as "readings" downplays the way in which such stagings might be considered "writings" or "rewritings" in themselves. To call stagings writings would be anathema within the white supremacy of operatic production and classical music programming that sacralize the authorial intent of the composer-genius's "masterwork" and consequently foreclose against critical interpretation through performance. This is indeed one, if not *the* central challenge in defining decolonial approaches to Western art music performance—to move beyond simply allowing space for Indigenous presence alongside the usual program of classical and operatic work, and toward new stagings of such work that make visible structures of settler colonialism and white supremacy that underpin art music's presentation and composition. To do so moves the work of classical music decolonization off the page and into other spaces for public engagement.

Material and Spatial Forms of Writing

Apposite methodology, as a methodology for writing and conveying intersubjective experience (as one among many forms of decolonizing the ontology of classical music experience), seeks to reflect the time and terms of intersubjectivity. How might this methodology spatialize a writing practice beyond the page, and within other artistic forms? One answer to this question would be to expand music scholarship toward applied forms of research-creation and dramaturgy. There is no reason why music scholars should not work with musicians to consider how the wide range of research that we do might be applied to twenty-first-century performance practices, that include staging ideas about the music and musical experience we write about. There is no reason why music scholars should not work collaboratively with scenographers, installation artists, architects, with collaborators from other disciplines in the humanities and sciences, and with Indigenous and other racialized communities to think about spatializing and materializing our questions about, and readings of, music as part of the musical event itself. There is no reason why music scholars should not consider the possibilities for transposing our analyses from the page to the concert hall, the gallery, the cinema, and site-specific contexts.

I can hear the voices of music colleagues asking: at what point does this stretch music scholarship too far from what is recognizable as the disciplines of musicology, music theory, and ethnomusicology? This question is often leveled against disciplinary change that is seen as diluting "disciplinary rigor" and standards. Yet, as I have been arguing, performative forms of scholarship do not necessarily eschew standards of disciplinary rigor; instead, they unsettle the normative scholarly formats whose ideological underpinnings we typically ignore. Here in particular, research-creation forms for conveying knowledge about music extend music subdisciplines into the Indigenous forms of conveying knowledge mentioned earlier in this chapter; song, oration, story, and dance and integrations of these are not simply primary forms for conveying knowledge; their forms allow us to uphold Indigenous epistemic values (and refuse epistemic violence of other forms). Additionally, we might remember that the choice of form our work takes is always a choice, whether we think of it this way or not. The formal and structural elements that we often imagine to merely frame the conveyance of our writing (language, cadence, sentence structure) are far from neutral aesthetically or politically. The choices we make for framing our scholarship and writing are more than signs that *contribute* to our perception of the ideas, histories, and knowledge we share; they are signs that *constitute* it. By recognizing this fact we might also recognize that there is a responsibility to aesthetically shape the signification of those signs that we would normally consider nonsignifying elements. When translating our experience of music in writing, we do not often allow the language of that music we encounter to transform the way we write about that music. Put more eloquently by Walter Benjamin: "The basic error of the translator is that he preserves the state in which his own language happens to be instead of allowing his language to be powerfully affected by the foreign tongue" (Benjamin 1996, 262). Apposite methodology demands that we understand writing as a methodology for understanding the subjects and intersubjectivities we study. As one form of apposite methodology, arts practice–based "writing" prompts us to further consider before beginning any scholarly project: what space, form, or media is apposite to the information I want to convey about the work? What language should I use? How should I spatialize this experience of intersubjectivity?

Yet there are formidable challenges in adopting apposite reorientation of scholarship. Primary among these is the learning of new languages and syntax—the craft—of whatever forms this writing is to take. This holds both for the readers of those languages and for the writer. In learning to read practice-based musicologies that emerge from apposite methodology, the reader must not only "read" for meaning but for sonic, material, and kinaesthetic import, and the "carnal stereophany" (Barthes 1975) of knowledge. Such reading challenges the assumption that the exclusive intention of text is to explicate meaning (Rancière 1991). As with most forms of performative writing and research-creation, the reader is not simply served up knowledge on a plate, but is put to work in preparing the meal. This work refuses hungry modes of perception and demands relationship of co-constituting meaning. Readers must equally be open to parsing a variety of aesthetic strategies that may frustrate the impulse for clear explanation. Those using apposite methodology to engage in performative writing or research-creation will most likely entertain some level of deliberate opacity in their aesthetics; they will ask readers to entertain the element of play, and they will take as a given that readers do not presume these choices to be *merely* stylistic.

It is equally challenging to learn to use apposite methodologies in ways that result in compelling performative writing and research-creation. It is not simply a matter of deciding to write a poem, orate, or develop an immersive installation. As with any form of writing, one needs to develop the skills and technique of such forms. The same could be said for entering into another disciplinary discourse or new language. Performative writing and research-creation practices that strike readers/spectators as precious, self-indulgent, "trendy," or "clever" (Pollock 1998, 65)—rather than provoking that disturbance of the ineffable encountered in the performance experience itself—might be understood as the result of insufficient time spent immersed in learning the craft of that artistic medium. It would come as no surprise that a poem written by a musicologist (or scholar in any other discipline) who has not written poetry before might convey a facile or naïve quality. In recognition of this fact, this book incorporates relatively few poetic interludes, event scores, and performative writing throughout, rather than relying on these for its overall form. To do so would be presumptuous for my current stage of expertise and craft that I continue to refine.

Conclusion

This chapter has emphasized the work of non-Indigenous writers who seek forms of writing otherwise to convey sensory experience about the intersubjective relations between sound, song, listener, and space. An Indigenous reader and reviewer of this book before publication noted, "I came away from this chapter feeling like I had been returned to graduate school seminars where we discussed someone else's way of understanding the world." It is likely bad form to conclude a chapter with a less-than-positive review of one's work, but I do so here in order to situate this chapter within the context of citational practice and epistemic power relations that have not only continued to be a central debate in critical Indigenous studies and Indigenous resurgence theory, but also in black, feminist, queer, Latinx, and in other disciplines where Indigenous scholars and scholars of color have to justify their very presence. In 2020 there remains a continuing pedagogical prevalence across disciplines for historical, theoretical, and methodological surveys to avoid even raising questions around racist, setter colonial, and heteropatriarchal foundations of disciplinary values and histories. Even worse, the experience of being in a class ostensibly focused on Indigenous perspectives where there is little if any actual writing or work by Indigenous people has been a common experience for many Indigenous scholars, myself included. Upon first reading the statement above I was returned to my own memories of being in such seminars, and moreover, of leaving a music composition program at the university I was enrolled in as an undergraduate student in the 1990s. In that instance, the context of education was one wherein musical exoticism was discussed as positive intercultural influence without any sense of the appropriative and racist underpinning of this exoticism. These educational experiences for Indigenous people are ones in which Western theory and history have been wielded against us as part of a descriptive stultification and "explicative order" (Rancière 1991) that maintains a Western epistemological hierarchy and perpetuates epistemic injustice (Fricker 2009).[10] It is an understatement, in the intergenerational legacy of the Indian residential schools and Indian boarding schools, to say that Indigenous people remain triggered by "education," given that such systems of supposed education have been used as forms of violence intended to eradicate Indigenous epistemologies, languages, and forms of perception. Put most simply, writing *about* rather than *by* Indigenous people both actively dispossesses knowledge from Indigenous knowledge holders in our communities, and naturalizes Indigenous knowledge resource extraction as simply "knowledge mobilization" and dissemination. To combat this continued knowledge extraction, Indigenous scholars have adopted practices of citational politics that center our knowledge by privileging Indigenous writers and knowledge keepers in our work.

This critique of *Hungry Listening* by an Indigenous reader was a call to reexamine the intersectional aim of the chapter—to understand how performative, feminist, and queer writing in particular might provide models for conveying sensory experiences of music in ways that do not blunt such experience through language and form that unintentionally quiets and flattens musical life. In considering this critique, I asked myself why this chapter did not feel, as I wrote it, like a form of perpetuating Western theoretical privilege (or worse, epistemic violence). Foundational debates in Indigenous studies have focused on the imperative for Indigenous writing and theorization to focus on nation- and community-specific knowledge systems rather than drawing relationships between Western and Indigenous knowledge. These debates have continued to have relevance in the more recent work of Indigenous resurgence.[11] But to see Indigenous and Western theoretical discourses as mutually exclusive and to refuse all that is not essentially Indigenous is to impoverish our work as Indigenous writers and scholars, not to mention to assume that we do not make critical choices and repurposings of non-Indigenous theory in ways similar to how we have always repurposed non-Indigenous tools to advance our work. In the case of the chapter you are currently reading, I propose that intersectional relationships between nonnormative forms of writing (performative, feminist, and queer) provide other tools that we as Indigenous scholars can use in privileging musical life and subjectivity.

It is far from unique for Indigenous writers to draw extensively upon non-Indigenous theoretical perspectives, engage directly with the canon of Western theory (Coulthard 2014b; Byrd 2011; Byrd and Rothberg 2011), and cogently articulate how transnational (Warrior 2009) and theoretically promiscuous approaches (A. Simpson and Smith 2014) might benefit Indigenous people. Far less work, however, has been done on the ways in which *structural* choices made in writing and creative practice by Indigenous people express Indigenous logics regardless of the degree to which they are made explicit as such. I am guided here by the artistic and writing practices of artist Tanya Lukin Linklater (Alutiiq) and scholar Eve Tuck (Unangax̂) in particular, who, in my reading of their work, bring Indigenous and non-Indigenous language, theories, and gestures into new relationships through structural logics that are often not easily legible or even explicitly recognizable as Indigenous. The structures and aesthetic choices that Tuck and Lukin Linklater use in their writing and artistic practices do not participate in the Western imperative to explicate their Indigeneity. While each brings Indigenous and non-Indigenous voices and discourses into relationship through forms (the glossary, epistolary, contemporary dance) and aesthetic structural choices that are centrally grounded within their own Indigenous experience (whether made explicit or not), these exist outside of the legibly Indigenous, an "Indigenous essentialism," or what we might otherwise call Indigenous narratocracy (Panagia 2009). This chapter has followed a similar path of intersectional relationship that is not mutually exclusive of resurgence but rather seeks to walk alongside it. As with my understanding of Linklater and Tuck's work, my work is guided by Indigenous structural logics that are purely my own as a xwélmexw thinker and writer and that are irreducible to essentially Stó:lō values while being guided by these at the same time. To Indigenous readers who continue to read, my hope is that you might find some use in the intersections between these perspectives, or repurpose something presented here as a tool again for your own use.

Figure 8. Still from the video *Report*. Copyright 2015 by Raven Chacon.

XWÉLALÀ:M, RAVEN CHACON'S *REPORT*

I.

let's clear the air:
listening to land is not a pristine act
that finds the quiet wild
not the breeze stirring leaves,
not the falling snow as your heart beats
not the clairaudience[1]
that filters out all but buzzing insect and rustling reed
that filters sound, that is, from land

hear the word sound   scape
built upon the word landscape—
its colonial gaze, its hungry designs
—separating heartbeat from heart
hear the word sound   scape
collect the resonance of lands, waterways, skies,
collect whispered breath and life that dwells therein

hear
síwéltset te tèmèxw
síwéltset te shxwelí
the sounds of this land are not resources
nor messages to be deciphered for danger and delight,
for xwelítem mining sound from site
to listen without extraction, selchí:meleqel
what does this sound like?

not as affective collection, selchí:meleqel
what does this sound like?
what does this report do
to clear the air,
to let us hear
what does this do
as each gunshot disquiets segregate sense
now, again, again
what does this do—
this orchestration of weapons,
of varying calibers
scored for precision
—to the settled ear

what else does gunshot reverberate
leave behind
through muzzle blast
as the crack, sound-shock
of bullet from barrel
breaks upon this place
sound-marks the listening land
while here inside this room
the firing line
together charges the body
again to hear

II.

xwlálám, to witness
xwlálám, to listen
shxwelméxwelh attention, xwélalà:m listening+witnessing
refuses listening without limit
ravenous gathering of murmur and hum
to line the shelves with sense content
xwélalà:m remembers our history
xwélalà:m, éy kws hákw'elestset te s'í:wes te siyolexwálh
xwélalà:m, síwél
pricking ears with sense

finds ways to listen not driven by use,
not by accumulative desire
xwélalà:m, listening beyond insular sense,
toward téméxw shxwelí,
the mountains, the plants, the water,
to practice this sense connects us
to everything
around us
our ancestors
as well as ancestors transformed
into those mountains.[2]
xwélalà:m, a practiced attention
sets a crisis for listening's settled state
to become uncertain of what listening is
xwélalà:m, the willful act
to kick colonial listening habits,
to shift structures of feeling
xwlálámethò:m
to remember relationality
you are listened to by the land

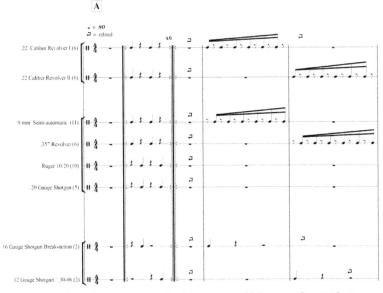

Figure 9. Page 1, from the score *Report* (for firearm ensemble), copyright 2001 by Raven Chacon, Dineyazhe Music (ASCAP).

III.

me stáléqep
eháléqep
tlesu th'átsem kw'el q'ô:l

a distant sound comes
faint and carried by the air,
then rings in my ear

Figure 10. Still from the video *Report,* copyright 2015 by Raven Chacon.

THREE
CONTEMPORARY ENCOUNTERS BETWEEN INDIGENOUS AND EARLY MUSIC

> Imagine a nativity scene in which the chanting angels are the singers
> of the chronologically and geographically distant 12th century
> Notre Dame Cathedral, while the shepherds are the natives of arctic
> Canada, the Inuit. This is the image which has inspired *Viderunt
> Omnes*, a utopian image perhaps, but then the historical interaction
> between the Europeans and the arctic natives of North America has
> been for the most part one of cooperation, not confrontation, unlike
> the relationship between the Europeans and the more southern
> natives of the American continent . . .
>
> —Christos Hatzis, *Viderunt Omnes*

At the turn of the millennium, on December 31, 1999, close to midnight, Christos Hatzis's electroacoustic composition *Viderunt Omnes* was broadcast across the fifty-six nations (including North America and Australia) who were members of the European Broadcasting Union. Hatzis's work combined a number of prerecorded sources: a recording of the Toronto Consort performing Pérotin's twelfth-century organum *Viderunt Omnes*; a recording made in Iqaluit, Baffin Island, of Inuit throat singers Angela Atagootak and Pauline Kyak; and recordings of "other distinctively 'Canadian' sounds, such as the sounds of the loons" (Hatzis, n.d.). That Canada inaugurated the turn of the millennium sonically with a composition that integrated loon calls, Inuit throat singing, and a twelfth-century organum might give one pause. That such a striking convergence of pre-1750 European art music (often referred to as "early music") and First Nations and Inuit cultural practices has taken place with increasing frequency in Canada in the twenty-first century is yet more unusual.[1] As the following timeline demonstrates,

114 Contemporary Encounters

however, these encounters evince an interest by First Nations, Inuit, and settler composers alike to return to and reconsider the sound worlds of first contact:

- March 18, 2001, Sty-wet-tan Longhouse, xʷməθkʷəy̓əm lands, University of British Columbia; and March 19, 2001, Squamish Nation Recreation Centre. Spakwus Slolem, the Sḵwx̱wú7mesh Nation Eagle Song Dancers share the stage with the Pacific Baroque Orchestra and baroque dancers Paige Whitley-Bauguess and Thomas Baird.

- 2003 to 2007 (various dates) and March 2014, across the United States and Canada, Macau, Hong Kong, and China. The Tafelmusik Baroque Ensemble presents a concert titled *The Four Seasons: A Cycle of the Sun,* a project that adapts Antonio Vivaldi's Concerto No. 4, "L'inverno," from *The Four Seasons,* to include Inuit throat singers Sylvia Cloutier and June Shappa of the group Aqsarniit, Jean Lamon playing violin, Aruna Narayan playing the Indian sarangi, and Wen Zhao playing the Chinese pipa.

- March 31, 2005, Canadian Broadcasting Corporation (CBC) Television's *Opening Night* broadcast. The documentary *The Four Seasons Mosaic* premieres. It chronicles the development of Tafelmusik's *The Four Seasons: A Cycle of the Sun* and "takes viewers on a world tour of European, Inuit, Chinese, and South Asian music traditions" (Tafelmusik 2007). It is subsequently broadcast internationally on BBC, PBS, TV5, and ARTV and is released commercially as a DVD in 2007 on the Analekta label.

- November 3–11, 2008, the Smithsonian National Museum of American Indian, Montgomery College and University of Maryland. Mohawk cellist and composer Dawn Avery performs *Both Worlds.* This piece places the Sarabande from J. S. Bach's Suite No. 5 for cello in C Minor, BWV 101, alongside an improvised vocal line sung in a traditional Mohawk falsetto style and accompanied by Buffalo drum. The work is performed by Avery and Steven Alvarez (Mescalero Apache, Yaqui, Upper Tanana Athabascan).

- March 13–14, 2010, Église du Précieux-Sang, Winnipeg. A concert titled *Medieval Inuit* is presented by Camerata Nova, a choral ensemble specializing in the performance of Renaissance music. At this concert throat singers Madeleine Allakariallak and Sylvia Cloutier present songs passed down from elders Elisapie Ootova and the late Minnie

Allakariallak, Madeleine's grandmother. The concert brings Nordic folksongs and art music together with Inuit throat singing and drum songs to stage an imagined historical encounter between the Vikings and the Dorset peoples.

- April 8–24, 2010, Theatre Passe Muraille, Toronto. Native Earth Performing Arts Inc. and An Indie(n) Rights Reserve coproduce *Giiwedin,* an opera co-composed by Spy Dénommé-Welch (Anishinaabe) and Catherine Magowan. The opera follows an Anishinaabe woman's struggle to protect her ancestral land in the Temiskaming area of northeastern Ontario from railway expansion. The work is written largely in a neo-Baroque style and integrates Anishinaabe song and references to French Canadian folksong.

- May 15, 2010, Glenn Gould Studio, Toronto. The Aradia Baroque Ensemble and Kwagiulth mezzo-soprano Marion Newman present *Thunderbird,* a concert that features performances of Kwagiulth songs, dances, and stories in alternation with Baroque works for chamber ensemble based on supernatural themes. The concert is restaged at the Music Gallery in Toronto on June 17, 2015, with Aradia Ensemble, and on May 12, 2017, with Thirteen Strings Chamber Orchestra in Ottawa.

- March 7, 2015. The UCLA Early Music Ensemble performs "Imagining the New World," a concert organized by ethnomusicologist Ryan Koons and professor and director of the Early Music Ensemble Elizabeth LeGuin. The program explored "repertoire from interactions between North and South American Native Americans and Europeans during the colonial era. Included were the first transcriptions and settings of Native American music in existence, period Indigenous Christian liturgical music by Indigenous composers, and European baroque operas with Native American characters and themes" (UCLA 2015).

- February 3–4, 2017. *Kanatha/Canada: First Encounters* is produced by the Toronto Consort. In its promotional materials, the organizers note that the concert seeks to "imagine new musical encounters between European and aboriginal nations" and features Canadian composer John Beckwith's *Wendake/Huronia* and "music from the early colonists." The concert also includes "First Nations performers Marilyn George, Shirley Hay, with Wolastoqey singer Jeremy Dutcher, and special guest, Wendat Traditional Knowledge Keeper Georges Sioui" (Toronto Consort 2016).

At first listening, early music and Indigenous music aesthetics might seem to share little common musical ground. They cannot be said to have related social functions either in the past or present; nor would we understand them to address similar listening communities. Yet despite their difference, Indigenous composers and non-Indigenous composers and ensembles have found it productive to bring these musics together. This has sometimes happened for the simple reason that composers and ensembles have understood them as the music of first encounter. Yet this conceit falls short given the fact that the music that would actually be played by crew members of Cartier's, Cook's, or Esteban José Martínez's voyages (or by the on-land company of Simon Fraser and Sir Alexander Mackenzie) would not likely be the refined music heard in these collaborations. Instead, non-Indigenous musicians would more likely have shared folk music of the time, and in the case of the Nuu-chah-nulth people to be discussed later in this chapter, the songs of first encounter were welcome songs. Despite the reality of music shared in historical encounters, this chapter seeks to understand what the imagined re-encounter of these sound worlds holds for composers and ensembles who choose to place them alongside one another or to integrate them. More specifically, I will ask to what extent are these musical encounters heard as symbolic expressions of reconciliation. Do they offer models of reconciliation through their structures, in both their limitations and potential? To what extent, that is, might we perceive the *physical* encounters occurring within the collaborative process and performance event, and hear the *aesthetic* encounters taking place within the meeting of musical forms, to model or enact various structures of reconciliation?

Since Canada's Truth and Reconciliation Commission on the Indian Residential Schools (TRC) was officially established in 2008, the aims, extent, processes, and politics of what "reconciliation" means has been a particular subject of scrutiny by Indigenous scholars, artists, and community members (Alfred 2009; Younging, Dewar, and DeGagné 2009; Corntassel, Chaw-win-is, and T'lakwadzi 2009; Robinson and Martin 2016).[2] Critical engagement with what the word "reconciliation" and its processes mean has been offered by those who challenge its Western foundations, its assumption that there was, in fact, a period of good relations to begin with that might be returned to, and its focus on symbolic rather than material restitution including the return of land (Robinson and Martin 2016).[3] During the five years that the TRC took place, a wide variety of symbolic gestures occurred, many of which were focalized through artistic practice.[4] While some initiatives were a direct outcome of the TRC, taking place at national and regional events, others were supported by initiatives such as the Canada Council for the Arts'{Re} conciliation program (2015–2017). Still others have been initiated by Indigenous artists and communities at arms-length from state funding bodies. As with reconciliation's tendency to elide dissensus (Rancière 2010) through forms of coming together to resolve difference, inclusionary performance between Indigenous artists and Western classical music ensembles and composers has similarly emphasized seamless integration that in more politicized terms models forms of assimilation rather than rough aggregates of difference and sovereignty. Each of this chapter's case studies examine what politics of aesthetics this body of inclusionary and Indigenous+early music models, particularly given its topical orientation to colonial history and the imaginary of first contact.

To examine the politics of aesthetics in these works, the chapter proceeds by questioning how we listen to the sounds of interaction, integration, and negotiation taking place within inclusionary music's aesthetic structures and forms, and the ideological underpinnings expressed through genre. By situating these forms of meeting within a political framework, I seek to respond to Geoffrey Baker's critique of the very term "encounter" to describe colonial meeting. In the context of writing about music and colonial Latin America, the term "encounter," says Baker, can depoliticize the "great imbalances of power between colonizers, colonized, and imported slaves, and by extremes of domination, suffering, deprivation, and violence. Many musical developments in the New World thus took place in contexts that were far less neutral than the word 'encounter.'" Consequently, "encounter" is here used as a placeholder that will gain greater precision through interrogation of the specific power dynamics in the meetings each musical work or performance engenders. Examining a range of relationships from the extractive impulse of integration to dissensual agonism, the chapter

118   Contemporary Encounters

assesses the extent to which inclusionary music and Indigenous+art music make audible the rough edges of difference.

As the first of three chapters that feature close listenings of particular works, this chapter seeks to render inclusionary music's easily consumable forms of recognition and difference less palatable. This chapter and those that follow offer unpalatable and indigestible accounts intended to suspend hungry listening's starving desire to hear Indigenous participation in art music as musical forms of multicultural enrichment or conciliatory resolution.

Colonial and Contemporary Encounters

In examining the dramatic rise in collaboration between early music ensembles and Indigenous performers, it is important to understand two contexts: the historical context of encounter and the present-day context of métissage. Turning to the context of historical musical encounter provides a foundation for understanding the terms and stakes of structural encounter. Two of the earliest musical encounters between colonizers and Indigenous people—Marc Lescarbot's adaptation of a Mi'kmaw song and Captain James Cook's physical encounter with the Nuu-chah-nulth people upon his arrival in Yuquot—here provide a starting point. Turning to the contemporary context of métissage in Canada, we are better able to understand a current, and particularly problematic social and political context of recognition in Canada that undercuts Indigenous sovereignty through inclusion. To exemplify this second context of contemporary métissage, we will turn to John Ralston Saul's writing about Canada as a nation founded on the values of Indigenous people and the claim he derives from this, that "Canada is a Métis nation."

In 1606 Marc Lescarbot transcribed a Mi'kmaq song that exists as one of the first extant copies of Indigenous music to be collected in Canada. Thirty years after this in Mi'kmaq territory on the east coast of Canada in 1636, Gabriel Sagard-Théodat arranged Lescarbot's transcription into a four-voice homophonic setting. Olivia Bloechl has written that Sagard-Théodat's setting "represent[s] a more radical process of transformation than [Lescarbot's] earlier monophonic transcriptions." She continues, "the borrowed melodies quoted in the body of Sagard's

Histoire du Canada were already twice removed from Mi'kmaq . . . performance worlds, and the arrangements in the *Histoire du Canada* further distanced the transcriptions from their sources. The arranger altered the melodies by adding rhythms, and he also changed certain pitches, presumably to accommodate the new harmonies" (Bloechl 2005, 367). This transcription by Lescarbot and subsequent composition by Sagard provide what is arguably the first musical representations of First Nations culture to Europe. Bloechl notes, "The *Histoire du Canada*'s metamorphosis of the Mi'kmaq . . . transcriptions into austere harmonized settings was part of the same impulse toward musical reform and, as a result, profound cultural transformation" (372). We can note this relationship of "musical reform" to our previous discussion on the reform of Indigenous listening. Yet the harmonized settings are also consistent with what is to become a common practice in the inclusion of Indigenous voices and musicians into Western composition: the imposition of Western temporality through "clock-defined time," regimented through time signatures and meter, and the application of capitalist teleology upon the sounds (as well as peoples, voices, and bodies) of the New World. We will return to the implications of these changes later in this chapter and elsewhere in the book, but for now it is important to note this originary instance. As the "New World's" first example of appropriation of Indigenous song, Sagard-Théodat's adaptation and Lescarbot's transcription situate extractivism as a foundational aspect of Canadian musical identity. Contemporary musical extractivism is, then, unremarkable as merely an extension of this historical moment.

Perhaps more remarkable as an example of musical contact is the Nuu-chah-nulth meeting with James Cook and his crew in Yuqot (now named Friendly Cove, Nootka Sound) in Nuu-chah-nulth territory on the west coast of Canada over a century later. Writing in his journal while aboard Cook's 1778 voyage to Nootka Sound, Lieutenant James King gives an account of "musical exchange," a musical dialogue that precedes any attempt by Cook's crew to communicate with the Nuu-chah-nulth through language:

> The greatest number of the Canoes remained in a cluster around us til ten O'clock, & as they had no arms, & appeared very friendly, we did not care how long they staid to entertain themselves, & perhaps us: a man repeated a few words in tune, & regulated the meaning by beating

against the Canoe sides, after which they all joined in a song, that was by no means unpleasant to the Ear . . . A young man with a remarkable soft voice after ward sung by himself, but he ended so suddenly & unexpectedly, which being accompanied by a peculiar gesture, made us all laugh, & he finding that we were not ill pleased repeated his song several times . . . As they were now very attentive & quiet in list'ning to their diversions, we judg'd they might like our musick, & we ordered the Fife & drum to lay a tune; these were the only people we had seen that ever paid the smallest attention to those or any of our musical Instruments, if we except the drum, & that only I suppose from its noise & resemblance to their own drums; they observed the profoundest silence, & we were sorry that the dark hindered our seeing the effect of this musick on their countenances. Not to be outdone in politeness they gave us another song, & we then entertained them with French horns, to which they were equally attentive, but have us no more songs in return, & soon after went away, excepting a few boats that kept paddling around us all that night. (Beaglehole 1967, 1394–95)

King's perception of the decorum of the moment, the gestures of "politeness" and light entertainment in the encounter, are amusing. However, the musical encounter is also remarkable for the way that both parties engage in sustained listening to the other and for the reciprocity of

Figure 11. Nuu-chah-nulth canoe, drawn by John Webber, April 1778. Courtesy of a private Australian collection.

response in their exchange of gestures and music. It is not a leap of logic to describe this meeting as one of nation-to-nation diplomacy. While these two models of extractive integration and of exchange ground our discussion of encounter in colonial history, a more complete picture requires addressing the the concept of métissage and the extractivism it engenders through a politics of recognition.

In *A Fair Country: Telling Truths about Canada* (2008), philosopher and public intellectual John Ralston Saul argues that Canada is "a Métis nation" and in doing so reinforces the recognition and inclusion of First Peoples' cultural practices as central to the exceptionalism of Canadian national identity. Saul declares that Canada's national identity and core multicultural values are founded upon First Nations principles of governance, and he claims that Canadians have internalized such principles over centuries of interaction with First Peoples. He redefines Canada's founding multicultural principles as based upon First Nations concepts of inclusion and the "ever-widening circle." When he "digs around in the roots of how we [Canadians] imagine ourselves," what he finds is "deeply aboriginal" (Saul 2008, 3). Continuing this litany of claims to the essential métissage of Canadian identity, Saul cites celebrated Canadian novelist Guy Vanderhaeghe, who states, "We have a subconscious Métis mind" (quoted in Saul 2008, 9). Most emphatically, Saul declares in the very first sentence of *A Fair Country,* "We are a Métis civilization" (3).

Saul uses "we" and "our" in these instances to refer to all Canadians, while his use of "Métis" co-opts the distinct cultural identity of the Métis as shorthand for "multicultural." *A Fair Country* here celebrates First Peoples and positions our cultural values at the center of what it means to be Canadian. Ultimately, Saul claims, "the fundamental influence of Aboriginals on our civilization is revealed in the ease with which we have adopted their art as an expression of ourselves" (16). It is apparent from Saul's litany of Indigenous foundations to Canadian identity that he feels no uneasiness with this adoption, but rather pride.

Saul's argument is, of course, another index of the present moment in Canada where one strand of reconciliation takes part in a representational politics aimed at increasing Indigenity across state-funded institutions. Representational inclusion of Indigenous content, peoples, and art is understood as central to the process of redressing the history of colonization and its impact on First Peoples in Canada. Yet viewed through the framework advanced by Glen Coulthard, this representational politics claims First Nations, Inuit, and Métis values for their contribution toward the state, as with Saul's revisionist narrative of Canadian national identity. In its primary address to the Canadian public, *A Fair Country* asks settler Canadians to recognize the historical elision of First Peoples in Canada's history, through advancing a nationalist narrative that insists on the use of First Nations principles to reconceptualize *Canadian* identity. Saul here supports his claim of the deep influence of First Nations' principles on Canadian culture by citing principles such as the Mohawk concept of tewatutowie ("sovereignty as harmony through balanced relationships") and the Cree concepts of witaskewin ("people of different nations living together") and miyowicaytowin ("happy, respectful relationships"). But his words (or rather the Mohawk and Cree words he uses) speak instead to the ease with which such concepts might be mobilized for Canadian nation building under the sign of multicultural enrichment. Indeed, Saul's citations provide only a cursory explanation of how these words embody Cree and Mohawk values and cosmologies. This remythologizing of Indigenous culture as the foundation of Canadian identity takes part in a larger history of "love and theft" (Lott 1993) that undergirds the multicultural extractivist complex at the heart of Canadian exceptionalism. Its inclusionary framework—set out by Saul but long practiced through nationalist forms of recognition—conscripts Indigenous worldviews as contributions that Indigenous people have freely given to the enrichment of the state.[5]

A Taxonomy of Musical Encounter

I began with an extended historical context of encounter and the contemporary context of Saul's métissage for the purpose of defining a partial taxonomy for examining the structures of inclusionary music and Indigenous+art music. This taxonomy includes four models. The first is *integration*, following the examples of Gabriel Sagard-Théodat's *Haloet* and Saul's narrative of métissage; the second is *nation-to-nation music trading and reciprocal presentation*, following the example of Captain James Cook's encounter with the Nuu-chah-nulth. To these two models I add a third, a model that *combines* the two modes of encounter, enacting a progression that begins with extended musical trading and concludes with a single composition that demonstrates integration. Finally, a fourth model avoids integration in favor of structures that allow for a coexistence of difference that refuses integration. In focusing on these four models, my aim is not to provide a compressive accounting of structures of musical encounter. Instead, I use this taxonomy to illustrate hungry listening's depoliticization of musical encounter as the simple coming together of difference. To do this necessitates paying particular attention to the ways in which First Nations and Inuit musical self-determination is undercut through compositional structures of recognition and inclusion, and, alternately, attending to the structures through which Indigenous musicians claim musical sovereignty. The next three chapters will not only consider how musical structures follow patterns of integration and trade, they will detail how these models of encounter influence concert presentation and the physical encounters that occur between the actors in these collaborations: instrumentalists, singers, and composers.

I begin this examination of categories of musical encounter with two works that fall within the model of *integration*: *Giiwedin* and *Viderunt Omnes*. I follow this by addressing an example that represents most fully the category of musical *nation-to-nation trade and presentation*: a collaboration between the Pacific Baroque Orchestra and Spakwus Slolem. I subsequently turn to a concert that bridges these two models to enact a progression from presentation toward integration: Tafelmusik's DVD *The Four Seasons Mosaic*.[6] While this third model of progression might be understood as a positive framework for learning and building trust over time, I will show how its integrationist end goal continues to subsume Indigenous values on the terms of Western art music. To conclude, I discuss Mohawk cellist and composer Dawn Avery's "Sarabande," which eschews all three models and refuses integrative listening.

Integration: *Giiwedin* and *Viderunt Omnes*

In speaking of the encounters between actors in any Indigenous+art music or inclusionary performance, the tendency is to turn first toward those who occupy the space of the stage rather than the space between performers and audience. Yet, for all performance there is what might be called an accountability of form to its imagined public. In generic terms, the word "experimental" is sometimes appended to performance to signal that this accountability might be under question. In financial terms, the very programming of performance literally takes part in performance accounting (if not accountability); those works that are not accountable to the desires and expectations of the audience whom the arts organization seeks to reach (or maintain) are less likely to be programmed. To better understand this space between composer and audience, between intention and reception, I ask "to whom are *Giiwedin* and *Viderunt Omnes* accountable?" This question seeks to trace how these works' aesthetic choices address their respective audiences, and how I, as a member of these audiences, am alternately moved, alienated, or left cold by their address. To trace relationships of accountability toward imagined audiences and centralize my own particular reception of these works runs contrary to musicology's largely unspoken value of generalizability, where to be valuable as musical knowledge experience needs to be generalizable beyond the writer herself. In contrast with this value, my approach within this chapter and book is unapologetically singular in its refusal to extrapolate experience to generalized reception. Reception at the level of the individual does not discount the relevance of particular experience to a wider audience that does not hold similar experience as equally as it refuses the assertion of speaking for "the audience" or "a community."[7]

Notwithstanding the similar ways in which these works integrate Indigenous music and history within an early music aesthetic, the audiences these works address, and the compositional approaches they take, are significantly different. Whereas Christos Hatzis's *Viderunt Omnes* voices a millennial proclamation of Canadian identity to a global radio audience, Spy Dénommé-Welch and Catherine Magowan's *Giiwedin* addresses a local community of largely non–opera specialists by employing a musical language largely unrelated to the Classical- and Romantic-era genres that dominate the operatic canon, and to the dissonant and post-tonal language of much contemporary classical and new music. As my own reception of this work demonstrates, however, audiences are far from the cohesive entities they are imagined to be or feel like;[8] they are composed of multiple overlapping communities and of individuals who may disidentify with the primary audience to which programming organizations may consider themselves accountable. For both *Giiwedin* and *Viderunt Omnes,* I will attempt to tease out the multiplicity of these relationships between what could be called the organization's "primary audience"—the audience to which a musical ensemble considers itself accountable—and the individual, in this case myself, who may feel alienated from or identify with the values of the "primary audience" addressee. Speaking of a "primary audience" is admittedly problematic and quickly becomes generalizing in any attempt to establish a set of values or constitution. This notwithstanding, it is useful to engage with the imagined audiences that music organizations envision, or with the public they seek to constitute through the work's beacon. Such is the very foundation of marketing.

In the co-composers' choice of an early music aesthetic as the ground upon which *Giiwedin* stands, issues of audience engagement and alienation were central.[9] In conversation with Joseph K. So, Dénommé-Welch and Magowan describe their choice of an early music aesthetic as the predominant sound world for *Giiwedin* as a choice to engage an audience with less tolerance for dissonance than one might encounter in a contemporary opera: "we choose to write accessibly in a way that pleases us, and others. We've listened to everything—from Gilbert and Sullivan to Hildegard von Bingen to madrigals, early music, rock 'n' roll and jazz" (So 2010, 5).[10] As So observes in response to Dénommé-Welch and Magowan, "there is some snobbery in classical music circles about music that is very accessible, for example, music with hummable melodies" (5). Conversely, the choice for accessibility might be understood within an ethical framework of responsibility to the presenting organization's typical audience. In particular, Native Earth Performing Arts's significant urban Indigenous audience is an audience with whom atonal musical languages would find less resonance.

This choice for musical accessibility is also revealing in another way: it suggests that the creators understand *Giiwedin*'s audience's tolerance for visual and verbal dissonance to be higher than their tolerance for musical dissonance. *Giiwedin*'s story focuses on particularly violent events that include the lobotomy of the opera's protagonist, Noodin-Kwe, and the killing of Noodin-Kwe's allies. The brutality of these events is represented in strikingly dissonant ways both verbally and visually in *Giiwedin*'s libretto and staging. As a spectator for this performance, the question of balance of representational and auditory dissonance was central to my experience. One might assume that the relative accessibility of the music in *Giiwedin* is an aesthetic choice based on balancing the brutality represented visually and verbally, and thus providing what might be understood as a representational care in service of avoiding the re-traumatization of its spectators. Contrary to this reading, *Giiwedin*'s relative consonance instead served to elide and undermine the disruptive potential of the narrative to unsettle the received history of violence against Indigenous people and the strength of Indigenous resistance to this violence.[11] *Giiwedin*'s use of an early music style as a "pleasing" aesthetic avoids alienating its audience, but in doing so allows hungry listening to ingest Indigenous trauma without prompting reflection upon what it means to aurally consume such violence.

That the contemporary semiotics of an early music aesthetic remained underconsidered by Dénommé-Welch and Magowan is particularly curious given that they are in fact keenly aware of the signification of musical genre. For example, in their musical characterization of the French Indian Agent, Jean, they use a flippantly stereotypical "French Canadian"–sounding jig. As Magowan notes in an interview, this genre quotation represents "this whole idea of ridiculous, fun themes, and turning the convention on its head and sort of flipping it. Everyone else has serious, beautiful, lush themes, and these colonizers enter with music that is evocative of a completely different place, which, although [it] is completely appropriate to the character, seems really silly set in northern Ontario in the 1890s" (Dénommé-Welch and Magowan in discussion with the author, November 29, 2009). Although Dénommé-Welch and Magowan pointedly invert the gaze of musical stereotypes and quote musical styles for other characters and historical contexts (notably the "girl group" sound of the 1950s), their more general use of an early music aesthetic remains particularly incongruous. Given the importance Dénommé-Welch and Magowan place on the semiotics of musical genre to signify eras and stereotypes, it is similarly relevant to question what the choice of early music might express. Moreover, what does the tradition and sound of early music connote for the nonspecialist audience or, more specifically, for the Indigenous (and allied settler) community in Toronto who regularly attend work presented by Native Earth Performing Arts, the organization that produced *Giiwedin*?

By way of answering these questions, we might turn to the contemporary reception of Baroque music and the mood-regulating function of such music since the rise of "easy listening" *barococo* beginning in the 1950s and continuing into the present.[12] In this context, I question the ramifications of making *Giiwedin* musically accessible through the use of both a predominantly early music aesthetic and the associations with such an aesthetic. Historically, Baroque music's frequent function as *Tafelmusik* (literally "table music" or background music at social gatherings) and its contemporary function in an everyday context as "easy listening" or, worse, as Muzak, should be considered, particularly given the specific audience of nonspecialist listeners in attendance. To be clear, I am not in any way attempting to conflate Baroque music with Muzak, but instead emphasizing that, for a large portion of audience members who do not attend early music concerts, such music is perhaps most often encountered as background music, where it codes the atmosphere as pleasant or calming. Moreover, even with my own experience of Baroque music as a pianist, university-trained listener, and infrequent Baroque music concert-goer, I too find myself lull-listening, letting the undeniable sonic pleasure of contrapuntal play wash over me. By drawing attention to the public experience of Baroque music as background music, it is not my intention to deride the quality of the composition through this association. Rather, my aim is to consider the implications of musical accessibility and to question how such accessibility in *Giiwedin* inadvertently smooths over the more dissonant political aspects of the opera. It does so at the cost of allowing such violence not only to be heard as well as seen but to be engaged with reflexively, asking listeners to contend with what it means to consume violence. The contemporary, quotidian use of early music, as an object of mood regulation consumed in contexts from spas to elevators, co-opts attention through a mode of listening where *Giiwedin*'s Indigenous history of resistance satiates hunger for damage-centered Indigenous narratives (Tuck 2009). If the concept and practice of dissonance is a measure of the irreducible alterity of agonistic difference, then *Giiwedin*'s sound world quiets the strident call for resistance embedded within its own narrative. And yet, the question posed remains unanswered: what is dissonant art music's relevance as a strategy of aesthetic engagement for Indigenous listeners more broadly? The question is not asked rhetorically. Given the social and political relevance other strikingly dissonant

128 Contemporary Encounters

Indigenous music has found—for example in the work of Tanya Tagaq, in the sharp stride of some powwow singing vocality, and in noise music such as that by Raven Chacon—to what extent can we imagine Indigenous community-relevant art music composed within the wider range of more dissonant and experimental compositional practices including serialism, and spectral, aleatoric, or new complexity approaches, for example? Is the dissonance of contemporary classical music irreconcilable with Indigenous culture and politics?

In contrast to *Giiwedin*'s predominantly local audience for its Toronto premier, a much more diffuse audience is addressed by Christos Hatzis's international radio broadcast of *Viderunt Omnes*. Hatzis was commissioned by the CBC to compose the Canadian contribution to the multinational Millennium Project, a radio project of the European Broadcasting Union. The project guidelines stipulated that all national entries were to be based on the organum *Viderunt Omnes* by Pérotin.[13] Hatzis's resulting composition manipulates samples from a recording of the Toronto Consort performing Pérotin's organum, recordings Hatzis made of katajjaq (throat games), and a song by two Inuit throat singers (Angela Atagootak and Pauline Kyak). Hatzis describes the piece as

> the bringing together of the colonial and native elements, the primary building blocks of Canada's culture, into a celebration of the 2000th birthday of Jesus of Nazareth ([represented by] "Viderunt Omnes," a Christmas chant . . .). Imagine a nativity scene in which the chanting angels are the singers of the chronologically and geographically distant 12th century Notre Dame Cathedral, while the shepherds are the natives of arctic Canada, the Inuit. This is the image which has inspired *Viderunt Omnes,* a utopian image perhaps, but then the historical interaction between the Europeans and the arctic natives of North America has been for the most part one of cooperation, not confrontation, unlike the relationship between the Europeans and the more southern natives of the American continent. Furthermore, present day Inuit culture is deeply Christian, in spite of its animistic origins. So this representation of the nativity scene as a virtual meeting place between two musical worlds that have not actually "met" yet, is not as inappropriate as one might originally imagine. (Hatzis, n.d.)

As with Saul's narrative of Canadian métissage, Hatzis's *Viderunt Omnes* understands Indigenous culture as part of the "primary building blocks" of Canada's musical culture. *Viderunt Omnes,* as the Canadian contribution to an international project created to celebrate the turn of the millennium, is framed by the Canadian myth of peaceful encounter between First Peoples and settlers, a myth that understands Canadian history as a history of nonaggressive settlement and tolerance for First Peoples in contrast with the United States history of Native American forced migration. Scholars have sought to disentangle the Canadian history of contact from the "mythology of white settler innocence" (Mackey 2002, 39) and the "peacemaker myth" (Regan 2010, 14), yet despite this work, a prevalence remains for understanding "the historical interaction between the Europeans and the arctic natives" as "for the most part one of cooperation, not confrontation." Given the forced removal of Inuit communities to remote and uninhabitable areas of Grise Fjord and Resolute with the express aim of serving as "human flagpoles" to demonstrate Canadian sovereignty in the north; the residential schools which were some of the last to close in Canada during the 1990s; and the qimmiijaqtauniq / sled dog slaughter between the 1950s and 1980s that threatened Inuit hunting and ways of life (and the resultant community activism that led to the *Qikiqtani Truth Commission*), Hatzis's reference to the Inuit's history of "cooperation" cannot be understood as anything other than one of "cooperation" while under the duress of the state.[14] The settler fantasy that Hatzis perpetuates also goes by the name of "white settler innocence."

In her book *The House of Difference,* Eva Mackey cogently details how this myth prevails in the settler imaginary:

> from the early days of Canadian historical writing, historians liked to portray the colonizers of Canada as more generous than those of the USA. According to these histories, while the Americans violently and brutally conquered their "Indians," the Native peoples of Canada never suffered similar horrors of conquest. . . . [T]hese claims . . . indicate a push to construct a settler national identity perceived as innocent of racism. (Mackey 2002, 25)

Speaking back to Hatzis's conception that "present day Inuit culture is deeply Christian," in the documentary component of *The Four Seasons Mosaic,* throat singer Sylvia Cloutier candidly notes that while it is true that the Inuit are now deeply influenced by Christianity, this influence was often the result of missionaries' efforts to "crush" her people's spirituality. Cloutier's description does much to redress the myth that portrays the settlers and missionaries as generous and tolerant. Countless testimonies of survivors of the Indian residential schools also attest to the contrary; if there was any "cooperation" by Indigenous people, this was most often a forced cooperation under the threat of physical abuse.

Hatzis ends his description of *Viderunt Omnes* by noting that the piece "is dedicated to all those who view contemporary culture as the reflection of a borderless global human identity; a culture whose elements are constantly cross-referenced, but are never dominated or usurped by any particular contributor" (Hatzis, n.d.). The language "never dominated or usurped by any particular contributor" imagines an ostensibly democratic model of voices in relationship, and perhaps a sharing of power between contributors. Upon even the slightest amount of scrutiny, however, this perspective holds little import for an analysis of *Viderunt Omnes*. Like other compositions by Hatzis, his sampling of throat singing and loon song are used exactly as "building blocks" in an architecture of Canadian nationalism where any agency of his Indigenous "contributors" is entirely absent. Hatzis's practice of musical extractivism—what others may call "musical pastiche"—is consistent with his larger position on the cultural pluralism of a postmodern musical aesthetics outlined in his lecture "Footprints in New Snow: Postmodernism or Cultural Appropriation?" (1998). There he claims that such "borderless global human identity" entails a kind of free access to musical resources as part of a compositional practice of citation and pastiche. While compositional forms of pastiche and citation have their earlier predecessors in appropriation art in the 1980s, and musical precursors including Berio's *Sinfonia* (1968), Salvatore Sciarrino's *Anamorphosi* (1980), and John Oswald's plunderphonic works, Hatzis's lecture is unique in its advocacy for Indigenous music to be included within a postmodern citational aesthetics. While Hatzis claims that he is "against cultural appropriation," he suggests that "no one at the time knew exactly where to draw the line between it and a genuinely creative enterprise." Hatzis's proposed binary of "cultural appropriation" and "genuinely creative enterprise" of course implies that the latter is exclusive of the former. In the remainder of his lecture, Hatzis elaborates his distinction between an unethical use of cultural material that is "parasitical" and an ethical use of such material that produces new meaning:

The difference between (genuine) postmodern practice and cultural appropriation, or even plagiarism, is that the latter parasitically feed on the meaning and significance of the borrowed material; in fact they have no meaning and significance of their own apart from the borrowing. Conversely, the former re-contextualizes the borrowed material in ways in which it reveals a startlingly new meaning and significance in its re-articulated state. (Hatzis 1998)

Under such a distinction, appropriation is that which doesn't add new meaning to the material cited. Hatzis's views stand in sharp contrast with Indigenous perspectives on cultural sovereignty, and the ways in which Indigenous ontologies of songs as law, healing, rights, and history, mean that they are much more than merely sonic resources and material. Simply put, the quotation of Indigenous song might in many cases not be merely a quotation of song: it may entail an abuse of power through the theft of family/community/personal history, an improper use of medicine, and in doing so a violation of Indigenous law and protocol. Without understanding Indigenous ontologies of song, the issue of song appropriation will exist merely within a Western framework of copyright and fair compensation/credit rather than within a context of inalienable human rights and moral rights. Hatzis does raise the important question of "how [his] borrowing is going to make a difference to [Inuit] communit[ies] and/or their culture, in other words, what are the checks and balances of this cultural trade which makes it equitable for both trading parties" (1998). Yet other than gesturing toward how such music may result in "exposure" for the artist, no accounting is given for how such reciprocal action might occur in more-than-financial terms—and on the terms of those he worked with—for the knowledge that was shared with him. In both Hatzis's lecture and work, music is treated as aesthetic material rather than as a cultural practice that has more-than-aesthetic significance.

As I listen to the opening of *Viderunt Omnes*, the sampled voices of the Western choir speed by though pitch bending that renders them as cars speeding by. There is no attempt to conjure any representational sense of place beyond the sound of the loon, either the place that Hatzis refers to as a nativity scene or a depiction of Inuit lands and life. Instead, the sound sources are treated formally, with the majority of the throat singing remaining untransformed and spliced and layered together with Pérotin's organum to add a regular rhythmic pulse. At the three-and-

132　　Contemporary Encounters

a-half-minute mark a four-second Inuit song fragment emerges that is striking as the first instance of melodic singing not from throat song practice. The fragment is also conspicuous for its melodic contour and use of Inuktitut. In an e-mail correspondence, Hatzis noted that "most of our recordings were of *ayaya* songs and throat songs, but this particular one is neither. The reason I used it was because it confirmed rhythmically and tonally the *Viderunt Omnes* section against which it sings" (Christos Hatzis, e-mail to author, June 11, 2010).

Hatzis's separation of the sonic qualities from the cultural significance of this fragment's text is noteworthy. Although he acknowledges in the program notes that Angela Atagootak and Pauline Kyak are the singers of the katajjaq (throat games) he uses in *Viderunt Omnes* (Hatzis, n.d.), he gives neither an indication of the cultural meaning of the recorded material nor any translation for the text. The fragment, used because "it confirmed rhythmically and tonally," again emphasizes the value Hatzis places on throat singing as a compositional resource. As with many of the inclusionary works this book examines, the parameter used to determine what Inuit song to include is that it "fit" within Hatzis's Western compositional practice. More striking, however, is that this "fit" of Inuit song within a liturgical context sits uncomfortably close to the model of missionization and church-led residential schools that similarly attempted to fit Indigenous peoples into "civilized" life.

The formal "confirmation" of Indigenous song to the Western temporality of Hatzis's work is a compositional choice that may seem removed from the continuum of Indigenous relationships to the state. This assumption could not be further from the truth given colonialism's foundations of "fitting" Indigenous bodies and practices into Western forms. From the confinement of Indigenous bodies on reserves, the restrictions of movement through the pass system and potlatch bans, and the carceral context of residential schools, this "fitting" is a hallmark of settler colonialism that has a parallel within inclusionary music. This larger structure of fixity operates in both state policy and aesthetics.

Although it is expected that writers be held responsible for the ways that they represent other cultures, Hatzis's work raises the question of to what degree composers should be held responsible for an ethics of *formal* musical choices (in addition to narrative and representational choices). That is, to what degree should composers prioritize an engagement with or be held responsible for the politics of their works' *aesthetics*, including the structures of musical inclusion and cultural encounter their works enact? Classical music composers, by nature of their artistic practice, are concerned primarily with the aesthetic interweaving of musical materials. The manipulation of musical form—along with the "confirmation," dis-integration, and simultaneities of forms—is precisely the focus of composition training in music schools across the globe. Their training focuses upon learning how different sounds, timbres, and rhythms might be uniquely combined. And this training often excludes consideration of the aesthetic relationship with gender, sexuality, and race, not to mention questions of ethics and collaboration that are a part of social arts and community-oriented artistic practices. The effect of this near-exclusive focus on the formal qualities of music in compositional training results in a lack of opportunity for composers to question the ethical implications not just of the "postmodern aesthetics of cultural pluralism" (Hatzis 1998) but, more generally, the cultural and social significance of the musical languages they use. Given the increasing interest in socially and politically engaged forms of composition and collaborative alliance from arts funders and presenters alike, composition programs need to significantly rethink curricula in order to reflect these changing priorities. In order to move beyond a "reserve model" of composition, where Indigenous artists are given a place and not the agency to determine the parameters for their engagement and placement in the composition and performance, the normative and foundational assumptions for compositional training and practice must give way to decolonial transformation. Both the Pacific Baroque Orchestra's collaboration with Spakwus Slolem and the Aradia Baroque Ensemble's collaboration with Marion Newman move in this direction, each rethinking how the parameters for concert performance might change to reflect Indigenous values.

"Nation-to-Nation": Presentation and Exchange

In contrast to the model of integration *Giiwedin* and *Viderunt Omnes* follow, the presentational model employed in the Pacific Baroque Orchestra's (PBO) collaboration with Spakwus Slolem, a dance group comprised of members of the Sḵwx̱wú7mesh nation, alternates between musical performance by each group and situates the ensembles as equal partners in a meeting that takes the sharing of traditions as its aim. In an interview, violinist and PBO director Marc Destrubé noted that "the idea wasn't in any way to meld the two things, it was simply to say here are two ancient traditions . . . existing at pretty much the same time" (*First Story* 2001). In turn, S7aplek Bob Baker, leader of the Spakwus Slolem dancers, described the dances they presented as those "that would be given to [presented by] visiting nations at a potlatch" (*First Story* 2001). By introducing the metaphor of the concert as a site for visiting nations (here with the PBO and Spakwus Slolem representing those "visiting nations") to present their cultural practices to each other while visiting each other's "territory," S7aplek situates early music and Skwx̱wú7mesh cultural practices as a practice of nation-to-nation contact, similar to the cultural diplomacy enacted by the Nuu-chah-nulth upon encountering Captain James Cook and his crew. The method of concert presentation is founded upon protocol for how Northwest coast nations affirm the sovereignty of nations whose lands we are guests upon. The premise of this concert format is not to merge music and cultural practice but to allow audience members to engage in comparison of "protocol" and story for each group.

The concert began with Spakwus Slolem presenting a welcome song, a "Canoe Journey Song," in which the dancers arrive from behind the audience. The PBO, along with Baroque dancers Thomas Baird and Paige Whitley-Bauguess, in turn presented "Fête Marine." As Baird describes, the piece begins on a boat caught in a tempest, which strands Prince Acis on an island where he meets and falls in love with Galatea the sea-nymph. Completing the love triangle is the Cyclops Polyphemus, who regularly eats those visitors unfortunate enough to land upon his shores and who is also enamored with Galetea. In response to the introduction of Polyphemus, Spakwus Slolem presents the dance of qálqaliḷ (or Kalkalilh), the wild cannibal woman of the forest who steals children in her basket. "We call them smiylelh, in our language. We believe some of them are still with us today, out in the various places in the mountains" (S7aplek, quoted from *First Story* 2001). The alternation of these dissimilar musical languages—the agile counterpoint of the PBO's strings against the intensity and solidity of the Skwx̱wú7mesh voices and drumming—are linked by their shared focus on myth and

Contemporary Encounters 135

legend but also by their focus on protocol. Whitley-Bauguess describes the focus on protocol in seventeenth-century European court balls as another link between the two traditions that emphasizes the importance of protocol in dance (*First Story* 2001).

This idea of sovereignty enacted through the structure of "visiting nations" deserves further unpacking, given the concert's location at two different venues: Sty-wet-tan Longhouse at the University of British Columbia on the lands of the xʷməθkʷəy̓əm nation, and at the Squamish Nation Recreation Centre in Sḵwx̱wú7mesh territory. As a conceit, the idea of "visiting nations" situates the relationship between the two ensembles within a framework of guest and host, where presenting songs for the other underscores the differences between their respective worldviews, stories, and protocols. Yet what happens when this conceit of visiting nations is enacted in a territory in which *both* groups are in fact visitors? In the first location, at Sty-wet-tan hall on the lands of the xʷməθkʷəy̓əm nation, both groups are effectively guests of the xʷməθkʷəy̓əm people. Presenting to each other as if taking turns being guest and host here undercuts the relation to territory that both groups should have as visitors on xʷməθkʷəy̓əm lands. In sharing this framework for nation-to-nation presentation with Tsimshian scholar and friend Dr. Mique'l Dangeli, whose work centers on protocol and dance, she noted how

> the idea of "visiting nations" results in the flattening of difference for the sake of projecting "equality." It also trivializes the politics of Nationhood. As though being recognized as a distinct Nation is as simple as a grouping people with common interests (i.e. the PBO are all musicians . . . therefore they are the PBO Nation?). (Dr. Mique'l Dangeli, e-mail message to author, April 22, 2014)

Such critique takes the politics of the concert's "visiting nation" conceit seriously and holds up the ontological difference of "protocol": song and dance have regulatory power for Sḵwx̱wú7mesh people, whereas in seventeenth-century court culture they are imbued with a sense of propriety and social logic that governs Baroque courtly music.

Returning to the question of place and protocol, in the concert's second location it is Sḵwx̱wú7mesh Nation protocol that should be followed by *both* groups. In Sḵwx̱wú7mesh lands that are now called North Vancouver, the Sḵwx̱wú7mesh Nation is the actual host, and for them

136   **Contemporary Encounters**

to "play guest" would be to undercut their own sovereignty. While the metaphor of visiting nations works within the context of musical diplomacy and nation-to-nation dialogue, it ignores the fact that each group is presenting their work upon Indigenous lands, and as such requires actual protocols to be enacted and respected. This deeper analysis of the differences between host and guest in the concert structure in actuality allows us to engage in ontological comparison, and understand this as a missed opportunity for the audience to learn of the importance of protocol as a practice of affirming sovereignty. Indeed, to hear audience response following the concert is to hear the misunderstanding of these foundational differences and the slippage back into discourse of integration. "It's been blended very, very well," noted one audience member, while Whitley-Bauguess affirmed how "it was really lovely to be here with the other dancers—they were supportive, we were supportive, and it really did feel like a family once we all came into the longhouse" (*First Story* 2001).

Perfect Every Time: Tafelmusik's *Four Seasons*

In the third model we continue with the structure of alternating between traditions, with the additional difference that such concert structures of sharing conclude the concert with a final instance of integration: a new work that brings together shared forms. This model offers a narrative of progression where increased familiarity (the sharing of different music over time) *leads* to integration. Similarly implicit in this third model is the narrative structure of reconciliation that demonstrates the development of trust between Indigenous and non-Indigenous communities over time. But on whose terms does integration take place?

In her critique of the inclusionary nature of Canadian multiculturalism, Eva Mackey notes how inclusion reproduces hegemony by maintaining an imbalance of power between those who decide the terms of inclusion and those who must meet those terms (Mackey 2002); moreover, the act of inclusion maintains the dominant structure while finding space for that which is included within it. The word "inclusion" thus expresses a hegemonic position at odds with models of structural change that ask how dominant and normative structures are to be remade. When models of integration are applied to compositional and concert format structures, inclusionary structures of power are once more at stake. As detailed earlier in the Introduction, the political gesture of renaming what many scholars commonly call "intercultural" performance as "inclusionary" performance is done not to acknowledge the positive aspects of inclusion but to critique inclusionary hegemony. In the case of Hatzis's *Viderunt Omnes*—and Mychael Danna's *Winter*, discussed in the next section—we see how best intentions of integration continue to reinforce and maintain the hierarchal dominance of art music as the genre to which other music must conform.[15] It is taken as a given that Indigenous performers should seek to follow the musical time set out by the composer, rather than the inverse. Similarly, integrative forms of composition and concert programming mean that the improvisational play and flexibility fundamental to Indigenous cultural practices are infrequently encountered, despite the wealth of aleatoric methods at the composer's disposal. Here also the degree to which art music composers are asked or expected to change their habitual methods of collaboration has been relatively small. Unlike the typical art music performance practice where musicians are expected to actuate music from scores, rarely do we find an orchestra asked to play an entire work from memory or learn it by repeating it from another performer, as takes place in Indigenous oral traditions. Instead, Indigenous people and our cultural practices are included in art music as long as composers can find ways to script those musicians (who frequently do not read Western music notation) into the genres within which the composer works. Moreover, this scripting of only the musical aspects of a cultural practice enacts a form of symbolic violence upon that cultural practice itself, recognizing and including it within a system of Western music rather than understanding its ontological difference as having a more-than-aesthetic function.

The presentation of the concert *The Four Seasons: A Cycle of the Sun*, of which Mychael Danna's adaptation of Vivaldi's "L'inverno" was part, took place in a variety of locations across North America and Asia. I will first confine my analysis to the film documentary of *The Four Seasons Mosaic*, which in large part recreates the format of the concert, and follow this with a discussion of a performance of the work I attended in Toronto in 2014. As with the other concerts I have considered within the third category of combined presentation and integration, the *Four*

138   Contemporary Encounters

Seasons concert and documentary provided a forum for the musicians to present their music and to contextualize it by discussing their cultural traditions. At the conclusion of the concert and documentary, the musicians present Danna's *Winter,* an adaptation of Vivaldi's Concerto No. 4, "L'inverno" from his *Four Seasons,* in which all of the participants take part. Perhaps the greatest strength of the documentary is how it features the musicians traveling to their "homes" and how they describe the process of learning their musical traditions from their mentors or Elders. Although the documentary provides space for the musicians to contextualize their music as part of a larger cultural tradition, this context is unfortunately elided in Danna's adaptation of Vivaldi's "L'inverno."[16] Despite the documentary's rich explorations of East Indian musical traditions, as related by Aruna Narayan, and of Chinese musical traditions, as described by Wen Zhao, I primarily limit my remarks here to the section of the documentary that focuses on Inuit throat singers Sylvia Cloutier and June Shappa and on their involvement in Danna's adaptation.

Of central importance in Cloutier and Shappa's segment of the documentary is the history of throat singing and wider expressions of Inuit spirituality. As with Narayan and Zhao, Cloutier tells stories about the important role that Inuit cultural practices play in her community and explains her community's desire to pass its knowledge on to younger generations. Cloutier discusses the nature of throat singing as play, the way environmental sounds are imitated in the songs, and the effects of colonization on Inuit cultural traditions: "Unfortunately, missionaries came up and banned many things in our culture, and our spirituality was sort of [pause] *crushed* in many ways, and throat singing was part of that. My mother's generation didn't learn how to do that because people stopped having pride in throat singing in those days, so they didn't pass that on to their kids" (Cloutier et al. 2005, Cloutier's emphasis). Moreover, Cloutier emphasizes the value she feels throat singing has in empowering young people in Inuit communities:

> It's something that I can't be selfish with because these songs really don't belong to me; they belong to our people. Young people feel so powerless and they feel so . . . troubled and they don't realize that their problems are just temporary and they take their own lives. It's *so* hard because everyone's been affected by suicide. Every single person living in the North has been affected by suicide. What I really try to work

Contemporary Encounters

139

hard at is trying to work with young people and trying to find ways to empower them through the arts. I'm going to teach those songs. I'm not just going to keep them to myself. I'm not just going to share them with my audience, but I'm going to share them with young people that want to learn. (Cloutier et al. 2005)

Cloutier's presentation highlights the relationships between the singers and the Elders as well as the continuance of Inuit cultural practices through teaching the younger generation. Despite the emphasis on Inuit culture in the interview portion of *The Four Seasons Mosaic,* the cultural significance of throat singing is exscribed in the video's final scene, a performance of Mychael Danna's *Winter.*

The first movement of *Winter* opens with an extended two-minute solo passage for the sarangi, demonstrating the unique pitch-bending capabilities of the instrument and Aruna Narayan's intricate technique, in which her fingernails control the subtle glides and embellishments that are characteristic of Hindustani music. This opening segues into "L'inverno" proper, in which the violin, pipa, and sarangi exchange solo passages, while the film shows Cloutier and Shappa looking on from the background in anticipation. Finally, three minutes into the performance, Cloutier and Shappa enter for the first time, singing a remarkably metered throat song that remains unaccompanied for three seconds before they are joined by the string section for a total of twenty-one seconds. It is clear from this initial introduction that Cloutier and Shappa are part of the orchestra, rather than soloists. The first movement continues with soloistic exchanges between the violin, sarangi, and pipa, with Cloutier and Shappa singing one final time with the same throat song as before for twenty seconds. This formula is repeated in the second movement of *Winter,* in which the violin, pipa, and sarangi again exchange virtuosic phrases with one another. In this movement, Cloutier and Shappa perform only twice, for between ten and twenty seconds each time, in contrast to the almost constant soloistic presence of the sarangi and pipa parts. Visually, in its focus on the aesthetic finger dexterity of the violinist, saragni player, and pipa player, the documentary reinforces the high degree of virtuosity evident in string instrument capability against what might be perceived as the aesthetic limitations of throat singing.

One might argue that Danna's work conscripts throat singing and its performers to the background, the former sonically and the latter

140 Contemporary Encounters

spatially, thus visually and sonically marginalizing the throat singers' virtuosity. Yet this argument would misrepresent the orchestral part of Vivaldi's "L'inverno" as somehow being of less importance than the solo parts in the work as a whole. Instead, I suggest that Danna's inclusion of the throat singers in *Winter* neglects the wide variety of forms that throat singing often takes and thus the extent of the virtuosity that it requires. Throat songs demonstrate both extreme diversity and virtuosity in their incorporation of vocables, names of ancestors or elders, animal names, terms designating an object seen while playing the game, animal cries (often goose calls), sounds from nature, the melody of an aqausiq (an affectionate song composed for an infant), or the tune of a drum dance song or religious hymn. Moreover, in the competitive and ludic aspects of throat singing, the singers demonstrate an improvisational vocal virtuosity when exchanging vocal motives. The omission of these aspects of throat song virtuosity in *Winter* is ironic: the same basic features expressed in Vivaldi's *Four Seasons*—call and response, fluidity of response, and even the virtuosity of improvisation—are also features of throat singing. Danna's adaptation of "L'inverno" ultimately uses the singers' traditions more for their timbral color and rhythmic pulse, rather than taking into account the cultural tradition of throat singing itself.

I do not, however, suggest that Inuit cultural practice is intentionally marginalized either by Tafelmusik or by Mychael Danna (or, for that matter, by Hatzis in *Viderunt Omnes*). Rather, I want to foreground that a question of primary significance in any intercultural work must be how the semiotics of inclusion function in the formal encounters between musical languages and epistemologies. In *Winter* it is important to question the ways in which sonic and visual virtuosity may unwittingly be framed as the singers' lack of ability to integrate or as an aesthetic limitation of throat singing and thus as an aesthetic devaluation of that cultural practice. Such a reading is only further reinforced by a statement of violin soloist and Tafelmusik artistic director Jean Lamon in the interview portion of the documentary: "In the case of the Inuit throat singers, they said they just needed to 'feel it in their gut.' At first I thought they're never going to feel it in their gut, they're so far off . . . [but eventually] they got from being totally off to being completely on and totally reliable and perfect every time" (Cloutier et al.

2005). Lamon's statement is revealing, for to expect any Inuit or First Nations performer to acclimatize to the highly controlled and literally "measured" language of much Western art music is to curtail the inclusion of the cultural practice itself. To expect Inuit throat singers to be "completely on and totally reliable and perfect every time" is to overlook the very nature of throat singing as play and the flexibility of time in play. It also participates in the stereotype of unreliability of Indigenous people and returns us to Anna Jameson's characterization of Indigenous people's "wild, restless habits" that hindered "fixing their attention." Much Indigenous music is referred to as following the heartbeat of the drum. Yet while the regularity of the drum may seem a defining feature of much Indigenous music, to force Indigenous performance into an unvarying meter misconstrues the life-giving force of the heartbeat as having its own rhythm and relative variation from moments of exertion to rest.

From March 6 to 12, 2014, Tafelmusik remounted their concert, *Four Seasons: A Cycle of the Sun,* in Toronto, which presented me with an opportunity to invite a small group of audience members for a group interview on their listening experience. One of the premises of the "encounter" that Tafelmusik attempts to stage is to take the audience on a round-the-world tour using Vivaldi as transportation:

> Our concert, "The Four Seasons: A Cycle of the Sun" is a musical journey around the world in 1725, the year in which Antonio Vivaldi's set of four violin concertos called *The Four Seasons* was published. We will travel to Vivaldi's Italy, to eighteenth-century China, to the far north of Canada and to India. (Tafelmusik 2007)

This narrative here prioritizes a kind of audio-tourism, a cruise in the comfort of the luxury liner, with ports of call in three locations. But what if we understand it, as we have other encounters considered in this chapter, as a meeting of people upon a common meeting site? What, moreover, if we reverse the colonial narrative of Western explorers arriving in the "new" lands, and entertain the plausibility of intercultural contact in Venice? Such was the suggestion of one of the interview listeners:

> **Audience Member 1:** It seems like it's plausible to think, at least in some way, that Western orchestral music could somehow coexist with Chinese

142 Contemporary Encounters

music, especially in Venice. Chinese people came to Venice . . . Inuit though . . .

Audience Member 2: It happened!

AM1: Really?

AM2: Well not Venice exactly. There were Inuit who were captured in the late 1500s. . . . Three Inuit were taken by Martin Frobisher from Baffin Island. A man, and a mother, and her infant. They were taken to England, where they were to be claimed by the Queen as royal subjects. But they all died before the Queen was able to reaching them. The infant is buried somewhere in a London graveyard, but the grave is unmarked.

AM3: So if they really wanted to do a historical thing . . .

AM2: This is the thing! The kinds of narratives that are told. We tell these lovely stories about the plausibility of cosmopolitanism and the influence of other cultures, but are we going to mention a captivity narrative in 1586? Because that is part of the historical encounter with the Inuit. But that's off the table I think.

AM4: . . . they basically saved all the interesting political comments to brief things in the talkback. They talked about their work with young people relating to suicide prevention. They were talking too about the removal of throat singing for sixty years through residential schools. And why they save these things for the people who are interested in coming to talk after the concert rather than on stage is that it would damage the politeness of the stage to be talking about violence in its various forms. (Audience members, interview with author, March 13, 2014)

This is indeed one of the key differences between the film documentary of *The Four Seasons Mosaic* and the concert performance. In the former, as the performers bring the audience to their homes—to their families, communities, and musical mentors—we gain some understanding of the social and political context of which these musical practices are a part. Yet in the concert situation, the contextual material is limited to historical notes about the instruments while the larger social and political context is saved for a postconcert talk that a small fraction of the audience stayed for.

Also unlike in the video recording, the throat singers for this live performance—Beatrice Deer and Sylvia Cloutier—did not align to Lamon's fixated standard of being "totally reliable and perfect every time." While the throat singers' entries were fairly consistent with the orchestra, within the tempo set by the orchestra, the singers were "off." To consider this from the perspective of the art music listener, like Lamon, might be to interpret this lag as lack, and yet from the perspective of asserting cultural difference, one might instead assert that this lag refuses integration. As noted by one listener, "it was a very cool, compelling phasing thing that you wouldn't get any other way, that I now realize was maybe a 'mistake' in terms of what they were directed to. It's very interesting that it can't fit" (Audience member, interview with author, March 13, 2014).

The Agonism of Non-integration

To further explore this resistance to "perfect fit," I turn to one final example: Mohawk cellist Dawn Avery's piece "Sarabande," first listed on a 2007 concert program as by J. S. Bach/Dawn Avery. The piece consists of the Sarabande from Bach's Suite No. 5 for solo cello in C minor performed alongside an improvised vocal line in a traditional falsetto style and a Buffalo drum line composed by Avery and performed by Steven Alvarez (Mescalero Apache, Yaqui, Upper Tanana Athabascan). Avery has elsewhere titled the piece "two worlds," a title that fittingly describes the way the two aesthetics occupy the same space but nevertheless do not fuse together into a seamless amalgamation. This choice not to integrate cultural aesthetics might be understood compositionally as avoiding the structural work of integration prioritized by non-Indigenous composers. Much intercultural art music is concerned with adapting the structures of non-Western music, perhaps to demonstrate an understanding of the other culture, or perhaps instead to demonstrate a mastery of musical alterity. Avery's piece here maintains a sharpness of difference and in doing so reminds me more specifically of the principle of "non-interference" represented by the Two-row wampum belt. The pattern of the belt, two rows of wampum beads against a background of white beads, signifies the courses of two vessels—an Indigenous canoe and a European ship—traveling down the river together, parallel but never interfering with the other's navigation. Avery's work does not aim to fully integrate the rough edges of difference and instead sets out a model for the listener to herself experience the push and pull of musical

144 Contemporary Encounters

alterity, while foregrounding irreducible difference that enacts Indigenous sovereignty.

Avery's choice for the non-interference or nonengagement of musical difference here stands in sharp contrast with metaphors of counterpoint that have had particularly significant purchase with musicologists and cultural theorists. Edward Said, who cofounded the West-Eastern Divan Orchestra with conductor Daniel Barenboim, took counterpoint as a model for both his methodology of "contrapuntal criticism" (Radhakrishnan 2012, 23–28) and for dialogue between the voices of Israeli and Palestinian musicians of the orchestra. Drawing upon Said, Ajay Heble discusses how Glenn Gould's radio documentary "The Idea of North" necessitates a responsible, contrapuntal listening (Heble, Pennee, and Struthers 1997) through the co-presence of multiple historical voices. Yet to look at the actual definition of the word "counterpoint" and its practice is to understand it not merely as a model for the co-presence of difference. "Counterpoint," from the Latin *punctus contra punctum,* translates as "point against point" or "note against note," and refers to the movement of musical voices against each other. In contrapuntal writing, each voice must stand independently, but all voices are considered of equal importance and no single voice dominates. From this description one can easily understand the appeal of using counterpoint as a metaphor for democracy. As Rajagopalan Radhakrishnan notes, to engage in contrapuntal listening also meant for Said that

> two modes of listening need to be exercised: modes that recognize each other as mutually vital even as each "does its own thing" within the structured totality. Recognition does not mean a bland and uncontested recognition, just as antagonism does not spell a breaking away from the opponent in implacable difference and irreconcilability. (Radhakrishnan 2012, 25)

Despite Said locating antagonism at the heart of democratic dialogue, the description of contrapuntal listening resembles Charles Taylor's politics of recognition model based on a humanistic understanding of the mutual recognition of the other. This model, while promoting the equality of difference, would foreclose upon the necessary primacy of Indigenous sovereignty and the necessity of spaces that allow for incommensurability and irreconcilability, spaces that refuse the epistemic violence recognition in its appropriation of alterity.

Musical models of nation-to-nation dialogue might, like my experience of Avery's work, expand practices of agonism of "vibrant clash" (Mouffe 2000) within which we need to listen with care. Despite the compositional potential agonistic dissensus offers to the compositional interplay between innumerable settler Canadian, arrivant/immigrant, and Indigenous positionalities, we need to remain attendant to the way that our everyday listening habits might still seek to reconcile irreconcilable auralities ("Sarabande" / "two worlds"), and temporal mis-fits (*Four Seasons*). These listening habits, influenced and framed by Canadian discourses of multiculturalism, sanitize the sharp edges of difference unless we are aware of how such habits are oriented toward the certainty of resolution.

EVENT SCORE FOR THOSE WHO HOLD OUR SONGS

Take everyIndigenoussong you've cited, you've used, you've scored
Take everynativerecordcylindersound in your collection,
Take everyIndianvoice pinned down upon the stave
Take these songlives trapped
Take them back

Bring them back to the people who sang, who sing—
    our aunties, mothers, selsí:le, siya:m
Bring them back in legacy—
    for your ancestors (voice gatherers, song-catchers, listeners) who
    cannot
Bring them back to the millions who still carry forward
    our histories,
    our laws,
    our families
    through song

Carry them back to our children
Carry them forward to those who don't know what you hold
Carry this life you hold, carry it in your arms across land and water
    to us
Let go your holding-on, let go your safe-keeping, let-go

FOUR
ETHNOGRAPHIC REDRESS, COMPOSITIONAL RESPONSIBILITY

> For impressiveness nothing approached the song of Skateen, the Wolf head-chief of the Nass River tribe. The lament of the mourners rose plaintively and fell in descending curves, like the wind in the storm. It was the voice of nature crying out. For Modernity it went beyond the moderns. The intervals sounded strange, at times like quarter-tones. I heard Dr. MacMillan say, when he was trying to transcribe it from the phonograph: "Those things can't be written down on our stave, they simply can't." But they could, our stave being a rack upon which to pin down sounds and rhythms whatever they are, at least approximately.
>
> —Marius Barbeau, "Songs of the Northwest," 1933

Barbeau's description of the five lines of the musical stave as a rack upon which to pin down sounds is not simply an evocative metaphor; it is consistent with the Western system of zoology aimed at capturing, "preserving," and categorizing specimens. As the capture of "nature calling out," of "the wind in the storm," the history of gathering Indigenous songs by ethnographers is a history of "pinning down" that which is alive, like the wings of butterflies. In 1929 Barbeau writes: "Indian songs from every part of Canada are . . . heavily represented in our national collection; about three thousand of these are filed away at the museum." Important song repatriation initiatives have been initiated by Trevor Reed (Hopi) and Aaron Fox, who lead the *Hopi Music Repatriation Project*; Robin Gray (Ts'msyen/Mikisew Cree) with her community of Lax Kw'alaams, and Kathryn Bunn-Marcuse who leads the project *K̲an's hil̓ile (Making It Right)* with members of the Kwagu'ł community including Yakawilas Corrine Child, Musgamdzi Kalerb Child, and

149

150   Ethnographic Redress, Compositional Responsibility

Namsgamkala Tommy Child.[1] Yet despite these initiatives thousands of Indigenous songs remain "filed away" in the Canadian Museum of History and other museum collections, disconnected from the Indigenous communities, families, and individual hereditary rights holders to whom these songs belong.

During the height of ethnographic song collection in the early twentieth century, many Indigenous leaders were convinced that sharing their songs with ethnographers would keep them safe for future generations. Many agreed to have their songs recorded, feeling the impact of the Indian Act's censorship of performing songs and dances. From 1880 to 1951, under Section 3 of the Indian Act, the Canadian government considered singing and dancing in potlatch and winter dances an offense: "Every Indian or other person who engages in or assists in celebrating the Indian festival known as the 'Potlatch' . . . is guilty of a misdemeanour, and shall be liable to imprisonment" (Hinge 1985, 93). Residential schools, where Indigenous children were similarly prohibited from speaking in their languages, from singing, and from other cultural forms of expression, further compounded this feeling of precarity around the potential for large-scale cultural loss. Under duress of these policies that explicitly sought to erode Indigenous cultural strength and eradicate our systems of law, medicine, teaching, and historical documentation, our community knowledge holders were persuaded by ethnographers to have their songs recorded. Little did they know, however, that upon sharing their songs with ethnographers for safekeeping, these songs might also become "pinned down" in contemporary compositions without their consent. This chapter sustains critical pressure on inclusionary art music that appropriates Indigenous songs and represents Indigenous people. It does so by following two lines of inquiry on compositional ethics and responsibility.

In the first instance, the chapter turns to the history of ethnographic recording and transcription of Indigenous song in Western notation, to examine how settler Canadian composers attempted to use these recordings and transcriptions as a resource to develop a uniquely "Canadian" national music. I assess the damage done (beyond appropriation) when Indigenous songs are embedded within art music against Indigenous protocol, and how Indigenous people have begun to address such breaches of protocol. The chapter outlines the different responsibilities

Ethnographic Redress, Compositional Responsibility   151

and opportunities we—and particularly museum curators, composers, and Indigenous people—have to the life of Indigenous song, incarcerated and trapped against its will in its current locations within the archive and within other classical music compositions. This chapter asks what, moreover, are the different means by which we as Indigenous people— sí:yá:m, hereditary chiefs, and Indigenous scholars and artists—might address this misuse of our songs. To provide one answer to this question, I turn to an example in which Nisga'a dance group leaders Wal'aks Keane Tait and G̱oothl Ts'imilx Mike Dangeli address the misuse of Nisga'a songs first transcribed by Ernest MacMillan in 1927 and subsequently used in his composition *Three Songs of the West Coast*.

The primary issue as stake here is not merely that such recordings and transcriptions were made in the first place. Although Indigenous people shared these songs under duress, in the face of great adversity and precarity resulting from the Indian Act's "Potlatch Ban" and cultural genocide resulting from the Indian residential school system, recordings such as those made by Barbeau have in some cases been reconnected with the descendants of those who entrusted them to ethnographers for safe keeping. Rather than focus on the history of ethnographic collection and the salvage paradigm that underpins this work, this chapter instead focuses on a number of interrelated questions regarding the legacy of ethnographic collection, and current actions and lack thereof to address histories of misuse. If the presentation of Indigenous material culture behind museum glass constitutes a kind of "life support," as Mique'l and Mike Dangeli note, then this chapter asks what it means when the songs and voices of First Peoples are held in the archive in other material forms from wax cylinders, to reel-to-reel tapes and mp3s. When songs are not firstly songs but forms of doing (healing, law, and sovereignty), how does this "doing" change on their transfer from an oral to material medium? What remains when the integral ancestral and familial lineages of these songs become disconnected from our communities, leaving younger generations without knowledge of protocol surrounding their use? In the absence of such knowledge and context, should these songs then be left in the archive, given that potential misuse of their power in the world may lead to significant damage when they are performed outside of the appropriate contexts? A new generation of Indigenous artists has begun the challenging task of singing these songs anew, of reconnecting severed ties between songs and their lineages, as they configure their work as a form of dialogue with ancestors. In this re-sounding, choices are sometimes made to break protocol, or move forward where knowledge of protocol is absent or only partially known. Here Peter Morin's performances find new protocols for the use of Tahltan songs collected by James Teit, while Maliseet/Wolastoq singer Jeremy Dutcher works with recordings of Wolastoqiyik (Maliseet people), collected by ethnographer William H. Mechling in 1913, and brings this work into contemporary formats. I situate the work of these artists in relation to visiting, as a practice that understands song not as an object but as a form of affirming kinship.

This leads to the second line of enquiry this chapter pursues: compositional responsibility. Composers who make works that represent Indigenous history, culture, and people have consistently failed to enter into a long-term practice of relation with the very people they create work about, as well as with the larger political history and present-day contexts of the communities they represent through their music. Beyond the exigencies of Indigenous representation, this chapter outlines the necessary shift from compositional models of writing *about* to models of writing *with*. In particular, I will address settler composers' representations of dogsled travel in the north in ways that perpetuate an idyllic image of the north at the cost of addressing the larger Inuit history of qimmiijaqtauniq, that translates to "'many dogs (or dog-teams) being taken away or killed,' and [is] frequently translated now as the Mountie Sled Dog Massacre or, more simply, 'the dog slaughter'" (*Qikiqtani Truth Commission*, 24; quoted in McHugh 2013, 150). In particular, this second half of the chapter critically examines the representation of the north in Alexina Louie's *Take the Dog Sled* for chamber ensemble. The chapter is followed by an event score that proposes one model for how compositional responsibility might entail more than being accountable to offering nuanced representations of the social and political histories and current realities of those people and places we write about. What this "more" entails, I argue, might be located in reparative models of artistic practice that move beyond Tuck's critique of "awareness raising." In this instance, my approach offers a decolonial staging of Louie's composition. This model not only demonstrates how art music presenters might engage in decolonization through restaging inclusionary music but how scholars who write about and research music (myself in this case) might move from critique to redress by providing dramaturgy for such restagings.

Indigenous Song Ethnography and Cultural Advocacy

To address responsibility in the context of early Indigenous song collecting in Canada, it should first be acknowledged that ethnographers, folklorists, and anthropologists undertook such collection under the auspices of feeling a responsibility to document and preserve songs for fear that they would vanish in the onslaught of modernity.[2] The intertitles of the ethnographic film *Nass River Indians* (Barbeau and Watson 2001) justifies this need to document through its description of "the vanishing culture, the rites and songs and dances of the Indians" where "Mr. Barbeau and Dr. MacMillan record the songs and chants fading away with the advance of the white man." What is today understood as the "salvage paradigm"—a false ascription of the inevitable extinction of Indigenous cultural practices and the resultant desire to save them— was at the time motivated by a sense of ethnographic responsibility, a similar practice of best-intentionality that led to the establishment of the residential schools and the sixties scoop.[3]

Figure 12. Frank Bolton recording songs for Marius Barbeau and Sir Ernest MacMillan on the Nass River, 1926 or 1927. Harlan I. Smith, United Church Archives, Toronto. 93.049P/520.

An increasing number of studies have begun to critically reappraise the history of song-collecting fieldwork in First Nations communities (G. Smith, Jessup, and Nurse 2008; Wickwire 2006; Coleman, Coombe, and MacArailt 2009), and provide important context on the relationships ethnographers had with their "informants" and Indigenous communities. A conspicuous absence in this research, however, is how ethnographic recordings and transcriptions have acted as a resource. In addition to countless Indigenous material objects including poles, regalia, musical instruments, and other ceremonial and everyday objects that fill museum storage rooms and display cases across the country, it might come as no surprise that an equal number of songs are contained in the physical and electronic archives of museums across the globe. Yet these songs do not merely rest in museum archives; unencumbered by the same materiality as their object cousins, they have retained a certain mobility. We might hope for a future in which this mobility may yet facilitate their return to the families and communities of those Indigenous composers who created them, but this is hardly the norm at present for many, if not most, song collections. Rather, the relative mobility of these songs has allowed for another kind of use: their repurposing as aesthetic resources. While it would be unthinkable for anthropologists and curators to give Indigenous masks to settler artists so that they might repurpose these in the creation of new artistic works, this was exactly the kind of reuse advocated by several ethnographers who collected First Nations songs.

From the 1920s through to the 1980s, ethnographers offered songs to composers predominantly without the larger consent and support of the communities the songs originated from, or from the specific families or individuals who owned the songs. Ethnographers' advocacy to use Indigenous songs as a resource for nationalist music composition dates back as early as composer and song collector Ernest Gagnon. In a 1911 letter to Marius Barbeau—recently appointed to the National Museum of Canada—Gagnon outlines what he considers the foundation for defining a unique Canadian musical identity:

> I have spent my life studying and documenting the history of our country. It has always been my belief that the "discovery" of our roots would help establish a sense of national identity. With particular reference to music, I intended my work on our folksongs and the music of

our native Indians to lay a foundation for a musical language based on these repertoires. Perhaps you will continue to encourage Canadian composers to seek out these sources in their musical works. (G. Smith 1989, 32)

Gagnon's view of the "Indigenous roots" of Canadian identity bears resemblance to John Ralston Saul's centralization of Indigenous values defining features of Canadian identity discussed in chapter 2, but his view is also consistent with other artists and critics who were contemporaries of Gagnon who wrote about the Canadian "inheritance" of Indigenous culture and of being artistic "descendants" of Indigenous people. A particularly striking example of this is the response to a 1927 Group of Seven exhibition in Paris, where the arts critic Charles Chassé noted how, "in seeking to be themselves, they were surprised to discover that they too had become followers of tradition; they saw that they were sons, not in blood, but in heart, of those dusky foes of their forefathers, the Indians" (quoted in Dawn 2006, 87). Chassé goes on to describe how "Canadian artists are looking for inspiration, not to the English school of the 18th Century, nor the French School of the 19th, but to that primitive art of the Indians, the direct descendants of which they feel they are" (87).[4] This identification of settler artists as the artistic heirs to Indigenous people is a historical precursor to more well-known and continuing instances of "going native" that have been a staple of Canadian and American culture from Grey Owl to more current false claims to Indigenous identity (Leroux 2019). While the language of these reviews distinguishes between "feeling like" the descendants of First Peoples and being descendants, no such distinction is present in composer R. Murray Schafer's advice to Canadian composers on how to create uniquely Canadian music:

Task number one, forget where you came from; only then will you find out where you are . . . When you finally realize you come from Canada (with no strings attached) you find yourself brother and sister of the Indians and the Inuit. All your life you had denied this possibility based on ethnic grounds . . . now you discover that it is right and inevitable. (Schafer 1984, 89)

Although Shafer is writing nearly sixty years after Gagnon and Chassé, the trope of native family "inheritance" is just as strong in Schafer's

156   Ethnographic Redress, Compositional Responsibility

celebration of cultural amnesia that will allow composers to take their rightful place as not simply heirs to the culture but as "part of the family."

This supposed "inheritance" of Indigenous cultural wealth goes well beyond the metaphors circulated by Chassé. In addition to the thousands of Indigenous songs collected by Barbeau that remain in the Canadian Museum of History, other ethnographers including James Teit, William Meechling, and Ida Halpern similarly amassed collections of Indigenous songs that have become—from a Canadian copyright perspective—the property of museums. While such collections have not explicitly been referred to as the inheritance of the Canadian public, the granting of permission to non-Indigenous composers by Gagnon and, as we shall see, by Ida Halpern operates under the presumption that it is the collector who holds the right to song use, and has a responsibility (like the museum) for circulating Indigenous culture and knowledge to the public.

Halpern is best known for her work with Northwest coast First Peoples, and in particular for recording 86 songs by Laichwiltach Kwakwak'wakw hereditary chief Billy Assu in 1947 and 124 songs by Kwakwaw'wakw carver and hereditary chief Mungo Martin, the latter most controversially including Hamatsa songs and songs Martin had been gifted by the Haida, for which his community reproached him for singing.[5] In collecting songs, Halpern, like Barbeau, saw herself as a cultural advocate operating in opposition to the prevailing belief that Indigenous people and cultural practices were uncivilized and in need of reform. One of the ways ethnographers tended to promote the value of Indigenous song was by encouraging its use by composers in the more "elevated" aesthetic form of art music. As such, this advocacy promoted by ethnographers was not so much a break with the residential schools and Indian Act's moral reform, but an extension of a civilizing paradigm in which Indigenous song was recast in a seemingly more sophisticated form. In a *Vancouver Province* newspaper article titled "Native Songs Saved," Halpern is quoted saying, "'perhaps some young composer will use the music as the foundation of his own music . . . It is there to be used. And what could be more Canadian,' she asks with a wry smile" ("Native Songs Saved," *The Province,* November 30, 1986). This promotion of Indigenous song for the establishment of "Canadian music" is exactly the course of action Halpern pursued, taking on the role of "music consultant" for several composers, including Alex Pauk for his composition "Totem Spirit" (1976) and Imant Raminsh for his work "Nootka Paddle Song" (1984), among others. In several instances, her role as an Indigenous music consultant entailed granting composers permission to use Indigenous songs for their compositions:

> Theo Goldberg was very taken by my Raven songs (which are beauties, really, he made a very good choice!) and so he asked permission, which my publisher gave and which I gladly gave . . . Alex Pauk was another composer . . . he wrote a very beautiful composition called "Totem Dreams." [sic] He fell in love with some Nootka music and I again very gladly co-operated with him. (Interview with Jurgen Gothe, n.d., Series 2, Research and Private Records, Ida Halpern Fonds, Royal BC Museum)

Halpern's possessive use of "my Raven songs," and her repeated emphasis on her granting permission for composers to use these works, or "cooperating with their requests," contradicts the significant emphasis Halpern consistently placed on acknowledging the names of the singers whose songs she recorded. In Halpern's record liner notes, she gives prominence to the voices of those singers she worked with by including their descriptions of the stories and cultural context for song performance rather than translating such accounts in her own words.[6] Yet despite Halpern's approach and overall intentions, Coleman, Coombe, and MacArailt have noted how, in a legal context, once these songs are deposited in archival collections, "Halpern is the only individual whose artistry is recognized" (2009, 192).

Halpern's emphasis on Indigenous songs that are "there to be used" by non-Indigenous composers baldly illustrates the discrepancy between Indigenous and settler understandings of ethnographic collection. The aim of Indigenous people in sharing songs with ethnographers was to ensure they were kept safe for future generations—generations who today continue to hold the hereditary rights to the presentation of these songs. In contrast, from the perspective of ethnographers, gathering Indigenous songs was done under the auspices of knowledge sharing for the Canadian public. This use of Indigenous culture takes part in the museum's explicit aim "to enhance Canadians' knowledge, understanding, and appreciation of events, experiences, people, and objects that reflect and have shaped Canada's history and identity, and also to enhance their awareness of world history and cultures" (Government of Canada 2013). As is the case in many museums across the globe, the metadata on Indigenous material and intangible culture is fragmentary, entirely missing, incorrect, or at best filtered through a Western ethnographic perspective. Given this fact, the museum's project to "enhance awareness" is built upon the fraught ground of misunderstanding Indigenous life and culture. Halpern and Barbeau's promotion of Indigenous song to settler Canadian composers for use in constructing a national arts identity is particularly egregious, given the simultaneous policies aimed at severing Indigenous people from our cultural wealth, systems of law, healing, and teaching. Yet it in fact exemplifies just one aspect of a much larger museum system where Indigenous cultural wealth is understood as having its primary benefit for the settler Canadian public, in which settler Canadian hunger—coded here as "enhancing awareness"—is centered.

The museum's instrumentalization of Indigenous knowledge as the basis for public education forecloses interrogation of its premise because of an assumed public benefit that makes imperative the sharing of any and all knowledge. Knowledge access is here taken as a "good" even as it disregards Indigenous protocol that guides the specificity of when, and by whom, knowledge might be shared. In contrast, the use of Indigenous song as a foundation for Canadian music has been overlooked more simply because of a lack of awareness that such appropriations have even occurred. An important distinction exists here between such music and visual art that similarly represents, adapts, and appropriates Indigenous cultural iconography. From the early paintings by Paul Kane to modernist work by Jack Shadbolt and Emily Carr, the representation of Indigenous culture by non-Indigenous artists circulates quickly in the public sphere, and indeed has generated a whole a subset of Canadiana for sale in airports and gallery gift shops. This quick circulation and high visibility of Indigenous visual culture has allowed for an attendant critique on the terms of its inclusion. Unlike the public prominence of Indigenous visual iconography, the life of contemporary classical music that includes Indigenous songs is comparatively idle. Once performed at its premiere to a relatively small audience that consists largely of those already working within contemporary music, it is the rare piece of contemporary classical music that receives subsequent performances. As a consequence, the uses of Indigenous song in contemporary compositions remain hidden in their scores, largely out of circulation in the public sphere. This lack of circulation is significant not only because it forecloses the possibility for the general public to hear these compositions, but because it conceals knowledge of Indigenous song inclusion from Indigenous families and individuals with whom hereditary rights continue to reside. The very unpopularity of contemporary art music here protects the secret of its appropriations. Not only does its unpopularity prevent knowledge of its appropriations, it prevents the discourse surrounding appropriation from becoming a topic of public discussion and scholarship.

A case in point is the 2010 production of Harry Somers's 1967 opera *Louis Riel* by students in the University of British Columbia's (UBC) opera program. To coincide with this production, UBC organized a conference on the leader of the Métis rebellion, Louis Riel, that situated the opera in its broader context of Riel's history, Indigenous relationships to opera, and Métis culture more generally. I presented at this conference, and as part of my presentation I mentioned the fact that Somers had used a Nisga'a song as the basis for an aria sung by Riel's wife, Marguerite. As musicologist Colleen Renihan notes, Marguerite's aria, that elsewhere exists as the stand-alone song "Kuyas,"

> is based on a five-note motive from the "Song of Skateen," a Nisga'a song from Northern British Columbia—not of the Montana Métis, as the opera implies. . . . The "Song of Skateen" was collected and notated by Sir Ernest MacMillan and Marius Barbeau. In an interview about Somers' composition of the opera, his wife, Barbara Chilcott recalls the choice of the piece for this scene, explaining how she convinced Somers to use it because of "the Indian connection; it's in Cree; and it's talking about long ago." Incidentally, Somers did not feel that this was problematic.

Elsewhere, Somers's wife, Barbara Chilcott, relates the story of how the Kuyas aria was written differently:

> I said, well, you know, "what about the Kuyas?" I mean, there is the Indian connections, that it's in Cree, and it's talking about long ago. . . . Anyway, after this second bottle of champagne, Kuyas was the opening. (Cornfield, 2006)

Figure 13. Simone Osborne *(foreground)* as Marguerite Riel and *(back row, far left)* Justin Many Fingers (Mii-Sum-Ma-Nis-Kim) with members of the Land Assembly (Virginia Barter, Bizhiw, Joan Chalifoux, Michael Dennis, Robyn Grant-Moran, Verlin Lloyd James, Reno King, Chelsea Krahn, Ashley Lloyd, Cullen McNabb, Glenn Neshkiwe, Kimberly Sanderson, Janice Sanderson-Wilson, Autumn Therrien, Laura Therrien) in the Canadian Opera Company and National Arts Centre new co-production of *Louis Riel*, 2017. Conductor Johannes Debus, director Peter Hinton, set designer Michael Gianfrancesco, costume designer Gillian Gallow, lighting designer Bonnie Beecher, and choreographer Santee Smith. Photograph by Michael Cooper.

My presentation at UBC that day included much of the same information I have noted above. At the question period, an audience member raised their hand quickly to ask the first question. It was the Métis dancer Yvonne Chartrand. What I remember clearly from the opening of her question were four words: "How did this happen?" These words expressed her simultaneous incredulousness, shock, and anger to learn that Marguerite, a Métis woman, was engaging in a form of musical self-identification by singing a song belonging to another First Nation. Noting that this opera had not only misrepresented the Métis but perhaps also had broken protocol, Chartrand responded to Somers's misuse of a Nisga'a song by asking what could be done to rectify this offense. Could the song be removed and replaced with an actual Métis song, for example? The room viscerally bristled at the idea. With no small measure of condescension, some of the composers in the room, and without any sense of irony, reminded everyone that Somers's opera was a *musi-*

cal work, a copyrighted document, and any alteration to the composer's work would essentially destroy the opera. One woman, with what I perceived as a particular desire to educate those few of us Indigenous presenters about what opera was, noted that since opera represented a fictitious world, this misattribution was really only a minor offence, if one at all. "It's just poetic license," she said. Despite my presentation and Chartrand's passionate response that day, there was little sense that this was an issue that needed to be addressed either then or in the future.[7] Like Justice McEachern, who could only hear the limx oo'y as aesthetic rather than as law, this presenter's response demonstrates the same adherence to the Western ontology of song as "just song" rather than the more-than-aesthetic Indigenous ontologies of song as law, historical documentation, and medicine. The misuse of the limx oo'y takes place as equally through its misrecognition as song as it does through the settler entitlement to Indigenous songs as cultural resources for the building of a nationalist music. As Coleman, Coombe, and MacArailt argue, "if a constitutive proof of the validity of [Indigenous] law is a song's correct performance by particular people in a particular performance, then its use as a resource in the 'musical' creativity of others strips it of its most significant power" (2009, 194). Given this fact, the ongoing performance of Indigenous song within art music (as in *Louis Riel*) is not just an issue of appropriation but one of the continued subjection of Indigenous law and sovereignty.

This instance of a Nisga'a song gathered by ethnographers and subsequently used in art music is not an isolated instance. Other Nisga'a songs recorded by Marius Barbeau and transcribed by Ernest MacMillan—in addition to a range of other songs from other First Nations—have similarly become part of music by non-Indigenous composers. Since 2015 I have been in discussion about Nisga'a songs incarcerated in art music compositions with el q̓ó:ltheteq siyáye Mike Dangeli, a Nisga'a artist and co-leader of the Git Hayetsk dance group; Dr. Mique'l Dangeli, a Tsimshian scholar and co-leader of Git Hayetsk; and Keane Tait, a Nisga'a artist and leader of the Nisga'a dance group Kwhlii Gibaygum Nisga'a Traditional Dancers, who is a direct descendent of the family who holds the traditional rights to sing some of the songs collected by Barbeau and MacMillan. Through the years, our discussions have focused on the ethics and protocol that guide our responsibilities as individuals to address these misuses publicly, even when we might not be descended from the House or family who holds hereditary rights to the performances of these songs. The following transcription is taken from one such discussion, held as part of a closed gathering for primarily Indigenous artists, musicians, and scholars called *Doing Sovereignties,* July 25–28, 2016, and co-organized by myself, curator Candice Hopkins (Carcross/Tagish), and settler scholar Kelsey Wrightson. At this event, the Dangelis and Tait not only addressed the misuse of Nisga'a songs in composer Ernest MacMillan's piece *Three Songs of the West Coast* but enacted Nisga'a protocol as part of the redress for this appropriation within what they called the "temporary longhouse" of the Western Front Artist-Run Centre.

A Temporary Longhouse for Ethnographic Redress

[Mike Dangeli and Keane Tait open by singing the Nisga'a song "Aguhlen hagweeyaha"]

Mike Dangeli: I realize that this isn't a potlatch—we were talking about potlatching earlier. We're very public people, and I have some contributions today, both the tangible and the intangible, before we finish our session. . . . *[Dangeli takes out a drum, about two feet in diameter]* I brought my little drum today. *[laughter]* This is my potlatch drum and I brought it out for a specific reason today, because, like I said, I'm very honoured to be here but I also have a little bit of Potlatch business to take care of as well, towards the end.

[Dylan plays a recording of composer Ernst MacMillan's "Three Songs of the West Coast," where each piece is based on ethnographic recording of different Nisga'a song collected and transcribed by Barbeau and MacMillan]

Dangeli: *[gesturing toward Keane Tait]* We're both over here trying not to turn our backs because that's something we do at our potlatches when we don't agree with something. . . . But we're over here dying laughing, too. *[laughter]*

When Keane and I and Dylan were having a quick talk yesterday, the discussion wasn't about the songs being sung, and how they've been used in classical music, because I actually have an affection for all music, including one of my favorite groups called Gibal who sing speed and thrash metal in Sm'algyax. *[laughter]* Our ways of being go into everything we do, including hip-hop and rap, and it's all beautiful. We don't have an issue with Nisga'a using other forms to express our history and culture. What we have issue with is being written out of the history, when composers use Western copyright against us. How can Western copyright supersede our law, though, when we've been potlatching these songs since time immemorial? These songs Dylan played have been changed to create something else, they have been made to fit into part of the "Canadian mosaic." But hearing these songs have been changed by MacMillan—it's like getting a punch in the stomach. Our songs are something that we grew up hearing and knowing and respecting from our Sim'oogit and Sigidimnak'—our chiefs and matriarchs—these songs have been passed down throughout our lineage.

So my naks, my wife *[Mique'l Dangeli]*, is going to be distributing something . . . I have some gifts, for two reasons. It's been wonderful for my other brother here *[gesturing toward Keane Tait]* and I to be able to share our understanding and where we fit in the cosmos, to be able to have this conversation with like-minded people, people of good hearts. And we may not always agree, but we're coming together with a mutual respect. So I have an intangible and a tangible gift. The tangible gift that my wife and my wak are sharing is a print that I did a while back called "you're #1 one in my books." *[laughter]* I'm a combat veteran. I served ten years as a U.S. Army airborne ranger, and I jumped out of perfectly good airplanes. And before we jumped, we used to flip each other the bird, the finger, whatever you want to call it, and say 'you're number one in my books,' and that was just kind of a good luck thing. And this gesture also doesn't mean anything to us and at the same time it's meant so much to so many people, including my dad, who's the Chief Councillor of the Kitsumkalum band as well as a hereditary chief; he wears that t-shirt when he's in talks with the government. He's usually wearing his suit, but then all of a sudden things get heated, he starts unloosening his tie, and starts unbuttoning his shirt, and next thing you know you start seeing 'you're #1 one in my book.' *[laughter]* There's also a face in here, which represents something that my grandfather used to always do: blow a raspberry. *[blows raspberry]* So that's what this being is in the center of the image, and it's about having fun. Because in our culture what we do is to work so hard at having that balance of both: the humor and the seriousness; looking at the light and also looking at the darkness; and walking in a balance between these. So, this work is the tangible gift for all of you.

Figure 14. "You're #1 In My Books," print by Michael Dangeli, 2007. Courtesy of the artist.

The intangible gift is a song. I heard you *[speaking to one participant]* talk about being so far away from home and needing a song to bring you back. That spoke to me. That's when I was like, "oh," *[snaps fingers]* a light bulb came on, and I knew I needed to do this. It's been awesome to share so much with all of you and it was such a beautiful moment the other day with Cheryl L'Hirondelle, walking through what I call home, as an uninvited guest here in Coast Salish territory, unceded territory, and thinking about all the songs that I've written here in Vancouver. So I am sharing this song with all of you. This song has a history, and if you're going to sing this song you have to explain that history. I'm laying this down—I've paid all of you with this tangible gift—and the intangible gift is remembering this history. This song was actually a very old song and it comes from one of our Haida relatives, Lily Bell. The Reverend Lily Bell sings this song, and it's about thanking the Creator. My Uncle Mackie who holds a high-ranking name, samaget-wiisagawan, or

Ethnographic Redress, Compositional Responsibility

chief mountain . . . niisambalada, our two Nisga'a high-ranking individuals from my village of Gingolith. Because we're so close to Alaska, on Gingolith, oftentimes Gingolith is left out. In fact all of our anga'asks that my wak *[Keane Tait]* talked about, our traditional territories, no longer exist or belong to us.

And so Mackie and Mercy have been taking not only our government, the Nisga'a government, but the provincial government and the federal government to court. Seventeen Court of Appeals over thirteen years. When my wife and I stepped in to support and stand with them and sing songs for their strength, Mercy and my Uncle Mack had one lawyer and one assistant. Our Nisga'a nation, who was countersuing them, our own people, had five lawyers and three assistants. The provincial government had ten lawyers and five assistants. The Canadian government had over twenty and just as many assistants. As I said, I'm a combat veteran. I know what an ambush looks like, I know what it's like to be outgunned and outnumbered. And I looked at these odds, and I was always taught never to retreat but to fall back, regroup, and attack another day. And I literally had to sit down looking at these odds, looking at my Uncle Mack and this whole process that has aged him, and Mercy— she's an Elder and she's on a limited pension—watching her fight, and I asked them both, "how can you guys continue?" And they said it wasn't about them. "It's not even about you, Michael," they said. "It's about your children, and your children's children." It's incredibly humbling, and I'm actually moved with lots of emotion even about this thought now. Yes, we all have to deal with difficult things. Huge decisions that we sometimes don't know how to make, can't make, or that are being chosen for us. So how do we do that? We call upon a higher power, we call up—you can call them or her "god," or "creator"; I say wiiemligiilaha.

So this song is about hope. I have seen many parts of this world, and I've seen how, in some of the most beautiful places, how ugly as human beings we treat each other. But finding my way back home or forward to home, I've found hope. I have hope for us as people, as human beings, so it's with that that I give this song to you, however you choose to use it, if it's in a performance, that you remember that history. That if it's just being sung when you're far away from home, that it gives you the same hope that it's given us as a family. Even if it's just something that you sing in your studio, or in your home, or in your car, you can sing it when you are far away from home.

I include this transcription of Dangeli and Tait's presentation here in order to bring forward the history we were gifted and—as with knowledge shared in the longhouse—to share this with those who were not present, when the time is right. More importantly, however, I include this excerpt as an example of a sovereign practice for redressing the misuse of our songs and culture through Indigenous methodologies and protocols of gathering. The work Dangeli and Tait undertook in this "temporary longhouse" gathering involved paying those of us gathered there with something tangible and intangible to witness the truth of the lineage of the songs that they shared alongside the unauthorized inclusion of the songs in MacMillan's compositions. In this way, Dangeli and Tait enacted Nisga'a law to treat MacMillan's infringement of hereditary rights to use these songs in composing *Three Songs of the West Coast*.

However, it is not only the protocol of paying witnesses with a tangible and intangible gift to remember the true history of the songs that enacts Nisga'a law. There are other important markers that legitimate this sovereign work done within the Western Front "longhouse." One way in which this took place was through a small yet significant physical gesture. When referring to others in the room, Dangeli ensured never to point at the person, but instead gestured toward the ground in front them with his knuckle. For Salishan language–speaking people in particular, to point in the longhouse is to release negative spiritual energy. This seemingly small change may only have been recognizable to xʷməθkʷəy̓əm, Səlilwət (Tselil-Waututh), Sḵwx̱wú7mesh (Squamish) from the territory now known as Vancouver, as well as other Salishan language communities including Stó:lō. Despite its subtlety, this protocol "does sovereignty" as a legitimating marker; it is what makes the enactment of Indigenous law "felicitous," as J. L. Austin would say of performative utterances. Through the gesture's use, Tait and Dangeli not only asserted the rights and privileges to the songs through their oration, but effected the very situation of Indigenous law as practiced in the longhouse. Referring to the Western Front Artist-Run Centre as a "temporary longhouse," Dangeli and Tait were not merely deploying a rhetorical gesture or imaginative metaphor; they were confirming an emergent transformation of the space effected through gestures and protocol for witnessing.

Song Cleansing and Reconnection in the Work of Peter Morin and Jeremy Dutcher

In addition to the disconnection between our communities and ethnographic recordings of our songs that have become the "property" of archives, Keane Tait noted in the same presentation that such songs hold immense value as knowledge passed on to us from our ancestors. As it exists in museums, however, this knowledge is sometimes fragmentary and partial. It bears the traces of loss, including the loss of information about the singer and protocols for singing. For those communities and individuals who have had the ability to find their ancestors' voices incarcerated within the archives, being reunited with these relations comes with great joy but often also with a feeling of absence of connection to the histories, laws, and teaching that such songs convey. In the face of this absence, younger generations of Indigenous artists and singers have struggled with questions surrounding how and when these songs should be used. Additionally, in returning to this song-knowledge, and song-life, it is not only important to consider what functions these songs served but to what extent we need to uphold these functions, either in part or exclusively. Questions surrounding the ontological significance of songs prompt further questions about whether ontological shifts occur through the physical transfiguration of song into an object—a wax cylinder. Does this material shift result in a similar level of toxicity to the shift in museological "preservation" of our material culture where masks were treated by chemicals such as arsenic? Historically, the Western museological treatment of masks and regalia with chemicals has left its own toxic trace on our belongings, on our ancestors, and in those instances where repatriation is desired by our communities, often makes it infeasible for use in longhouse work. Is it necessary, or useful, to understand our songs' transformation into grooves upon wax as a kind of similar toxic transcription? Does listening to ancestors' voices on wax cylinder expose us to toxic grooves? If so, then perhaps we must develop new protocol for song cleansing. By "cleansing" I am not referring to a rendering of our songs in a more pristine form—this is not an argument for "cleaning up" scratches on wax cylinder recordings, for the pitch correction of voices, or for an audiophilic clarification of the voice. Instead, I understand the work undertaken by some of our artists and composers in song cleansing as another practice of "bringing to life" songs that have been kept in drawers, boxes, and servers of online archives. Mique'l Dangeli notes,

> The expression *bring to life* is used by Northwest Coast First Nations people to refer to the first time songs, dances, or ceremonial beings such as masks, robes, rattles, and drums, are brought out publicly at a ceremony such as a potlatch or feast. When a ceremony is held to conduct or revive a cultural practice, it is commonly described as "bringing it back to life." Sharing meaning, history, and ownership through oratory is an essential part of this ceremony. This knowledge is inscribed into the memories of the witnesses through gift giving and feasting. This description lays out some of the foundational principles only, as the practice of bringing to life is conducted differently within each Nation and community. (Dangeli 2015, 109)

What artists including Peter Morin (Tahltan) and composer/singer Jeremy Dutcher (Wolastoqiyik/Maliseet) effect through their work is exactly this: a form of bringing songs back to life. Far from simply finding new forms and ways to sing these songs, this work involves negotiation between protocol and contemporary art practice. The work of Peter Morin, in particular, has involved singing Tahltan songs (some learned from recordings made by ethnographer James Teit) both to British monuments in London and to Indigenous ancestors located there. This work, which Morin called *Cultural Graffiti,* was not, in the first instance, a performance directed to physically present spectators. Although tourists and the British public were often present at the sites where Morin sang, his intended public was one of ancestors and other-than-human relations. For example, in visiting Buckingham Palace, Morin spoke directly to the British ancestors who effected colonization.

In creating *Cultural Graffiti,* Morin visited two different kinds of site over the course of several weeks in June 2013. The first set of sites were British landmarks, many of them the support structures of colonial power and monarchy. These monuments, as Morin states, "cement colonial history, and are foundational to that history . . . they reinforce it" (Morin and Robinson 2013). Such landmarks included the Houses of Parliament and Big Ben, the Magna Carta monument, the Tower of London, Buckingham Palace, the Canada Gate at Buckingham Palace, the Memorial to Princess Diana, and a statue of Queen Victoria at Royal Holloway, University of London, which was Morin's first intervention

Ethnographic Redress, Compositional Responsibility 169

upon arriving in London. Morin describes his singing to sites of colonial power as an act of insurgence:

> buckingham palace. thousands of people. set up the blanket. put on your armour. sing the song. the song that is a tahltan river rushing inside of me. the drum speaks. it says "this drum supports indigenous voice." the drum beats are bullets. does anyone know this? (only me). sing the song. fall down and sing the song into the land. drum and sing around the monument. overheard conversations: 1. i think he thinks he's an indian, 2. shhh. this is an indigenous performance.
>
> walk up to the gate. wearing the amour. use your voice to write on the gate. the words "we are still here. we remain. we are still vibrant. you did not fucking win anything. today. you lose everything."
> (Peter Morin, e-mail message to author, July 19, 2013. Lower case in original.)

In contrast with his visits to British landmarks, Morin visited a second set of sites at which he used a different strategy of song intervention. These visits focused on lesser-known Indigenous monuments and sites of Indigenous presence in London, and included Pocahontas's gravesite in Gravesend and Kwakwaka'wakw carver Mungo Martin's totem pole at Great Windsor Park. In this visiting work, Morin's interventions enacted forms of Indigenous nation-to-nation contact with ancestors. Whereas it has become commonplace to use the phrase "nation-to-nation" to assert the necessity for sovereign forms of dialogue between the Government of Canada and First Nations, Métis, and Inuit peoples across the country, it is equally important to remember our longer history of nation-to-nation relationships, trade, negotiations, and solidarities between Indigenous communities. Building upon contemporary protocols of acknowledgment, Morin's interventions constituted forms of visiting in which he extended an ethics of care we have for ceremonial objects, drums, and other-than-human relations. Although he repeated the same phrases, "we are still here" or "we have not forgotten," as he did at colonial monuments, the meaning of these phrases differed significantly. Instead of declarations of survivance, when visiting Indigenous ancestors these phrases provided comfort. We were visiting with kin, reassuring our ancestors that "we are still here. We have not forgotten you. You are not alone, though you may be far from home." Our visit to Pochahontas's gravesite at Gravesend, for example, was a visit to "our

Figure 15. "singing to our auntie." Part of *Cultural Graffiti* by Peter Morin, Gravesend, UK, 2013. Photograph by Dylan Robinson.

aunty." In these visits with Indigenous ancestors, we approached "site-singing" through a nation-to-nation politics of care and solidarity of responsibility that did not differentiate between visiting kin at home in our communities and visiting with other Indigenous relations abroad.[8] Like the temporary longhouse work of the Dangelis and Tait, Morin's practice of visiting across distance in *Cultural Graffiti* is just one of many forms of Indigenous gathering that allow for anti-teleological, non-instrumentalizing forms of listening.

Gathering, Visiting

Under the bridge at lhq'á:lets we are eating and visiting. I sit with two friends—el siy:ám siyáye tel iwestéleq, language mentor, and artist Lumlamelut Wee Lay Laq from Tzeachten | Chi'yaqtel, and Dara Kelly from Leq'á:mel | Lakahahmen, a professor of Coast Salish economics. We are remembering and weighing words. I mix sentences with the English word "system" with Halq'eméylem words "a'ép," "sq'eq'íp," and "iyósthet." tel sqwálewel—my thinking+feeling—is about their value and values.

We sit together, my words trying to find form for instrumentalizations (self, strategic, or otherwise) within academic settings, and to xwèlmexw teachings and logics that operate aside state and institution. This visiting is a home, affirmed through small-form connections to these friends, el sí:yá:m sí:yá:ya. But for me this visiting also sits alongside alienation, a fissure between contiguous connection. Cracks and fissures open up around distance: that memory and lived distance grown up outside of Sólh Témexw as part of yé xwèlmexw áyel—a Stó:lō diaspora—and continuing to live at great distances from family. Even so, in the dissonance between belonging and alienation, the work of visiting has more importance than any words written on this page.

While spectators amble en masse through the museum and audiences sit silent in concert halls, Indigenous work—our gathering—at these sites is an exception. And yet, as an increasing range of Indigenous work demonstrates, spaces of visiting serve as a forum for intergenerational teaching and learning and move us away from normative settler cultures of display and hungry perception. Such is the case as with the *c̓əsnaʔəm, the city before the city,* discussed in chapter 1, where the closeness of family is visceral. A range of Indigenous artists have been exploring forms of what is often called social practice in visual arts discourse—and more simply "visiting" when discussed by Indigenous artists—that provide structure for knowledge sharing and transformation. Examples include David Garneau and Michelle LaVallee's exhibition *Moving Forward, Never Forgetting,* where three Indigenous Story Keepers were invited to speak with the artists in the exhibition to learn about their works and then share this information when gallery visitors engaged them. Moving away from institutional norms of the didactic panel and guided tour led by docents, these Story Keepers held greater responsibility to engage in dialogue with gallery visitors rather than merely interpret the work in the exhibition. Another instance of such visiting practice would include Garneau and artist Clement Yeh's collaborative work "Apology Dice" (2013), a set of dice that are used in groups to promote conversation about the Canadian government's 2008 apology to residential school survivors. The work is described by the artists as

> an artistic effort to stir emotional response, to help participants
> discover and express their feelings about this issue. For ambivalent
> participants, rolling the dice may prompt more certainty. To those

feeling decided, play may reinforce their beliefs or perhaps unsettle them. This work is not intended to make light of this dark legacy but to be a disarming vehicle to prompt discussion. Apology Dice will only be used in an environment of contemplation and conversation. Participants must be willing to share and discuss their thoughts and feelings.[9]

Wiisaakodewini (Métis) artist Dylan Miner has perhaps formalized this practice the most explicitly, naming it a "methodology of visiting":

> While conducting an oral history project with retired Anishinaabe autoworkers, elders shared the idea that "we don't visit as much as we used to." Because of urbanization and the necessities of wage labour, not to mention the effects of settler colonialism, many Indigenous people do not visit one another as frequently. In response, Miner wondered what it would mean to simply create a time and place to share tea and conversation within the context of the art gallery, museum, or Indigenous community centre. It is here that "The Elders Say We Don't Visit Anymore" emerges. Through this particular socially engaged artist practice, Miner organizes a tea time where people can stop by to share tea and conversation, creating and maintaining existing social relationships. (Kisynska 2016)

Such work—in addition to Morin's *Cultural Graffiti* work in London, Wilson's *sq̓ə́q̓ip—gathered together* installation in MOA's *c̓əsnaʔəm* exhibition, and Cheryl L'Hirondelle's ongoing *Why the Caged Bird Sings* project where she visits with groups of Indigenous women, men, and youth in prisons to collaboratively create songs about their experiences—demonstrates the ways in which visiting has inflected (or perhaps instead subtends) Indigenous social arts practice, or what Candice Hopkins and I have called "de-socialization."[10] Existing in as many configurations as there are Indigenous communities and nations, each with its own varying degree of formalized protocol for discussion, visiting also offers a method for developing ideas and doing work that has yet to be adopted in the realm of art music creation. And yet it would also be facile to understand mere conversation as holding the answers; simply setting up the parameters (a space, a table, chairs, some tea) does not constitute visiting. In the post-TRC era of reconciliation, it would be easy to understand dialogue as the new "talking cure." Dialogue in and of itself is increasingly instituted as a response to appropriation

Ethnographic Redress, Compositional Responsibility 173

Figure 16. David Garneau and Clement Yeh, "Apology Dice," 2013. Photograph by Sharif Mirshak. Originally published in *The Land We Are* by ARP Books, 2015.

(Cornellier 2016), while universities continue to respond to the white supremacy and racism that structures institutional culture by proposing further moments of dialogue with institutional leaders. I do not dismiss the potential for dialogue and visiting to incite action, yet the potential is high for these moments to simply serve as new spaces for extractive knowledge gathering, and for the spectacularization and essentialization of visiting when Indigenous talk is put on display within exhibitions. Such instrumentalizations undermine the efficacy of visiting as a sovereign political practice.

Indigenous practices of visiting (whether in the gallery, in private, or in public) do not effect "nicer" forms of talking together. Indeed, Indigenous spaces of gathering often result in alienation from agonistic debate or lateral violence. Such was the case at the gathering *Doing Sovereignties,* organized by myself, Candice Hopkins, and Kelsey Wrightson at the Western Front. As much as it provided an opportunity for the important "temporary longhouse" work carried out by Mike and Mique'l Dangeli and Keane Tait, it was also a site where Indigenous teachings and protocol overlapped and were in tension. One example of this emerged after the gathering concluded, in a discussion I had with singer Jeremy Dutcher (Wolastoq) regarding his performance of *Lintuwakon 'ciw Mehcinut,* a Maliseet death chant, as part of the gathering:

Jeremy Dutcher: . . . it gets tricky where we're talking protocol and ceremony. Especially with recorded material. That's something I'm always going to have to grapple with in the work that I do is finding that balance between what is appropriate and what is not. I think specifically as somebody from the east coast who's doing this work and because we've lost so much and in terms of that protocol. . . . we're at the point now where we're hanging on to whatever we can. Actually, at *Doing Sovereignties* I got some pushback from doing a death chant in that space. Someone had approached me and said, "we were so taken aback. We almost left the room because we couldn't handle it. It was just too much." The person started by framing it as a question, which was an interesting way to begin, by saying "So why did you choose to do that?"

Dylan Robinson: Did the person recognize it? I can't remember—did you frame it as a death chant during the concert?

JD: I did frame it as a death chant then. For her in that moment it was negating our sovereignty, she was basically saying to me "you should never have done that."

DR: I'm assuming—knowing the majority of the people who were there—that this person wasn't Wolostoq? But it sounds as if, from the person's response, that they know the protocol around what is appropriate to do from a Wolastoq perspective. A death or mourning song could mean something very different for Pacific Northwest First Nations, Cree, Haudenosaunee, and Wolastoq perspectives, for example. So, I think there are questions around who gets to enforce protocol here, the "you should never have done that." It makes me think about our earlier discussion of the term "protocop." I know it's a derogatory way to dismiss protocol, and I don't want to do that, but it's a term that gets used to point toward the enforcement of protocol outside of one's "jurisdiction" as it were. I know Peter Morin has been "protocopped" before and he gets this often, I think, because of the ways in which his practice operates between traditional work and performance art, and the way it brings together people and practices from multiple Indigenous communities.[11] The question is: how or when should protocol get suspended, changed, or ignored because of an artistic imperative?

JD: Yes, and I think Raven Chacon brought this up at the gathering as well. That's something I tried to echo in the room because I feel that's the role of the artist. To look behind the curtain, see the rules of the game and then say, oh yea, that's—not that it's bullshit—but just to play with it and tease out some of the absurdities and to maybe talk a little about the reasons for why we are doing it.

DR: It's a fine line between artistic innovation and protocol. Protocol is always relational, needing to respond and have relevance to the situation, location, people. And there is a balancing act that happens when protocol enters into relationship with contemporary artistic practice that seeks to question and push beyond those boundaries. How do you make those decisions?

JD: For me, the gathering was an interesting site of that cultural difference and someone being really upset about what I had done, despite not really having a way into my traditions or how that plays in my community. Because when people hear that in my community they're just so excited to hear the songs, period. For them, protocol maybe becomes a little less important and audience becomes less important. It's just about getting song out there and trying to revive it within and for the community.

DR: So, this person that pushed back and said, "I didn't want to be in the room when you were doing that," was this actually because they had familiarity with Wolastoq protocol?

JD: No, I don't think so. I think it's just because of what kind of song it was and what that would mean in their own territory. It was a complex site of that difference and really highlighted for me what we had lost. We are at such a stage in Maliseet territory that people are really hungry for it and are happy to hear in whatever form it comes. I spoke about this to my mother and she said, "yea, of course, we bore the brunt." We took it first and for the longest in terms of colonization and in terms of that cultural friction. When we're talking about the west coast we're talking about a much shorter time of contact. What does that mean for traditional song? It definitely has an impact. I think that protocol piece is just one of those things that's lost in translation. Because we're clinging to our culture in any way that we can. For you, protocol is so much a part of the musical practice.

DR: It's an ongoing jab at Coast Salish and Pacific Northwest people that we're "overly protocolled." *[Laughs]*

JD: Which is fine, and that's really exciting for ya'll. But, I think it's important to understand that not everyone has the same understanding of what protocol *is*. Maybe I didn't put it as eloquently then at the gathering as I did now. 'Cause I was stumbling. There's an experiential gap . . . I found myself apologizing for what I've done but at the same time I was (and am) really proud of what I had done. For me the death chant means something else entirely. It's an overcoming of that death narrative for me; that Indigenous songs are a thing of the past. Especially coming from the classical music world . . . near the tail of my degree I got interested in Indianist composers. These early twentieth-century American composers who were talking about and using content that belongs to Indigenous people. But it was always framed in a dying race and that's a narrative that still continues today. So for me, musically and culturally, I started to work on that death chant and started to think about what that meant. That piece in particular is one where I'm singing with the recording and doing that layered effect where the recording is singing it and I'm sort of in canon singing the same line. For me, this is a symbol of intergenerational teaching, that continuation of Indigeneity. Indianist composers, and all those anthropologists and ethnographers got it wrong—we're vibrant, we're here, we're young, we're doing it. For me, that was the story coming out of the death chant. So again, to experience this conflict between my intent versus the impact of how that landed on other Indigenous peoples' ears was interesting for me in a very gut-wrenching way.

DR: There's so much fractiousness within our communities. I feel like one of the things we're still struggling to figure out is how to have respectful critique and dialogue while still voicing disagreement, responding to disagreement. In that moment, as you were saying, of being simultaneously proud and embarrassed, maybe feeling called out, thinking "how do I respond to this?" There's a lot going on, and sometimes I don't think we make it to the conversation about differences between our perspectives as Indigenous artists, with varying involvements in communities, protocols, and practices. And I don't think we get there because we haven't until very recently had the opportunity to gather together and to actually figure out those ways of talking—

JD: We don't have the opportunities to be able to practice those ways of figuring out differences. And then that brings in questions of cultural hegemony and Pan-Indigeneity and whose cultures get privileged in that landscape of a Pan-Indigenous world. That's the reality that we're all facing. Whose voices are loudest and who has the legitimacy of tradition? That's really interesting to me. Especially coming from the east coast where our neighbors, the Mi'kmaq, they have maintained so much more than we have in terms of language, in terms of song, in terms of all of these things.

Our dialogue illuminates the ways in which gathering is not just a nice form of having tea and light conversation. Visiting is political work. Whether explicitly or implicitly, visiting is a process of affirming our varied responsibilities as Indigenous people to each other, our responsibilities to the communities we are part of, and asserting this, as Wilson notes, through a process that has careful listening at its core.

Like Peter Morin's singing of Tahltan songs originally recorded by James in new formats, Wolastoq singer Jeremy Dutcher's work of locating his community's songs recorded by William H. Mechling held by the National Museum of Canada and returning them to his community has also taken place through a re-visioning of the songs as contemporary conversations with his ancestors. Unlike Morin's frequent "transnational" practice of sharing these songs with non-Tahltan Indigenous ancestors in spaces far from the original context of their presentation, concert performance work like Ductcher's has fewer opportunities to be presented in spaces conducive to visiting. While it exists as a space of socialization, the space and class dynamics of the concert hall and classical music performance situate it far from the context of Indigenous visiting previously described. The space of the concert hall rigidly fixes what Marc Couroux calls the "proscenium–audience dialectic" that separates performer from audience. Although not referring to a settler colonial context, Couroux asserts the concert performance space as "one of the last vestiges of colonialism [sic], grounded in 19th century European concert practice. . . . Perhaps this ritual persists in order to reinforce or maintain our connection with European culture, which I have never felt to be necessary or desirable. The proscenium–audience dialectic, the basic social format of the concert, reenacts a basic colonial power-structure" (Steenhuisen 2001). While the rethinking of concert music performance and a shift in its basic power structure received significant attention in the work of John Cage (for example *Musicircus*) and in a large majority of R. Murray Schafer's work, Dutcher is one of the few Indigenous artists to resituate classical music performance using different formats:

> Jeremy Dutcher: . . . for me coming from my context, community was always involved in song making. When we were singing a song it was always at a community event or at a family gathering or something where it was very integrated. Everyone was raising their voice and

everyone was being heard and we were collectively coming together and sharing something. In the classical world, especially when we're talking about art song performance and singers, it's very much presentation. You stand up there. You'll have a pianist. We're going to watch you. You're going to awe us with your beautiful voice or whatever. The discord around those performance practices as well was really, really . . . I didn't realize how stark it was when I was in it. Because you just do it. Ok, this is how we do music now. Great, ok, I guess I'll do that. But once you get some space from it you can analyze or process it. Oh yeah, no wonder I was feeling so drawn in different directions and out of sorts with what I was doing, because it was so far removed from how I had understood musical practice growing up. But, no doubt, this new way, this classical way of doing things is a part of who I am now. So, finding that balance; ok, well, this is a part of me now too. How do I still keep music to be a communal thing but yet still within a framework of presenting works? Because so much of what I'm doing is as a solo performer as well.

I'll share a quick example. In Fredericton, New Brunswick, I did a concert at the Charlotte Street Art Centre in July [2016]. It's a nice venue, auditorium, beautiful piano. I think it was an old school, like an old gym that they turned into a performance space. It's quite beautiful. There's a huge stage and the auditorium is down here. That stage is probably about four feet up, or five feet, off the ground. That seemed so disconnected to be presenting my work in that space where I'm at that edge of the stage performing to these people out there. So what I did was include people on stage as well. Shifting that audience and bringing people on stage with me, I think really changed the mood of the performance. It really made the concert hall more of an Indigenous space in a way that I think doesn't happen often.

Dylan Robinson: This tends to happen in music that features Indigenous performers—everything about the performance remains the same as it normally would in a concert performance. The only thing that changes is the music. Those rituals of the concert hall are so deeply ingrained. But when you start to think about all of the many different formats of our own ways of sharing music in community formats, there's so much that can also be done. Your changing of the performance space reminds me of a piece Peter Morin did for the TRC where he had honored witnesses as part of the performance on stage that I was one of. He was bringing into the space a potlatch framework—where you have honored witnesses who witness what's going on, the work that's being done in the space. Their job is to be the first line of people to respond, to take that information they learn back to their communities; they are the book, the archive. That's not what's going on here in your piece, but it reminds me of that. There's also a witnessing or watching of witnessing that the audience does. They watch each other. That changes the dynamic.

JD: It does. I didn't realize it at the time. But in chatting with some audience members who were down here on the floor level afterwards. That was very much their experience. Also because my mentor, I was singing some of her songs. She was front and center, and with family all around. She was saying, for her, that part was as beautiful a show as what was happening on this side of the stage I was singing on. It's such a beautiful thing to see your people—again talking about that gaze a little bit—to see your people seeing you.

To "see your people seeing you" points toward a different form of relationality and accountability. As with the work that takes place in the longhouse and big house, it entails a public form of witnessing each other witnessing that is at the heart of how we affirm Indigenous legal, historical, and kinship systems, and thus is at the heart of Indigenous sovereignty. It brings the audience from an anonymous darkened space into a space of face-to-face relation, opening up the possibility for a new social contract where individuals become accountable in the act of witnessing, of face-to-face encounters. Indeed, to think of the concert music performance (dance, and theater) formats where audiences are submerged in darkness can be understood as erasing what Emmanuel Levinas calls the face-to-face encounter that absents the subject from the "pre-originary" responsibility to the other, an "exposure [that] precedes the initiative a voluntary subject would take to expose itself" (Levinas 1998, 180). Without this intimate co-appeal of mutual alterity, responsibility rests solely upon engagement with the work rather than those who join together in the emergent formation of social and political change.

Compositional Practices of Responsibility

The early 1990s saw an explosion of social art practice that was built upon forms of meeting, visiting, and other intersubjective encounters.

A wealth of scholarship exists on relational aesthetics (Bourriaud 2002) and dialogical aesthetics (Kester 2013), along with important critiques of such practices (Bishop 2006; 2012), and an examination of correlations between the rise of artistic efficacy and the erosion of the welfare state (Jackson 2011; Harvie 2013). Many of these scholars have critiqued how the mobilization of socially efficacious artistic endeavors (such as artists working with disenfranchised communities, and on issues ranging from the environment to homelessness) might, in fact, substitute "feel-good" artistic spectacle (Bishop 2004) for the necessary societal function of social work, environmental change, and political change. The social arts collective WochenKlausur, who has long focused on creating dialogical and relational art works has long positioned their work as an alternative to art that participates in consciousness raising. And yet, they note:

> It would be wrong . . . to expect that something like art can make decisive changes. Folksongs don't rescue whales; "Stop AIDS" posters don't stop the spread of the disease; and Klaus Staeck's agitprop posters have hardly hindered speculation in the housing market. Did Picasso's *Guernica* do anything for the tormented residents of that city? It remains a monument, a ritual of grief, and an admission that the power to effect anything with art is limited. (WochenKlausur, n.d.)

In the face of such debate on the political efficacy of social art practice, contemporary art music's comparative resistance to discuss such questions is remarkable. It would seem that these debates have emerged and receded over the past two decades with little if any impact on contemporary music practice.[12] Instead, contemporary music composition and programming, in comparison to other art forms, have vacillated between outright resistance to explicit social and political engagement that follows from Adorno's views on the autonomy of the arts[13] and embracing a politics of recognition model that prioritizes increased BIPOC representation and content that avoids attending to the deeply normative infrastructure of art music production and presentation.

Here it bears consideration that not all arts genres might be considered equal in their potentials for social efficacy. Non-representational forms of art, and contemporary art music in particular, find significant challenge in negotiating between aesthetic innovation's emphasis on formal abstraction, and social engagement's emphasis on direct action that seeks to effect substantive change. What is the potential for "difficult music"—music that is dissonant or challenging to listen to—to work in relation with "difficult" social and political issues? Outside of representational contemporary works (art songs, opera) with explicit political messages, instances do not yet exist where difficult musical aesthetics intersect with difficult practices of witnessing, or where formal structures and presentation formats seek to unsettle settler privilege and modes of perception. While the interlude that follows this chapter proposes one format by which to decolonize inclusionary music, other formats for decolonizing art music performance are sorely needed not just for explicitly inclusionary music, but more comprehensively with the Western art music canon.

Indigenous+art music and inclusionary composition often undertake what is commonly referred to as "community outreach" that fulfills arts councils' requirements for music organizations to demonstrate social and political engagement by taking the work to communities that do not have the financial resources to experience the work or cannot access it because of distance. Often such outreach work is premised on an assumption of the community's lack of artistic engagement, or a model that Grant Kester calls an "orthopedic aesthetic" wherein the viewer "is an inherently flawed subject whose perceptual apparatus requires correction" (Kester 2013, 88) provided by artistic experience. In another model of outreach, the programmer or composer assumes a role of elevating the social issue / community through consciousness raising. The composer or music organization in this scenario becomes "a tourist of the disempowered, traveling from one site of poverty and oppression to the next and allowing his or her various collaborators to temporarily inhabit the privileged position of the expressive creator" (123). Such models understand the viewer as "subject-to-be-transformed" (88) and "as a kind of raw material in need of transformation" (138) and also align with Eve Tuck's critique of consciousness raising as an ineffectual model for social change due to its reliance on the belief that it is merely information deficits that need to be addressed in order for change to occur. In this paradigm, the composer's role is to address the Western art music audience member's knowledge deficit of the other, while the other's knowledge deficit is addressed by providing knowledge about art music and how to play Western instruments. I turn now

182 Ethnographic Redress, Compositional Responsibility

to a piece of inclusionary music—Alexina Louie's *Take the Dog Sled*—that illustrates this model. This analysis will be followed, after the chapter concludes, with a set of instructions for the decolonial restaging of the work.

"I wanted to put you on a dog sled. Enjoy the ride!"

Forty-eight years after R. Murray Schafer's infamous pronouncement on the "marked similarity between an Eskimo singing and Sir Winston Churchill clearing his throat," we find Schafer sharing the stage of Koerner Concert Hall at the Royal Conservatory of Music in Toronto with two Inuit throat singers: Evie Mark and Akinisie Sivaurapik. Mark and Sivaurapik are there to premiere Alexina Louie's *Take the Dog Sled*; Schafer is there for the presentation of his composition *North/White,* originally written in 1979, for orchestra and snowmobile. The unintentional irony here is that Schafer's work incorporates the very technology used to help justify the culling of sled dogs in the north, the snowmobile. The concert's premise is to represent modes of transport in the north as if they are simply that: different forms of transportation.

What remains unspoken in this concert is the fraught political context of the change that was to a large extent imposed on Inuit people between 1950 and 1975 from dogsled to motorized travel, through what Inuit call qimmiijaqtauniq, or sled dog slaughter. Following a report from the Royal Canadian Mounted Police that "concluded that there was no evidence of an organized slaughter of sled dogs by RCMP during the time in question, under their own initiative or directed by government policy" (Qikiqtani Truth Commission, QTC), an Inuit-led commission was launched not just to assess the history of sled dog slaughter but to understand how policies of the federal government resulted in "immediate and tragic cultural, personal, and economic losses" (QTC) for the Inuit. Including prior interviews conducted by the Qikiqtani Inuit Association in 2004, the commission received testimony from approximately 350 individuals about how the killing of qimmiit impacted their lives, families, and well-being. The final report of the Qikiqtani Truth Commission (QTC), released in 2010, includes "government records, police patrol reports, scholarly research, newspaper and magazine articles from the 1950s, 1960s and 1970s [to] show that dogs were killed in the Baffin Region often without due regard for the safety of and consequences on Inuit families . . . because Qallunaat [settlers] were scared of dogs" (quoted in McHugh 2013, 153). Over a thirty-year period, Inuit sled dogs across the Qikiqtani region of Nunavik were either mandated to be killed by their Inuit owners or were killed directly by members of the Royal Canadian Mounted Police (RCMP). The QTC report notes the "undisputed fact that hundreds—perhaps thousands—of qimmiit were shot by the RCMP and other authorities in settlements from the mid-1950s onwards . . . under the authority of the *Ordinance Respecting Dogs*" (Qikiqtani Inuit Association 2010, 20–21; italics in the original). Scholar Susan McHugh notes that the QTC report describes "those Inuit who lacked *qimmiit* or snowmobiles to access the land felt that life in the settlements was a form of imprisonment" (quoted in McHugh 2013, 166; italics by McHugh). Focused on the Qikiqtani region (formerly Baffin Island), the report documents how hunters who depended on their dogs for hunting and travel were reduced to "lives of dependency and menial service in settlements in which they were effectively silenced by a combination of fear of reprisals and grief for dogs whose identities were intimately intertwined with their own" (McHugh 2013, 154). The era of qimmiijaqtauniq thus profoundly affected the lives of Inuit people, and its legacy continues to be felt today. The fact that this history remains silent in the face of compositions that portray dog sled travel as a fun pastime is one among numerous examples of how explicit political issues are elided in contemporary art music featuring Indigenous performers and those that use Indigenous songs. By focusing on this elision, I am not arguing that an explicit political approach must emphasize only the most unjust, most traumatic, and most victimizing narratives—it may equally set out to affirm those values, successes, and gains of Indigenous people that individuals and communities feel most useful to affirm. A compositional practice of political alliance where Indigenous peoples are partners in dialogue, creation, and production, works toward similar nation-to-nation structures called for in the realm of governance.

In late 2007, as Toronto-based composer Alexina Louie began work on a commission for chamber ensemble, *Take the Dog Sled,* the *Toronto Star* featured an article titled "Inuit Probe Sled-Dog Slaughter" announcing that "an Inuit truth commission is investigating long-standing accusations that Mounties slaughtered sled dogs in the 1950s and 1960s to force their owners to give up their traditional lifestyle, officials said yesterday" (September 20, 2007). Later, once the composition was complete, and as Louie and the Orchestra Symphonie de Montreal toured the work to small communities in Nunavik in 2008, a "tour" of a different kind was conducted: commissioner Jim Igloliorte and QTC staff traveled to all thirteen communities in the Qikiqtani region to gather testimony from those affected by the dog slaughter.

The synchronicity of these events is striking, but even more striking is the lack of relation between them, given their shared focus on the sled dog history and representation. Louie's work offers only a fleeting reference in the Esprit Orchestra program note to "how the sled dogs have been important partners and friends to the Inuit. It seems that the very survival of the people has been tied to the loyalty and reliability of these amazing animals." This representation paints a charming picture of human–animal companionship, which pairs easily with the main focus in Louie's words for the piece, "to capture some of the joy, tenderness, and energy of life in the North as well as the mystical quality of the land" (Louie 2013). Louie's description is consistent with an idyllic representation of the north as magical, which is not to say that these qualities are not actually present. This abstract vision of the north as a place of mystery does, however, work to displace the social and political realities as well as the achievements and cultural strength of Inuit people from Louie's musical representation.

While Louie's work shies away from representing the historical and contemporary social context of dogsleds, compositionally, her work closely follows an inclusionary model. In particular, Louie focuses on integrating the throat singers with the chamber ensemble and fully scoring the composition rather than allowing for improvisation:

> In this composition I didn't want to separate the Inuit songs from the Western instruments by allowing the singers to sing "solo," by having the instruments merely droning or playing sustained chords as back up to their songs, or by giving the percussionist the opportunity to improvise to their rhythms as they sang. (Esprit Orchestra 2009)

Notable here, as in the majority of compositions for throat singers, is the avoidance of improvisation, a key aspect of throat singing as a game.[14]

Louie noted that the singers performing the piece were unable to travel to Toronto to develop the work with Louie because of the signif-

Ethnographic Redress, Compositional Responsibility   185

icant cost for Evie Mark to travel roughly 2000 kilometers from the remote northern community of Ivujivik.[15] Becuase of this, Louie's compositional method involved obtaining recordings from Mark of previous throat song performances. In an interview, Louie clarified her rationale behind this choice: "I didn't know how long they could sing . . . what I decided to do was take those throat songs specifically . . . I took the songs that I found, and I wrapped the ensemble around the songs. I used the exact tempi because I knew those were the temp[i] they could sing the songs at. And I also used the pitch that they sang it on because I knew they could sing it on that pitch. Then there's the whole question of balance . . . the throat singers needed to be mic'd." Indeed, Louie also explains that she integrates the sound worlds by having the ensemble members themselves imitate throat singing by blowing over bottles, thus integrating throat singing technique into the composition. Through this integration of pitch, tempi, volume, and throat singing technique, Louie attempts to create a situation in which the throat singing and classical music are seamless. However, while Louie's choices might seem to provide a supportive musical environment in which the throat singers are able to perform to the best of their ability, they in fact have the opposite effect of making the singing sound less virtuosic than it actually is. This occurs for several reasons.

First, as with Danna's *Winter,* taking the tempo of a throat song as the tempo of a notated composition rigidly fixes that tempo against the relative flexibility of tempo in throat singing practice. Louie's music necessitates that the regular beat of the throat singing is as precise as that of her music. While the ensemble works to maintain that tempo, natural fluctuations in the throat singing may be perceived as "falling behind," given the precise rhythmic consistency of this music and indeed much of Louie's compositional oeuvre. We might, moreover, read both of these works in light of the history discussed in chapter 3 of precisely measured and regimented residential school time. This sensory regime of imposing regularity—"from being totally off to being completely on and totally reliable and perfect every time" (Cloutier, Narayan, Zhao, Lamon, Taflemusik Baroque Orchestra 2005)—sits uncomfortably alongside the carefully measured, inflexible time of Louie's and Danna's works.

Such precision continues as Louie asks the singers to begin and end as precisely as the musicians of the ensemble are asked to, thus avoiding the distinctive and typical conclusion to the throat singing when one singer loses the game, resulting in laughter between the two singers. Similarly, taking the pitch of the recording Louie received as a constant, and basing the ensemble's parts in relation to this pitch has the effect of casting any deviation from that tone by the throat singers as the inability to maintain tuning. Such aesthetic inclusions paradoxically disallow the flexibility and virtuosity of throat singing within a framework where the composer aims to enable it. As with other inclusionary work this book has examined, the terms of the throat singers' inclusion are here to "fit" into a Western art music setting that delineates a fairly narrow range of success and failure. Louie understands throat songs within a Western framework where songs are reproducible "works" that are defined by the relative stability and consistency of their performance.

A further integration of the throat singers into the composition occurs in their physical placement as members of the ensemble. In the staging for the premiere of the work in Toronto in 2009, the singers neither face each other, nor make eye contact or hold each other's arms and move together, as is typical in traditional practice. At another event associated with the premiere, Evie Mark joked when someone from the audience asked whether their performance of throat singing was different than it would be "at home": "We're 'cheating,'" responded Mark, "My grandmother would be angry if she saw us singing this way." As part of the ensemble, the singers stand at a right angle to each other, taking on the embodiment of the ensemble, restricting their movement and connection with each other. The result is that Mark and Sivaurapik look extremely uncomfortable. In comparison to the range of gesture and movement demonstrated by throat singer Tanya Tagaq (albeit extreme for most throat singing), Mark's and Sivaruapik's bodies have been constrained. In such a setting where the throat singers are remade in the image of the classical music ensemble, their voices become simply another aspect of the composer's palette, barely differentiated from the array of extended techniques employed by Louie throughout the piece.

Lastly, Louie integrates throat singing with Western art music by taking the original subject of the throat song and elaborating it. The role of Louie's composition here is to amplify the subject of the throat song as musical description. Louie notes: "I decided to write short movements depicting each one of the worlds that each one of the throat songs was depicting." However, while throat songs actively employ a variety of sounds from the environment, from the calls of geese to the sound made when sharpening the runners of the sled, Louie's approach magnifies the sound to such an extent that it becomes a caricature. An example of this is the movement titled "The Mosquito," where the original throat song that imitates the sound of a mosquito is theatrically elaborated by asking the percussionist to pretend to follow a mosquito around the stage and eventually kill it. In Louie's attempt to conjure these subjects with greater descriptive precision, she overwhelms the ways in which the throat songs themselves already re-present the sound. Such a view of "amplifying" culture is complicit with Louie's statement: "I wanted you to hear as much as you could about the culture through my music." Louie's composition announces: "You think that's a mosquito? I'll show you a mosquito!"

In a CBC Radio interview, Louie explained another aspect of the work's intention: "I wanted to evoke the sense of the land . . . how can I bring all of you who have never been up there, who have perhaps never seen the north, how can I bring you into the piece so you feel you're sitting right there in that twin-engine Otter with me?" She continues: "I wanted to put you on a dogsled." The final movement of the work, "The

Figure 17. *Take the Dog Sled* performance, Ottawa, 2012. Photograph by Fred Cattroll.

Great Dogsled," here attempts to bring some of this experience into the concert hall. Louie's description of wanting to put the audience on a dogsled similarly applies to composer Derek Charke's *Circle du Nord III*, written for the Kronos Quartet, complete with the yelps of the dogs set to the regular pulse of the music. About halfway through the composition, the composer introduces a recording of a dogsled trainer providing guidance to the person trying to lead the sled dogs:

> We're going to be just riding it like that. It's nice and wide so it's stable. Okay and, uh . . . and then say "Chi." That means turn right. And if you say "Cha" that means turn left. It's just paying attention, that's the main thing, just, just paying attention to your dog. Wanna do a turn with the dogs or, or for whatever reason your dogs up front might stop to sniff something on the trail or do a little peeing or something like that. So you're either going to go "Chi" or "Cha." [Sound of dogs fighting, then Woman says to dogs "No . . . No. . . ."] For sure you won't make it down the hill without going into a snowbank. The snowbank. For sure you won't make it down the hill without going into a snowbank. (Charke 2005, repetition in original)

Listeners might here live vicariously through Charke's and Louie's music, imagining the experience of working with qimmiit. In both works listeners may well feel the rush of exhilaration of dogsled travel or what they imagine dogsled travel to be. The Esprit Orchestra concert program note itself announces Louie's intention for listeners to "enjoy the ride!" Yet we might do well to compare the romanticized audio imaginary of exhilarating dogsled travel with the reality of sled dog aggression, the harshness of the north that such dogs endure, and the history of qimmiijaqtauniq. Louie's portrayal in particular sits uncomfortably against the history of sled dog slaughter that, although still central in the memories of many Inuit people, receives little if any attention in southern contexts. To place Louie's representation alongside Inuit sled dog history is to ask to what extent Canadian art music's representational strategies partake in the spectacle of sound tourism.

Toward Non-representational Action in Contemporary Art Music Composition

Louie's composition is far from unique in a history of Canadian art music that seeks to represent a leisurely view, or a delightful soundscape that is dissociated from Indigenous histories of the land, in addition to the continued activism against resource extraction and pipeline development. R. Murray Schafer's *Miniwanka, or The Moments of Water* (1971), for example, uses words from Indigenous languages including "Dakota, Wappo, Crow, Chinook, Achumawi, Otchipwe, Salish, Natick, Klamath and Luiseno" to "describ[e] the various states of water," (Schafer 1971). Schafer's opening lyrics, "The wise man delights in water," from Chinese philosopher Lao Tzu or Laozi, find a parallel in the composition's usage of Indigenous words as a delightful resource for representations of water, and with visual art's resourcing of representations of Indigenous lands for the development of a uniquely "national style." Representational landscape compositions resolutely depict (re-sound) the landscape, in contrast to Indigenous cosmologies previously discussed that think of song as being "for" the land, rather than "about" it. Nonhuman and intersubjective relations between song and land put into question those relationships between land and song in works including R. Murray Schafer's *Music for Wilderness Lake* (1979) and Paul Walde's *Requiem for a Glacier* (2013). These works that are ostensibly *for* lake and glacier do not in fact operate on the terms of reciprocal relationship wherein what is sounded is intended to have a material impact of sustenance for the lands, as gesture of thanks expressed to the lands. Despite the growing eco-musicological discourse and influence of new materialism and non-representational theory on artistic practice, composition is often still created for the benefit of the human subject rather than for nonhuman others, including the land.

What does this mean for a decolonial reconceptualization of compositional practice that demonstrates responsibility to First Peoples' historical and social realities and takes part in political activism? Given the investment in aesthetic innovation, to what extent is it possible for contemporary art music composers to develop compositional processes that would result in songs that *are* treaties (rather than representing treaties), songs that resist pipeline development, songs that serve as reparation, and songs that take part in harm reduction? With these questions in mind, the postscript to this chapter provides one example for a decolonial staging that addresses contemporary Inuit realities and histories, while providing a space for Inuit youth to advance resurgence.

EVENT SCORE FOR RESPONSIBILITY

"qimmit katajjaq / sqwélqwel tl' sqwmá:y"

Preface

The following event score varies from the other short, poetic event scores I have included elsewhere in the book. Like the other scores in the book, it is prescriptive. Unlike other scores, its form is more akin to stage directions. Similar to stage directions, this score might be considered as guidance for the realization of a work that is open to interpretation and variation. Although the event score exists in a form that is intended to be realized, as with some of Fluxus's and Yoko Ono's event scores, it may also be understood as a work that can be enacted in the reader's imagination.

Titled "qimmit katajjaq / sqwélqwel tl' sqwmá:y,"[1] the event score is manifest in two sets of pre-performance instructions for Alexina Louie's *Take the Dog Sled*, and one set of instructions for the performance of the work itself. In the first set of pre-performance instructions—the instructions for the preconcert experience—the instructions (in the right-hand page) are placed alongside a description of a preconcert experience that I had (in the left-hand page) that is also somewhat typical of preconcert experience.

The second set of preconcert instructions are production instructions for the presenting/producing organization that will result in the development of new artistic work to be included in the performance. In the third set of instructions for the concert performance itself, the performance instructions (in the right-hand column) are placed alongside brief descriptions of each movement that give the reader an intentionally partial sense and feel of the music (in the left-hand column).

191

Pre-performance Instructions, Part 1

Preconcert experience for "qimmit katajjaq / sqwélqwel tl' sqwmá:y"

Take the Dog Sled (2008)
Alexina Louie

A concert hall foyer.
Tickets claimed.
Coats checked.
Program note received.

Entering the hall and finding seats.
Musicians and throat singers enter onto the stage
and find their seats.
The throat singers avoid looking at each other
They avoid holding each other.

The audience:
Waiting. Looking. Reading.
Waiting.
The lights go down.
The concertmaster enters: Clapping.
Musicians tuning: No Clapping.
The conductor enters: Clapping.
Quiet.
Near-quiet rustlings.
A cough.
Another cough.
Several throat lozenge wrappers unfurled.

The conductor looks at the score

upon the lectern.

He raises his baton.

Music begins.

"qimmit katajjaq / sqwélqwel tl' sqwmá:y" (2018)
Dylan Robinson

A concert hall foyer filled with pairs of singers
playing throat games. Katajjaq.
Winning. Losing. Laughing. Having fun.
A foyer filled with Inuit sound and laughter.
With singers playing and players singing.

Audience members negotiate paths around players.
Entering the hall, a text projection:
>"We're cheating. My grandmother would be angry
>if she saw us singing this way"—Evie Mark.

And then, a recording of Alexina Louie:
>"It's all written down on the page.
>It's not like 'go have some fun.'
>You can hear that this tradition is totally oral;
>it's not written down. And orchestral musicians,
>they don't improvise. . . . So that was the problem.
>Because you could do the cop-out, which would be to
>have the singers sing and have the players play.
>Have the singers sing and have the players play.
>But that was not what the assignment was.
>Basically, I saw the assignment
>as bringing two worlds together . . ."

All musicians and conductor walk on stage at once.
>". . . so that when the piece is played
>in little tiny communities in the North
>they will hear something fantastic:
>a combination of two worlds.
>It's all written down on the page.
>It's not like 'go have some fun.'"[2]

A statement is projected behind the ensemble:
>"Each one of these movements is like
>a snapshot of the North."—Alexina Louie.

Take the Dog Sled begins suddenly.

Pre-performance Instructions, Part 2: Production

One year before the performance, the presenting/producing organization will be required to employ an Inuit filmmaker to spend a month working in a community with Inuit youth, teaching them filmmaking and film editing. These youth will film the physical location of the community they live in and/or daily events from their lives. They will film what they think is important. They will then edit eight short films— each matching the length of the eight movements in *Take the Dog Sled*. The films should not be made in order to match the themes of *Take the Dog Sled*'s movements but have their own internal logic and focus. The eight films will be presented simultaneously to the eight movements of *Take the Dog Sled* and will be screened in a separate room in the same building where *Take the Dog Sled* is being performed. The audience will make a choice.

Prior to the eighth movement of *Take the Dog Sled* (in one room) and eighth film (in the other room), excerpts from a number of documentary films will be screened about the sled dog slaughter that occurred from the mid-1950s until the late 1960s in the North. These film excerpts will be drawn from the testimony of Inuit people given at the Qikiqtani Truth Commission as well as interviews of Inuit and Royal Canadian Mounted Police conducted for the National Film Board documentary "Qimmit: A Clash of Two Truths" by Ole Gjerstad and Joelie Sanguya (2010), and the film "Echo of the Last Howl" (2004) produced by Taqramiut Productions for the Makivik Corporation. Should it be of interest, students are welcome to contribute to these excerpts from their own, their families', and their communites' perspectives. Community consultation will determine which excerpts should be screened prior to the eighth movement. Alternatively, communities may determine it is not necessary to screen these documentary excerpts.

Event Score for Responsibility 195

Concert Performance Instructions for "qimmit katajjaq / sqwélqwel tl' sqwmá:y"

The following describes the music for each movement of *Take the Dog Sled*.

During each movement, the following statements and images are projected on a large screen behind the musicians. Each quote or several-line statement should remain projected for at least thirty seconds. Individual words and several-word statements should be projected for at least fifteen seconds. There should be at least ten seconds of black background between each quote, statement, or word(s).[3]

1. Tundra

The sound of ice cracking is made by the percussionist hitting two rocks together. The sound of snow crushed underfoot is made by the trombone blowing into the instrument without producing a tone, and the percussionist using sand paper.

1. Tundra

"I wanted to evoke the sense of the land that I have actually seen from a twin-engine Otter. How can I bring all of you who have never been up there, who have perhaps never seen the North, how can I bring you into the piece so that you feel that you're sitting right there in that twin-engine Otter with me?"
—Alexina Louie, 2008

Playing.

Are they playing?

2. Sharpening the Runners of the Dog Sled

The orchestra plays with an unrelenting tempo.

2. Sharpening the Runners of the Dog Sled

"You're not just going to hear the singers and then the orchestra, the singers and then the players; you're going to hear them actually working together to make this

sharpening the runners on the dogsled, which is very rhythmic."
—Alexina Louie, 2008

Whose time?

3. Snow Goose

Alexina Louie: ". . . it is actually a traditional Inuit throat song. I evoke the sound of the snow goose for all of us." The sound is created by using violin glissandi.

3. Snow Goose

Are they winning?

Who's losing?

4. Cradle Song

Gently lilting, "Cradle Song" uses Balinese harmonies, soft trills, light bells.

4. Cradle Song

". . . this was inspired by a photo I saw of an Inuit mother in a traditional sealskin parka with fur. And she was holding her baby. And you can tell there was a great love between mother and child. It is a universal love. . . . I dug very deep inside myself to find music that would be very tender."
—Alexina Louie, 2008

Hundreds of photos:
children standing in front of
    residential schools
with hands clasped in front
posed sitting at desks,
their hands writing or holding
    books;
on beds, hands praying.
No photos of children being
    taken from their parents.
No photos of children at home,
    in bed.

5. Mosquito & 6. Bug Music

The throat song "Mosquito" is sung during the movement titled the same.

"Bug Music" follows directly after "Mosquito" without pause, the sound of a violin conjures a mosquito's flight around the room until it is killed by a percussionist striking two wood blocks together.

5. Mosquito & 6. Bug Music

"Onto a boy's arm came a
   mosquito.
'Don't hit! Don't hit!' it hummed,
'Grandchildren have I to sing to.'
'Imagine,' the boy said,
'So small and yet a grandfather.'"
            —Traditional Inuit Story[4]

7. The River

The throat song "The River" is
   sung.
The orchestra tries to sound like
   a river.
More trills and undulating repe-
   titions.

7. The River

Projection should include specific statistics on the disruptions to Inuit subsistence (hunting, fishing) caused by hydroelectric projects on Inuit territories that are embedded in a film that shows the construction of a hydroelectric station or other physical impositions upon or disruptions of Inuit lands.

~ Screening of Excerpts from Documentary Films on the Sled Dog Slaughter ~

8. Great Dog Sled Journey (Keep Going)

The orchestra blows into bottles,
   imitating throat singing.
A rhythmic journey by dog sled.

8. Great Dog Sled Journey (Keep Going)

"I wanted the orchestra to get in on the fun of this call and response . . . I'm thinking 'how can I bring these two worlds together?' So I have the wind players and the brass players find an instrument and they have to find bottles that resonate and I give them a rhythmic pattern to blow on. And it's a rhythmic, propulsive movement.

"I wanted to put you on a dog sled."

—Alexina Louie

"It would have been interesting if you'd written this as a competition."

—Evie Mark, singer

As the music concludes, the screen will cut to two written statements, each projected for twenty seconds, during which time the musicians exit individually:

No more snapshots

do you know
what do you know

Postlude

The projections alternate between explicit political critique and poetic gesture, between Brechtian distancing and subtle openings to reorienting perception. Like the forms of performative writing discussed earlier in chapter 2, "*qimmit katajjaq / sqwélqwel tl' sqwmá:y*" takes part in "showing, not telling" as a strategy. As such, I will not describe the individual intentions behind each movement's intervention, but want instead to note that the relative brevity and paucity of projected statements is intentional. The challenge for much inter-arts performance involving concert music is that the visual overwhelms attentional flexibility and overdetermines sound's multivalent meaning. To counter this, the paucity of image and brevity of text allows the viewer to attend to the sonic once visual and linguistic interest has been exhausted.

FIVE

FEELING RECONCILIATION

Against a background of a general, if differential, loss of belief
in formal modes of efficacy, and especially political engagement,
Western cultures are becoming increasingly prone to brief moments
of engagement tied to the affective texture of particular events.

—Nigel Thrift, *Non-Representational Theory*

It's over.
I'm sitting in a theatre.
Beyond Eden,
about "salvaging" poles from Haida Gwaii,
just finished
people clap, exuberantly
then people start rising, quickly
two by two; four by four;
entire rows of people rising
ovating
shouting
and now whistling
soon the whole theatre is standing
as I sit,
bristling
seething
not standing
I will not stand.
and then, suddenly
I feel myself crying
I wasn't alone

Feeling Reconciliation

In an interview Bruce Ruddell, *Beyond Eden*'s composer, notes: "We had audiences in tears every night."[1] Approximately thirty evenings of tears: one month of crying, more than a thousand people crying. To refer to the tears of audiences is to refer to the success, and some might say the transformative power, of performance.[2] The more tears, the better. Perhaps you yourself have witnessed intercultural music featuring Indigenous performers and felt moved; perhaps you have risen to your feet, propelled by the wave of movement around you or feeling its surge of peer pressure; perhaps you have cried.

But what, exactly, is at the heart of all this crying? What are the reasons, moreover, behind the strikingly consistent tears of audiences upon experiencing inclusionary music performances involving First Peoples, like the musical *Beyond Eden*?[3] This chapter examines the reception of inclusionary performance from a participant-observer framework focused on affect and "feeling reconciliation." I examine three performances presented as part of the Vancouver 2010 Cultural Olympiad: *Different Drum,* a performance that might best be described as powwow-bhangra-electronic music; *Hannah and the Inukshuks,* where a troupe of *Ilanaaq* (the Olympic-colored inukshuk mascot) come to life; and the rock musical *Beyond Eden,* about Bill Reid's expedition to Haida Gwaii to salvage poles, and among them mortuary poles. I follow this by considering a concert presented in a reconciliation context: the Truth and Reconciliation Commission of Canada's Victoria regional event in British Columbia on April 14, 2012, where the Gettin' Higher Choir performed a choral arrangement of Inuk singer Susan Aglukark's song "O Siem."

In examining these performances, I pursue two related aims. The first is to challenge the assumption that the shared affect—or "affective contagion" (Brennan 2004)—represented by an audience's tears indicates an experience of positive transformation that is similarly felt by audience members. Drawing on my own affective experience and observations of audience members around me, I situate this response alongside performance studies scholarship that has valorized the *communitas* of shared affect, and has read these shared physiological responses (crying, clapping, ovations) as signifying shared emotion (Dolan 2005). As the case studies in this chapter show, however, such responses may have strikingly different efficacies for Indigenous and settler audience members.

Feeling Reconciliation 203

My second aim is to examine how these inclusionary performances engender felt forms of reconciliation. I argue that performances involving First Peoples and non-Indigenous performers are not merely symbolic reflections of reconciliation—visual representations of working together by playing and moving together on stage—but a primary site for audiences to feel reconciliation's non-representational pull of resolution. Inclusionary music here acts as a site of affective investment where the push and pull of harmonic development and drive toward resolution arouse and sustain desire. While such arguments have had prominence since Susan McClary's *Feminine Endings*, this chapter's focus on inclusionary music's teleology seeks to show how repetitive, or "recombinant," teleological structures (Fink 2005) do not so much convince us of consensus as allow us to feel it.[4] In such instances, reconciliation takes the form of feeling a transformative experience.

This chapter differs from previous chapters in a few ways. First, the four performances I examine fall slightly outside of the art music category, although each maintains a connection with art music. *Different Drum* foregrounds Cree-Menonite cellist Cris Derksen's live performance as much as it does bhangra dancing. *Hannah and the Inukshuks* is a dance choreographed to orchestral music reminiscent of Aaron Copland. The Gettin' Higher Choir's performances of "O Siem," in turn, are a choral arrangement of Aglukark's pop song. *Beyond Eden* perhaps bears the least connection to art music, though as a musical it is a close cousin. With the exception of *Hannah and the Inukshuks,* none of these performances would find themselves out of place on a classical music concert or season series, particularly given the increasing embrace of the once-vilified popular music repertoire in an attempt to draw larger audiences from a younger demographic.

This chapter also differs from the others by foregrounding my experiences as a spectator through performative writing. As with the poetics of the opening page of this chapter, at various moments throughout the chapter I seek to give the non-representational aspects of these performances a greater measure of sensory imprint on the page. To convey the material impact of experiencing these works, the chapter will be punctuated by writing that, like affect itself, typifies the simultaneity of disorientation and intensity fundamental to such experience.

Non-representational Forms of Reconciliation

It is reasonable to expect that audiences might cry at performances that expressly focus on residential school histories, where trauma and abuse are represented on stage.[5] Yet to consider affect as derived solely from traumatic representation is to apply what Davide Panagia calls a "narratocratic" reading of sensory experience. For Panagia, narratocracy is "the organization of a perceptual field according to the imperative of rendering things readable" (Panagia 2009, 12). Narratocracy thus renders sensory experience as "making sense," as communication through narrative explanation. Rather than falling back on rationalizations for affect that rely on narrative explanation (i.e., "I cried because the piece related a story of injustice"), performances of works like *Beyond Eden* that do not trade in traumatic representation prompt questions of how the non-representational and formal qualities of performance engender affect.

This chapter offers two related perspectives that emphasize reconciliation's non-representational character, with the larger aim of understanding how audience experiences constitute affective forms of reconciliation. In contrast to the typical focus on reconciliation as the situation wherein two opposing groups or individuals come to "restore relations, to bring into agreement and establish peaceful co-existence" (Scott 2010, 206), what I offer here focuses on those moments where audience members' affective responses to music are experienced and described as felt forms of reconciliation. In such moments, audience members are affected by what might be called reconciliation's sensate qualities: its textures, its materiality, its atmospheres, and particularly its resonance.[6]

From the Latin *reconcilare*, "to bring together again," the first account identifies reconciliation as an experience wherein sound's materiality precipitates a heightened fullness, a feeling of abundance, in an exceptional moment of coming together. Anthropologist Victor Turner called such experience *communitas*, a collective state "where all personal differences of class, age, gender, and other personal distinctions are stripped away allowing people to temporarily merge through their basic humanity" (Turino 2008, 18). In the realm of music, experiences of *communitas* have been the subject of scholarship on ensemble music performance, with its shared sense of common goals. While performing, Thomas Turino notes, [musicians] are fully focused on the activity that emphasizes our *sameness*—of time sense, of musical sensibility, of musical habits of knowledge, of patterns of thought and action, of spirit, of common goals—as well as our direct interaction. Within the bounded and concentrated frame of musical performance *that sameness* is all that matters, and for those moments when the performance is focused and in sync, that deep identification is *felt* as total. (Turino 2008, 18; emphasis in original)

Drawing together Turino's observations with Christopher Small's well-known concept of *musicking,* which comprises the listener's participation in equal measure to the musicians' performing, Turino's description of coming together in sameness might also be extended toward the listening audience. Audience members, their sense of subjectivity temporarily suspended in what Turino would call an experience of "flow," may also feel this unity, this coming together.[7] The heightened connection audience members experience with those who perform—the identificatory aspect of listening—is also physical. The visceral qualities of sound as it moves through space and makes contact with listeners' bodies here effect what R. Murray Schafer calls sound's capacity for "touching at a distance" (Schafer 2012, 102). As an (im)material connective tissue, sound joins performers on stage with their audience. In another sense, we might describe music's affective and material collapse of distance as agglutinating.[8] This agglutinating not only effects affective connection; it has the additional ability, as musicologist Lawrence Kramer has argued, to make meaning "stick" to the music it associates with. Particularly in the case of absolute music that has no explicit representational content of its own, our heightened experiences combined with description in everything from program notes to commercial voice-over stick together to make such description all the more real. "To make anything more itself, or more anything," notes Kramer, "just add music" (Kramer 2002, 3). As this chapter's case studies examine, within a Canadian context, music agglutinates a preexisting exceptionalist belief in multiculturalism,[9] a universalist claim to transcending (negative) difference, and visual/musical representations of Indigeneity to produce reconciliatory affect. This reconciliatory affect conflates a collapse of distance with a collapse of difference.

Looking further into reconciliation's etymological origin provides a second non-representational reading of the term. Its root, *conciliare,* reminds us that the term stems from "to make friendly." At the heart of reconciliation then, at least etymologically, is a concern with "good" feelings of friendliness. The works examined in this chapter achieve their affective impact within this context of friendship. While the context of the Olympics (the site of *Beyond Eden*'s performance) is specifically concerned with principles of global peace and friendship, reconciliation as a return to positive feeling is also increasingly evident at TRC events themselves (the performance site of "O Siem").[10]

Between 2009 and 2015 I attended the TRC's national and regional events across Canada as part of the collaborative research project on the role of the arts in the TRC. It was at these events that I began to understand the use of the TRC as a site for survivors and intergenerational survivors to come together with their families and communities to share their experience of residential schools and the legacies of that experience. What also became clear at these gatherings was how the discourse of friendship circulated. Beginning with the 2012 Victoria regional gathering, each TRC event held a town hall gathering called "It Matters to Me."[11] The sessions at the 2012 Victoria and Saskatoon events were led by CBC Radio personality Shelagh Rogers and consisted largely of non-Native participants.[12] These forums were intended to offer space for the public to reflect on what they have witnessed and learned during TRC events, but also to discuss actions to be taken, individually and by Canadian institutions, in order for change to occur. Notably, a large number of those who gave public expressions at the Victoria and Saskatoon "It Matters to Me" sessions avoided making individual commitments or enumerating how they might be responsible for future change; participants seldom mentioned material reparation, restitution, or ways of giving over power, unless these were appeals to institutions (school boards, the government, the churches) to do so. Many of the contributions by settler participants addressed the need to cultivate harmonious relationships with First Peoples, while discussions regarding the need to establish political nation-to-nation relationships remained conspicuously absent. The language used by many of the "It Matters to Me" participants at sessions in Victoria and Saskatoon often dealt in the currency of friendship. On multiple occasions at the Victoria regional event Shelagh Rogers emphasized how "we're all part of the same great embrace," while the non-Indigenous poet Wendy Morton twice entreated audience members (whom she assumed to be settlers) to "please have a First Nations friend."

In spring 2013 the TRC expanded this forum, launching an online platform called "Reconciliation . . . Towards a New Relationship." As part of this website, users could create a personal "twibbon" (twitter-length virtual ribbon) of 524 characters or less; the intention was that the accumulation of these statements online would "represent a cross-section of Canadian society explaining why reconciliation matters to them" (Truth and Reconciliation Commission of Canada, n.d.). Linda Grimes commented on this forum, "It matters to me because continued feelings of sorrow, guilt, and mistrust are exhausting and unhealthy for everyone. We need to work towards replacing those feelings with joy, respect, and trust." While few would deny that sorrow, guilt, and mistrust might be exhausting, even paralyzing, the above statement also stands in for a much larger concern in the discourse of reconciliation, both generally and at TRC events specifically, with the elimination of negative emotion. Reconciliation as a return to good feelings privileges the public purging of sadness and anger associated with residential school memories that will supposedly allow survivors to "move on." The burden here lies with Indigenous people to "get over" our resentment and other negative emotions in order for reconciliation to occur and to make room for renewed friendship with the settler Canadian public and nation-state. The musical presentation of reconciliation-as-friendship, and the related need for First Peoples to "get over" negative emotions, were a feature both in settler music contributions to the TRC and also in the 2010 Winter Olympics in Vancouver.

Dancing to the Beat of *Different Drum*

Through the ideals of the Olympic Truce, the International Olympic Committee prioritizes "contributing to the search for peaceful and diplomatic solutions to the conflicts around the world" (IOC 2009). Established in Greece in the ninth century BCE, this truce enabled "athletes, artists and their families to travel in total safety to participate in or attend the Olympic Games and return afterwards to their respective countries." In present-day terms, this and other principles of peace are translated in the various symbols employed by the IOC, like the different colors of the interlocking rings on the Olympic flag, or the Olympic Truce symbol. As explained by the IOC, this symbol depicts how

> the Olympic flame has brought warm friendship to all the people of the world through sharing and global togetherness. In the symbol, the flame is made up of colourful effervescent elements—reminiscent of festivities experienced in the celebration of the human spirit. These elements represent people of all races coming together for the observance of the Truce. (IOC 2009)

The ideal of the Olympic Truce, as told through the symbol's various visual components, represents both a state of temporary reconciliation and also reinforces those qualities of reconciliation previously mentioned: warm friendship and togetherness. In 2010 the Vancouver Olympics sought to demonstrate these principles of reconciliation through its own symbols of Indigenous solidarity with the Canadian nation-state. This narrative of solidarity saturated all aspects of the Games, from the involvement of the four host First Nations (xʷməθkʷəy̓əm/Musqueam, Səlilwət/Tselil-Waututh, Skwxwú7mesh/Squamish, and Líl̓wat/Lil'wat) in planning the event itself, to the centralization of Indigenous performance in the opening ceremony. As the most prominent demonstration of inclusion, the ceremony began with each of the four host First Na-

Figure 18. "Olympic Truce Symbol." Copyright International Olympic Committee (IOC). All rights reserved. Reproduced under license from the IOC8.

tions welcoming the world to their lands and was followed by a dance where each First Nation across Canada was represented by one or more dancers. Performances by more than fifty Indigenous artists were also programmed in the Aboriginal Pavilion and other stages and venues across the city over the seventeen-day span of the Olympics. Such inclusion was not limited only to the Olympics, however; it was also scripted into those events leading up to the Olympics in the Cultural Olympiad and Olympic Torch Relay events.

On February 7, 2010, the Olympic Torch passed through Abbotsford, a suburb approximately 75 kilometers outside of Vancouver. Tourism Abbotsford's "2010 Abbotsford Olympic Engagement Report" noted an estimated 15,000 to 20,000 spectators took part in the Torch Relay Celebration event at Abbotsford Rotary Stadium. The event included the performance *Different Drum*, featuring two dance groups from British Columbia's Fraser Valley: The Good Medicine Dancers, including powwow Jingle Dress, Fancy, and Grass dancers, and Abbotsford's Sada Virsa Sada Guarav Bhangra Club (translation: "not only dance, but a way of being"), dancing to music by the Cree cellist Cris Derksen. Even before the process of devising the piece began, *Different Drum*'s choreographer Lee Kwidzinski noted there was considerable resistance to the idea for the performance from most of the powwow dancers she approached. Many were willing to perform on their own, or alternate between their dancing and other dance traditions, but almost none of the powwow dancers Kwidzinski approached were willing to experiment with blending it with other forms of dance: "They were quite open if I were to give each of them their own five-minute time slot and they were to do their own thing," Kwidzinski noted, "but coming together, they weren't interested in that" (interview with author, February 3, 2012). Once Kwidzinski was able to locate dancers willing to take part in the performance, such challenges continued from both groups, who were at first quite resistant to adapting their dance traditions into a single piece. Kwidzinski, along with arts programmer Kat Wahamaa who had the initial idea for the work, envisioned a piece that would both maintain a respectful relationship with dancers' cultural values and honor Kwidzinski's artistic values as a choreographer "to make it interesting artistically, and make it a fusion. We were very clear, Kat and I, that we didn't want them dancing their own dance separately; we wanted to blend them."

Figure 19. *Different Drum.* Courtesy of the Province of British Columbia and Creative Commons, 2010.

Figure 20. *Different Drum.* Courtesy of the Province of British Columbia and Creative Commons, 2010.

Musically, *Different Drum* incorporates two electronic dance works previously composed and recorded by Derksen but here performed live by her on cello and looping pedals. The first of these, "What did you do boy," was also the opening music for the Canadian Broadcasting Corporation's (CBC's) four-part miniseries *The 8TH Fire*, a series that "draws from an Anishinaabe prophecy that declares now is the time for Aboriginal peoples and the settler community to come together and build the '8TH Fire' of justice and harmony" (Canadian Broadcasting Corporation, n.d.). Although the show did not air on CBC until 2012, for viewers like myself who belatedly watched *Different Drum* on YouTube rather than at the Torch Ceremony itself, the anachronistic echo back to the focus of *The 8TH Fire* is unmistakable. In its focus on "Aboriginal Peoples, Canada, & The Way Forward" (Canadian Broadcasting Corporation, n.d.), *The 8TH Fire* was centrally concerned with reconciliation and often was explicit in its call for a social, economical, and political renewal of nation-to-nation relationships. Derksen's music, as the theme music for *The 8TH Fire*, bears the imprint of this discourse. For Kwidzinski, however, the music served a much different purpose:

> I knew that we needed *some* neutral ground somewhere to bring these two groups together. So when I thought, "let's go with neutral music," I had seen an ad for a performance in East Vancouver, which was where I saw Cris, so I went to the performance and saw her play and thought "this would work" . . . I thought it was music that was not too far . . . or not too odd for either of the cultures to listen to . . . so I thought it was something that we could come together on. (Lee Kwidzinski, interview with author, February 3, 2012)

As Kwidzinski explained later in the same interview, the rhythmic drive of Derksen's music was similar enough to both bhangra and powwow music that it offered the possibility of not having to sacrifice the core principles of either dance tradition. Derksen's music functioned as mediation that allowed cultural difference to comfortably occupy the same space. In doing so, the music was made to function as the agent of reconciliation in bringing the two groups together.

Choreographically, Kwidzinski noted the challenge of working with dance aesthetics that occupied space in dramatically different ways. While the bhangra dancing entailed dynamic, fast-moving patterns that traversed the entire stage, the powwow dancing—and the Jingle Dress dancing in particular—was defined by more static, in-place movement. "The Native dancers didn't take up space across the stage," emphasized Kwidzinski, "so how do we engage an audience for ten minutes when you're not taking up space?" Other than a brief opening segment where a Grass dancer performed on his own, Kwidzinski's solution was to choreograph the bhangra dancers' more dynamic movement around the powwow dancers. The assumption that a dancing body rooted in a single spot cannot command or sustain the attention of audiences prefigures a spatial politics that is not limited to the intercultural encounter onstage. Not all dance "travels." Nor do cultural practices occupy space in the same way. Kwidzinski's values of active versus passive spatialization, or what we might call "kinetic equality," conceptualize a choreographic filling of space that is commensurate with *terra nullius* judgments of uncultivated and unproductive land.[13] To understand powwow dancing as "not taking up space," is to misrecognize the dancers' use of space within a culturally situated framework. In another sense, Kwidzinski's observation that the powwow dancers "didn't take up space" is remarkably ironic, considering the extent of treaty settlement cases currently before the courts that are fundamentally concerned with First Peoples sovereign rights to the land now known as Canada. Even more curious is the fact that most powwow dancers will take up quite a bit of space moving through the dance arena, and from this perspective, "not taking up space" might instead signify a difference in not taking up that space in the way that Western choreography would. Indeed, their "lack" of filling the space might here be understood as the dancers reacting to an uncomfortable context where the correct "taking up of space" was premised on a non-Indigenous model of movement.[14]

It is useful to distinguish two aspects of *Different Drum*: its process of development and its performance. From the perspective of process, Kwidzinski's observation speaks to the choice of the powwow dancers to uphold an Indigenous model of taking up space. We can read the dancers' unwillingness to attune Powwow dancing to the dynamic quality of bhangra, or to the filling of space central to the principles of exuberant multicultural spectacle, as a desire to maintain spatial sovereignty. However, in reading the product of this collaboration, the performance itself, such a choice becomes less evident on stage. The bhangra dancers' movement across the stage and around the powwow dancers becomes a site of swirling activity that by and large subsumes the particularities of cultural difference. The diffuse fusion of bodies, materials, and colors as they spread throughout the space results in "kinetic equality," a choreography of neoliberal multiculturalism wherein one cultural practice takes up no more space than another. Kwidzinski's choreography might be understood to represent a spatial politics that dis-enables the recognition of Indigenous sovereignty. And yet, in itself, this representational reading of *Different Drum* is insufficient for grasping the reception of the performance's material and sensory politics; it reduces the work to a structural homology of assimilation. To understand its felt politics, we must also consider the non-representational aspects of *Different Drum*'s performance; we must account for the swirling experience of its materiality.

As noted, *Different Drum* offers an experience of community for its audience that hinges on the leveling of difference through an equality wherein space is filled up through exuberant dance. Its kinetic equality is redoubled through the vibrant flurry of bhangra scarves and powwow dance regalia that fills the space. Speaking to a similar fullness in film musical sequences like "Think Pink" from *Funny Face* (itself filled with swirling fabrics), Richard Dyer characterizes such exuberant display as "abundance." Although Dyer's work pertains specifically to the film musical genre, his application of the non-representational aspects of entertainment is useful for thinking about the spectacle of festivals more generally. The qualities of multicultural spectacle found in Olympic celebrations are apposite to Dyer's characterization of the utopian sensibility or feelings that musicals provide. Entertainment, Dyer says, provides "the image of 'something better' to escape into, or something we want deeply that our day-to-day lives don't provide" (Dyer 2002, 20). Entertainment's utopian sensibilities, he argues, attempt to compensate for inadequacies in society. The category of abundance in Dyer's framework here combats "scarcity (actual poverty in the society; poverty observable in the surrounding societies, e.g. Third World); unequal distribution of wealth" (26). The feeling of scarcity (though obviously not scarcity itself), Dyer claims, is alleviated through entertainment's non-representational quality of abundance.

In its response to anxieties over scarcity of resources (such as jobs) and social benefits (such as pensions) and the larger "uncertainty" of land claims in the resource economy (Mackey 2016), *Different Drum*'s abundance offers a space for coming together (onstage and in the audience) to occupy space *equally*, a space where Indigenous claims to sovereignty, demands for reparation, and efforts to publicly mark histories of colonial and contemporary injustice are temporarily suspended by the exigencies of the Olympic Truce. *Different Drum* here provides a role for Indigenous difference: to provide the energy, color, and vibrancy that model Canada's policy of "official multiculturalism" upon the stage. Canada's official multiculturalism, as Eva Mackey notes, "extends the state recognition of multiple forms of difference, so as to undercut . . . more threatening [forms of] difference" (Mackey 2002, 64). Yet *Different Drum* does not merely model a role for First Peoples in Canada as source of friendly diversity; in Rancièrian terms, it offers a redistribution of the sensible that counters the normative negative image of First Peoples as a drain on the welfare state. In sum, *Different Drum*'s (vibrant) "neutral ground" flattens both the lived inequalities of difference as well as difference's radical alterity. As such it provides abundance to counteract the scarcity of resources. Moreover, it provides a shared space that, in its openness to universal difference, is firstly comfortable. As with the majority of the music treated in this chapter, *Different Drum* bears only a marginal imprint of difference's alterity and inaccessibility, particularly with its orientation toward a model of fusion as indistinctiveness. In contrast, the relatively spare quality of a work like Dawn Avery's "two worlds" treated in chapter 3 would sit less comfortably in a space of celebration like the Abbotsford Torch Relay Celebration. The function of these performances, as with much state-led celebration, is to include their audiences with minimal threat of alienation.

This is equally the case in *Hannah and the Inukshuks*, the performance that followed *Different Drum*. In this performance the audience is introduced to a group of *Ilanaaq*, an inukshuk rendered in the Olympic colors, representing the central logo of the 2010 Olympics. *Ilanaaq*, translated as "friendship" in Inuktitut, is the literal embodiment of friendly difference. *Hannah and the Inukshuks*'s performance opens with a group of adult *Ilanaaq* jumping in unison to the accented off-beats of music that one might imagine accompanying a barn dance.[15] Dressed in marshmallow-like costumes of foam, the *Ilanaaq* wobble around the stage joyfully before being joined by a baby *Ilanaaq* (at which point a

Feeling Reconciliation 215

collective "awww" emerges from the audience), who we learn is about to embark on a journey on his own. As the baby Inukshuk wobbles toward the stage exit, the adult *Ilanaaq* wave farewell. But just as the baby *Ilanaaq* is about to exit, it hesitates (perhaps realizing it doesn't want to leave its *Ilanaaq* community behind) and returns to an enthusiastic welcome home. As a coda to the story, a young woman whom we assume to be Hannah joins the *Ilanaaq*. Dressed in full Olympic attire—a Roots-branded "Canada" written across her torso—Hannah gracefully dances across the stage. Her dancing is here in sharp contrast with the wobbly *Ilanaaq* who barely manage to coordinate jumping together in unison. Smiling from ear to ear, Hannah glides across the stage, picks up baby *Ilanaaq,* and spins it around (again resulting in "awww" from the audience) as they all bounce together happily to the music. Not only does *Hannah and the Inukshuks* literally soften cultural diversity though making Inuksiut into cuddly mascots, it takes part in the infantilization of Indigenous culture that historically considered First Peoples as wards of the state, and continues in the Canadian government's paternalistic relationship with First Peoples.[16] While infantilized depictions of Inuit are prevalent in National Film Board films, including Laura Bolton's 1943 "Eskimo Arts and Crafts" and the 1966 film "Tuktu and his Eskimo Dogs" (with music by Robert Fleming), paternalism continues today in instances such as Prime Minister Stephen Harper's 2008 apology to residential school survivors to see this discourse in operation through the acknowledgment "we apologize for failing to protect you" that is unintentionally ironic in its obliviousness to the fact that such "protection" was needed not as much *by* the state as *from* the state.[17]

The nonthreatening, friendly approach of *Different Drum* and *Hannah and the Inukshuks* claims a certain kind of respectfulness toward cultural difference by making such difference palatable and accessible. Such performances are unabashedly spectacular and celebratory. Their designs explicitly model and extend feelings of communitas outward to the public. The good feelings these works seek to engender here guarantee that hungry listening proceeds without pause, as desire for difference is redoubled through the literal sweetness of *Hannah and the Inukshuks*'s spectacle, and through the plentiful visual cornucopia of *Different Drum*'s display. Although it is unrealistic to expect that such mega-events program their performances otherwise, by critically

Figure 21. *Hannah and the Inukshuks*. Photograph copyright Jason Brown, Revival Arts Studio, 2010.

engaging with the utopian feelings of such work we might better understand how it is driven by satiate desire. The utopian feeling of such works' bounty acts to satiate the uncertainty of radical difference, an uncertainty of resource availability combined with challenges to entitlement that is felt increasingly by the settler Canadian public. Hungry listening not only has an appetite for abundant sweetness, however; it equally consumes the bitter spectacle of Indigenous injustice and trauma, as is the case in the musical *Beyond Eden*.

Beyond Eden

Like Olympic opening ceremonies, *Different Drum* and *Hannah and the Inukshuks* take part in the build-up of Olympic enthusiasm, provoking exuberant and uplifting responses from audience members. The collective power of these responses intends to raise audiences' "Olympic spirit" and to rouse feelings of national pride "with glowing hearts," as one of the 2010 Olympic trademark mottos (and Canadian national anthem) would have it. The experience of intense emotional response in reaction to Indigenous inclusionary performance is not exclusive to the realm of Olympic fervor, however. For those stories with less-than-celebratory narratives, like the rock musical *Beyond Eden,* we see an exuberant response of consistent ovation and audiences overcome by tears. According to Jill Dolan, we might understand these intense emotional responses as the result of what she calls "utopian performatives," those "profound moments in which performance calls the attention of the audience in a way that lifts everyone slightly above the present, into a hopeful feeling of what the world might be like if every moment of our lives were as emotionally voluminous, generous, aesthetically striking, and intersubjectively intense" (Dolan 2005, 5). Dolan's examination of how performance lifts audience members above the mundane and gives them hope draws on performative speech acts, which, according to J. L. Austin, enact the activities the speech signifies (i.e. "I promise") (Dolan 2005, 4–11). In extending Austin's theory, Dolan argues that utopian performatives are equally constituted through their uplifting hopeful narrative content as by their *non-representational* aspects (for instance, their celebratory atmosphere, buoyancy of movement, and even the teleological progression and resolution of song). Such non-representational content "inspire[s] moments in which audiences feel themselves allied with each other, and with a broader, more capacious sense of a public, in which social discourse articulates the possible, rather than the insurmountable obstacles to human potential" (164). This hope, in turn, "create[s] the *condition* for action; [it] pave[s] a certain kind of way, prepare[s] people for the choices they might make in other aspects of their lives" (169).

While I would agree with Dolan that a demonstration of hope witnessed in performance might then engender hope in the viewer, I contend that it is the physiological responses audiences experience—smiling, laughter, and crying—in themselves that afford a greater level of belief in performance's transformative power. Here affect, like absolute music, takes part in a kind of feedback loop *because* of its non-representational ineffability, because audience members cannot immediately identify what exactly such experience signifies. That is, affect allows an investment of belief in the sociopolitical impact of such work through a thinking-feeling of the work's "truth," or what I have elsewhere called its "sensory veracity" (Robinson 2012). Sensory veracity proposes that audiences cry (or have other sensory-physiological experiences) in response to performance, and from the intensity of this experience identify their response as apposite to the work's social or political truth. In sum, the intensity of affect when experiencing socially and politically oriented performance allows for a conflation of affect with efficacy. Audiences are persuaded, or more accurately *feel,* that something has happened; a moment (or more) of something ineffable that might best be called "reconciliation" has been witnessed because our affective response is irreducible, and as such does not lie. Moreover, this conflation of affect with efficacy is confirmed, and perhaps redoubled, when a consensus of response in fellow audience members is perceived. Yet I would argue that the strength of affective experience also allows for a mis-interpellation of collectivity and the consensual nature of shared physiological responses. Crying, in particular, does not necessarily represent the same emotional response for those who witness the same event.

> I sit,
> trying to control the flow
> of tears
> Surrounded by exuberant applause,
> I continue my willful exertion of sitting
> My ovation "sit-in."
> The words
> "has it really come to this?"
> (just the words,
> seeming outside
> the flow of continuous thought)
> puncture my disbelief
> as I sit stewing,
> seething. fuming.

We are at the end of *Beyond Eden.* The closing music, a refrain from the musical's title song "Beyond Eden," accompanies this applause. A sparkling of orchestral chimes harkens back to the mystical sense of place evoked throughout the musical. This title song returns us to the moment when we first heard the song: the expedition's arrival at Haida Gwaii during an idyllic morning sunrise following a storm that forced their boat aground: "Morning, and the calm on the ocean / Morning, and the silence in the forest / Morning, / Beyond Eden" (Ruddell and Henderson 2011, 42).

Calm upon arrival in Haida Gwaii.
We are reminded now: all is calm again upon our return.
We regain a sense of being settled.

The song, "Beyond Eden," shares both a melodic contour and intervals with the song "On My Own" from Claude-Michel Schönberg, Alain Boublil, and Jean-Marc Natel's musical *Les Misérables*. One might read into this citation a troubling intertextual reference to *terra nullius,* of being "alone" on the remote shores of Haida Gwaii, where the once-great presence of the Haida has, like the poles, faded away. In contrast, I read this musical intertextuality in relation to feeling settled. Here, the resonance and accessibility of this pattern of notes (in addition to the "soothing" piano accompaniment) from one of the most well-known musicals of our time engenders a sense of comfort and familiarity in the listener. It is toward the political stakes of this aesthetic accessibility to which I will now turn, in order to examine what it means to feel settled.

The Accessibility of Culture

Premiered as part of the Vancouver 2010 Cultural Olympiad, *Beyond Eden* is a fictionalized account of anthropologist Wilson Duff and renowned Haida carver and Canadian art icon Bill Reid's removal of twenty-three Haida poles and monuments from the village of Ninstints (SGang Gwaay) in 1957. Many of the poles removed were memorial and mortuary poles containing remains of the deceased within a cavity at the top of the pole. The justification of this removal was based upon salvage paradigm principles: that the Haida were supposedly unable to care for the poles, and their deterioration necessitated their removal and preservation.[18] While the musical explicitly treats this reason for the poles' salvage, the reasons for the Haida people's opposition remain veiled to the audience. The implication of cultural appropriation is present, but the musical omits specific information surrounding the cultural and spiritual significance of the poles, while the Vancouver production omits this information in its program.[19] *Beyond Eden*'s story instead focuses upon the poles' accessibility for the Canadian public and for Bill Reid as a source of inspiration and learning. The ethical dilemma faced by Reid to salvage the poles in the face of his community's opposition is counterposed with the argument that accessibility to First Peoples' culture will benefit the development of Canadian art. As the musical,

220 Feeling Reconciliation

program notes, and pre-performance talk make clear, the removal of the totem poles acted as the impetus for what has been called the "Haida Renaissance."[20] Housed in the Museum of Anthropology in Vancouver, BC, where they continue to reside, these poles became physically accessible objects of anthropological study and templates for Reid's study of Haida carving. Moreover, the institutionalization of these poles symbolically transformed them into objects of and for Canadian history. The crux of the argument put forward by *Beyond Eden* is that without access to these poles, Reid would not have become the renowned artist Canadians have come to embrace as "Native-Canadian." In his Act II solo in the song "Carving," Max Tomson (who in *Beyond Eden* is meant to represent Haida artist Bill Reid) sings:

> I must have them close to me
> I need them close to me
> To teach these hands to see
> I want them close to me
> I need them close to me
> Teaching these hands to see
> How this cut forms gently
> How this cut sweeps vertically
> How this cut arcs beautifully
> How this cut flows perfectly
> [. . .]
> Gently
> Beautifully
> Perfectly (Ruddell and Henderson 2011, 63)

Make no mistake, poles brought to life by carvers from Northwest coast nations *are* formed through the flow of beautiful cut and gentle arc, with a love that demonstrates care for ancestors. Tomson/Reid's imperative language of need, want, and "must have" here captures his hunger to possess this knowledge. Tomson/Reid's terms ("gently," "beautifully," "perfectly") additionally speak to the Western aesthetic of carving that sees totem poles as masterfully crafted aesthetic objects more than carrying life themselves. Moreover, here and elsewhere in the musical, Reid's expedition is predicated on the use-value of the poles to Canada's artistic heritage, while disavowing the value of the "nonproductive." That is, to more explicitly acknowledge the primacy of Haida poles as a materialization of family and community history, not to mention the cultural authority of the Haida's decision to let these poles return to the earth, would upend Reid's national labors.

Entertainment's Mystery

In scene seven of the first act, Louis Wilson, the anthropologist Wilson Duff's character, sings:

> Aroused by this moment.
> Excited by my fear.
> Knowing that I am moving
> Way beyond what's clear
> Don't know
> Where it's taking me.
> It's still a mystery.
> Like the feathers floating
> On the sea.
> A mystery.
> A mystery.
> And I am awakened,
> to this mystery that
> wants me.
> This mystery
> calls me.
> This mystery
> tempts me.
> This mystery
> flirts with me.
> This mystery
> embraces me.
> I want this mystery! (Ruddell and Henderson 2011, 29–30)

Arriving at the Vancouver Playhouse that day in the midst of the 2010 Cultural Olympiad to see *Beyond Eden*, I knew I was about to experience a spectacle in the form of a musical featuring the former lead singer of the band Spirit of the West, a popular folk-rock group in Canada in the 1980s and early 1990s. What I did not know was that I would stumble into a preshow talk in which Haida culture was to a significant degree still a "mystery" for the majority of non-Indigenous audience members who were present. In this discussion with composer Bruce Ruddell and Gwaai Edenshaw, a Haida carver and cultural advisor for the scenography and music, in a packed room of about sixty people, two different audience members expressed what was for them the confusion surrounding the ethics of the removal of the poles from Haida Gwaii. "If we didn't remove them, then how would anyone be able to see them?" said one member of the audience. "I think Bill Reid did an enormous favor for Canadians by saving those poles and Native culture from dying away," said another. Surely the best course of action for such valuable artworks, emphasized this second audience member, was their protection in the UBC Museum of Anthropology.

At the time I was astonished that these spectators were unaware of the cultural and spiritual significance the poles have for the Haida. I had assumed a greater depth of public knowledge about the role that poles have for Northwest coast First Peoples as physical manifestations of family histories and rights, or in the case of the Haida, that mortuary poles contain the remains of a chief or other high-ranking person. Yet even outside of this context, to remove a tombstone in order to display its aesthetic beauty in a museum would be to desecrate a gravesite. Why would removing a mortuary pole be any different?

In retrospect, we might understand such a view of artistic value as merely consistent with Bill Reid's iconographic status. The very fact that Reid's sculpture *The Spirit of Haida Hwaii* adorned the Canadian twenty-dollar bill from 2004 to 2012 points toward the status of his work as valued on (art) economic terms of Canadian identity export. In popular culture and artistic contexts alike, from the Olympic symbol of *Ilanaaq* to Reid's work more generally, Indigenous culture has increasingly become part of the branding of Canadian identity. This increased integration of Indigenous cultural iconography as the face of national institutions and civic infrastructure alike reframes such cultural practices as no longer a mystery but a constituent aspect of Canada's official multiculturalism that recognizes First Peoples' contributions as an enrichment to the identity of the nation-state.

> And I am awakened,
> to this mystery that
> wants me.
> This mystery

calls me.
This mystery
tempts me.
This mystery
flirts with me.
This mystery
embraces me. (Ruddell and Henderson 2011, 29–30)

At the end of *Beyond Eden* I sat, crying out of anger that these poles had been removed. I sat, crying out of weariness at how the spectacle of this rock musical elided important questions around public entitlement to Indigenous culture. I sat, crying at the crowd who had risen to their feet. Perhaps most of all I sat, crying in disbelief at the exuberance for mystery by those around me. The energy of the audience "aroused by this moment" as they embraced this story of salvage paradigm sat in tension with other less-palatable moments of mystery of which the general public remains ignorant—of the continued struggles of First Peoples who fight to repatriate our cultural wealth, including the songs that were taken from our families and communities. I cried in this instance for the lack of understanding that mortuary poles are not made for the aesthetic pleasure of the Canadian public nor for the celebration of Canadian identity. I cried from the cognitive dissonance between ignorance and affirmation. My crying, lasting mere moments, marked a transformative experience of resentment.

On Witnessing and Resentment in the Truth and Reconciliation Commission of Canada

Much of how one witnesses and listens at the Truth and Reconciliation Commission events depends on certain priorities of responsibility. I began attending the TRC as a scholar interested in the role that music and the arts played at these gatherings. But over the course of the TRC events I attended, my listening responsibilities shifted. At the beginning of each TRC event Justice Murray Sinclair, chief commissioner of the TRC, called on those present to bear witness to what they see and hear and to take the experience they have at the events back to their communities. For church officials this may have meant their congregations; for Members of Parliament this may have meant those in their federal ridings and other government officials; for residential school survivors and intergenerational survivors it may have meant those members of their families unable to face the brutality of history still viscerally present in their memories. For the settler attendees who did not attend TRC gatherings in significant numbers relative to the settler Canadian population, it may have meant their families, colleagues, and neighbors. For me, this call to witness has added significance as someone of Stó:lō descent. The role of witnessing is central to the longhouse work undertaken not just in Stó:lō communities but across all Northwest coast First Nations communities. Because audiovisual and written recordings of the proceedings are prohibited, witnesses act as our books, documenting our history in great detail through xwélalà:m. Such gatherings involve the host speaker calling selected respected members of the community to witness the work that is taking place, nominating them by declaring, "You are asked to witness the work that is being done here." The witness will sometimes respond to orators / siyá:m with the phrase "ô siyám" (a Halq'eméylem expression of thanks and respect). It is an important role to be chosen as an honored witness, and attentive listening within this context is imperative. Witnesses know that they may be called on in the future to recall what they have seen and heard accurately and truthfully. Witnesses bear Stó:lō history within collective memory, and within the heart and body.

Many of us whose parents did not attend residential school are still all-too-aware of its legacy of lateral violence and shame within our communities. We are in the process of reclaiming a history that our parents and grandparents strove to disassociate themselves from.[21] There have been many times during the TRC that I was moved, experienced a sense of heightened community, and felt empathy for survivors. But because of this history that intergenerational survivors from my generation have inherited, I have witnessed testimony and listened to music presented at the TRC events not as someone coming to this history for the first time. I have witnessed with the sedimented weight of knowing intergenerational loss. Often I witnessed and listened with resentment. I have experienced resentment at hearing such remarkably consistent experiences of emotional, physical, and sexual abuse. I have resented the TRC forum itself, where survivors were expected to limit their comments to a contained aspect of settler colonialism: residential school history.[22] I have resented the repeated "contributions" where institutional officials from the Government of Canada, Royal Canadian Mounted Police, and the Catholic Church have abdicated their responsibility. As Dene scholar Glen Coulthard notes, "resentment is often cast as the inability to come to grips with history. Resentment indicates an inability to let go." And yet "embracing one's resentment," as Coulthard contests,

> is not only an entirely defendable position, but actually a sign of our critical consciousness, of our sense of justice and injustice, and of our awareness of, and unwillingness to reconcile ourselves with the structural and symbolic violence that is still very much a part of our lives. Of course we should resent colonialism, as well as those people and institutions who are willfully complicit in its ongoing reproduction. (Coulthard 2014b)

While the majority of artistic and musical contributions taking place at the TRC have not induced such resentment in me, one in particular seared me with its offer of reconciliation.[23]

"O Siem" / We're All the Same

Unlike mere facts and statistics, the arts have the considerable potential to compel audience members to reflect deeply on colonial histories of genocide, on continuing injustices, and on their own accountability to these. For instance, the Métis scholar Jo-Ann Episkenew highlights Aboriginal literature's capacity to

> enable settler readers to relate to Indigenous peoples on an emotional level thereby generating empathy. By reading Indigenous literature, settlers come to understand Indigenous people as fellow human beings. Empathy, in turn, has the potential to create a groundswell of support for social-justice initiatives to improve the lot of Indigenous people. (Episkenew 2009, 190–91)

Music performance even more so has the ability to foster audience identification and empathy with a colonial history that non-Aboriginal Canadians may feel removed from. Where settler subjects' willful ignorance of their country's history of colonization persists, and many continue to resist individual intergenerational responsibility for civic decolonization, the participatory call of music may foment modes of identification that transform perspectives slowly over time. Many scholars have likewise emphasized the ways in which music affords agency for survivors of trauma (Pilzer 2012), provides a way to point toward what lies beyond trauma's representation (Cizmic 2011), and, as Episkenew notes, may provide the first step in settler subjects' future engagement with restorative justice (Episkenew 2009). These perspectives engage with music's *positive* impact on both survivors of trauma and those who are coming to learn about such colonial histories for the first time. And yet, while music and the arts may indeed engender all of these benefits, I am struck by the overwhelming presupposition of music's positive efficacy. I am struck most especially because as a listener I can rarely count myself among the audience that feels positively transformed or empathetically moved.

The different kinds of affect that music can generate for audience members became palpable at the Truth and Reconciliation Commission regional event in Victoria, BC, in April 2012. The first day of this event concluded with a series of performances that reflected First Nations cultural traditions from different Nations across Vancouver Island. A local Victoria choir also performed, the Gettin' Higher Choir, consisting largely of singers over the age of fifty. They concluded their portion of the evening with a version of Inuit singer Susan Aglukark's "O Siem," the chorus of which is familiar to many Canadians from its regular presence on easy listening stations across Canada since it rose to number one in the Canadian adult contemporary charts in 1995: "O Siem, we are all family / O Siem, we're all the same."

After eight hours of listening to testimony from survivors and intergenerational survivors, I listened to the Gettin' Higher Choir's contribution toward reconciliation. The concert was intended to lift peoples' spirits after hours of intense testimony from residential school survivors and intergenerational survivors, and it may have done so for some. Yet to sing this song after a full day's work of telling residential schools' overwhelming history of inhumanity felt not merely inappropriate but like an act of benevolent violence, or what Ghassan Hage calls racial mis-interpellation. Hage outlines racial mis-interpellation as

> a drama in two acts: in the first instance the racialized person is
> interpellated as belonging to a collectivity "like everybody else." S/he
> is hailed by the cultural group or the nation, or even by modernity
> which claims to be addressing "everyone." And the yet-to-be-racialized

person believes that the hailing is for "everyone" and answers the call thinking that there is a place for him or her awaiting to be occupied. Yet, no sooner do they answer the call and claim their spot than the symbolic order brutally reminds them that they are not part of everyone: "No, I wasn't talking to you. Piss off. You are not part of us." (Hage 2010, 122)

The irony in the choir's offering, sung with the best of intentions, is that the history of abuse and cultural oppression in residential schools was anything but "the same" history as that of settler Canadians. Nor is the present reality of Aboriginal communities "the same" as communities elsewhere in Canada. Canadians were not taken from their parents and beaten when they spoke English, were not forced to do manual labor in order to keep their schools running, were not called "dirty Canadian." Canadians, for the most part, do not feel shame at being Canadian, or learn to hide their past from their children.

To look at the faces of the Gettin' Higher Choir was to see belief. The choir's performance, both in message and in its atmosphere of enthusiasm, demonstrated a belief that to sing such a message was enough to make it better; a belief, as Jill Dolan puts it, "that beyond this 'now' of material oppression and unequal power relations lives a future that might be different, one whose potential we can feel as we're seared by the promise of a present that gestures toward a better later" (Dolan 2005, 7). The Gettin' Higher Choir's performance here operated within a framework wherein the harmonic resolution of popular song engendered a felt measure of resolution, where the difficulty of difference is absent, and where familiar tunes are made even more familiar through their standardized choral arrangement.

The familiarity with Aglukark's "O Siem" takes place, however, at a deeper level through its repetition on easy-listening broadcasts across Canada since its release in the early nineties. Its familiar reverberations, furthermore, do not end with a daytime-radio-listening audience. YouTube clips attest to an audience that is much more diverse:

it's like a tradition to sing this song on our remeberance day concert. all garade 6 and 7s sing it. I remeber doing it in grade 6 and 7
Were singing this song for my graduation
we have this song at skool every single morning . . . its stuck in

Figure 22. The Gettin' Higher Choir. Photograph by Lisa Kurytnik, EchoesWithin Photography.com, 2012. What is not visible in this black-and-white reproduction is that each member of the choir is wearing a vibrant-colored shirt.

> my head. EVERY MORNING. (YouTube comment on mishi45 2008, comments disabled as of October 17, 2018 [*sic* throughout])

> *"O Siem, we are all family. / O Siem, we're all the same."*

From Susan Aglukark's diverse public-speaking engagements as an Inuk spokesperson for First Nations and Inuit social issues, a listener might conjecture that "O Siem" is an Inuktitut phrase. They might, moreover, reasonably believe that the phrase translates somewhere midway between the two phrases of the song—perhaps as "we are all interconnected" or "we're all human"—the perfect message with which to begin a day of school or to mark those important events and celebratory transitions in life. In fact, Aglukark came to learn and use the phrase "O Siem"—or "ô siyám" as it is written in Halq'eméylem—from two Sts'ailes Nation (Chehalis) men at Banff:

> I first heard and witnessed the actions, the welcoming and honouring of guests, back in 1994 at a conference in Banff, Alberta. I was part of a head table and to my right were two gentlemen from the Chehalis First Nation, before they each spoke, they welcomed and honoured all

guests with the words, O Siem, Haitchka, Siem O Siyeya. I was very moved by this and asked for the definition and permission to use the words in a song.[24]

"O Siem"'s familiarity contrasts with the carefully delimited accessibility of "ô siyám" as a phrase spoken in the longhouse and at other cultural gatherings held by Coast Salish people. It is said to welcome or honor those who have assembled for a gathering. It affirms the work that is done, and the message that an honorable or high-ranking speaker gives.

> In elementary school we were forced to sing this song OVER and OVER again. Every assembly, every multicultural day, every grad, every special presentation, every guest speaker, on random days over the intercom and any other occasion we had this song was played. I must have sung it 100 times. (comment on mishi45 2008)

> O Siem O Siem
> A refrain of the Canadian curricula,
> Sung every day
> Over and over
> I did not hear ô siyám
> spoken every day,
> over and over,
> by my mother, by my grandmother
> spoken in everyday ways
> over and over, with pride

Remaining Settled

Indigenous music performance holds great power to transform, heal, and provide hope. But the performativity of diversity enunciated in the speech act "we're all the same" also enacts what Sara Ahmed has called the "non-performativity" of diversity. In her analysis of what she calls "diversity work" at British and Australian universities, Ahmed examines how "diversity language" and documents fail to bring about actual institutional diversity. By recasting Judith Butler's theorization of performativity in the negative, Ahmed describes non-performativity as

> the "reiterative and citational practice by which discourse" *does not* produce "the effects that it names." . . . In the world of the non-performative, to name is not to bring into effect. . . . Such speech acts

are taken up *as if* they are performatives (as if they have brought about the effects they name), such that the names come to stand in for the effects. As a result, naming can be a way of not bringing something into effect. (quoted in Ahmed 2012, 117; emphasis in original)

Likewise, in providing a system for affirming multiculturalism, a concert of inclusionary music affords audience members not just with a means of listening to and seeing diversity on stage but with an opportunity to participate in diversity. As a utopian non-performative, inclusionary music may here stand in for more significant forms of action and redress, ones that involve taking up a greater degree of intergenerational responsibility in the acknowledgment of Canada's history of colonization and the reverberations of intergenerational trauma as they play out in Aboriginal communities across Canada.

As Dolan suggests, audience members go to the theater, concert hall, and gallery in order to feel, to sense something different about the world, whether it is by viewing an exhibition of abstract painting or seeing the spectacle of a musical. Each represents a different model of politics, and perhaps in certain instances even micro-utopias, in their non-representational form. As Richard Dyer notes, the entertainment represented by the musical "does not, however, present models of utopian worlds . . . Rather the utopianism is contained in the feelings it embodies. It presents, head-on as it were, what utopia would *feel* like rather than how it would be organized" (Dyer 2002, 20; emphasis added). Dyer's conception of entertainment, says Linda Williams,

> also partly defines wants through its orientation of problems. . . . In order to be satisfactorily resolved, the real social problems that these categories of the utopian sensibility point to must first be aroused. Dyer calls this arousal "playing with fire." His point is that the utopian entertainment only plays with those fires that the dominant power structure—capitalism (and patriarchy)—can put out. (Williams 1989, 155)

The friendly, nonagonistic kinds of performance discussed here enact a particular kind of utopian performative for settler audiences—one of "settlement" itself. This feeling of being settled results in a certain ease of being together in which the equilibrium of colonization is maintained. As Tia DeNora's (2000) research cogently outlines, music's positive affordances allow us to gain equilibrium in our daily life (see especially 46–74). DeNora's *Music in Everyday Life* shows how listeners often turn music on to calm themselves after a particularly stressful day, to tune out the rest of the world in daily commutes across cities, and to increase focus while completing tasks. As utopian performatives of reconciliation, I would argue, such musical affordances may equally act to foreclose change. They may sustain the equilibrium of a daily life that allows settler audiences to remain settled. In this sense, Dolan's notion of the utopian performative in Indigenous inclusionary music becomes *constitutive of* reconciliation. The affective component of reconciliation engenders great hope, but may do so as an end in itself. Rather than galvanizing audiences to continued action for restorative justice, these works afford the feeling of friendship in place of fostering new alliances sought by First Peoples in nation-to-nation models of political sovereignty.

> O Siem the fires of freedom
> Dance in the burning flame

To celebrate diversity through the affirmation of singing, or to "dance in the burning flame" as Aglukark's lyrics describe more poetically, brings forth a solution to "Indian problems" as the mere recognition of inequality, or through ineffectual practices of awareness raising. The abundance of generosity in Aglukark's lyrics, of a common humanity, provides the solution: to dance together, to share moments where utopian performatives persuade us that a better future is imminent. As Dolan notes, "utopian performatives exceed the *content* of a play or performance; spectators might draw a utopian performative from even the most dystopian theatrical universe" (Dolan 2005, 165). Equally so, in the above instances it also holds true that utopian *non-performatives*, or even *dystopian* performatives, can be derived from the most utopian musical universes.

Conclusion: Toward Empathetic Unsettlement

For settler audience members, it may be a much easier task to embrace the mystery of Indigenous stories and aesthetics than to play a leading role in the eradication of another kind of mystery: the prevailing ignorance of Indigenous histories of colonization and their lasting effects on Indigenous people today. Similarly, it is much easier to believe in the transformative power of such work, to allow the feelings of being transformed to satisfy, rather than to unsettle and engage with the enormous amount of work that must still be done. In acknowledgment of this, we might do well to remain attentive to our own professional and disciplinary identifications with the music and theater we write about. We must not forget that we have strong investments in and hopes for the power of music and theater to effect positive change. We feel this change viscerally when witnessing, when listening, and when participating in music-making with those communities we work with. But in order not to conflate our own strong hope for change with the realities of struggle faced by Indigenous peoples, it is also imperative that we acknowledge the crudeness of empathy and affect alone.

As Cherokee scholar Craig Womack has noted, while "America loves Indian culture; America is much less enthusiastic about Indian land title" (Womack 1999, 11). It is not enough to note the function these performances have in fostering empathy with non-Indigenous Canadians that perhaps allow them to understand and even feel the weight of Indigenous histories in new ways. It is not enough to embrace the mystery of difference. It is not enough to let the embrace of sound surround. It is necessary to move beyond the position of intergenerational bystanders. It is necessary to acknowledge the privilege and power that we hold within our artistic and working communities, and then find ways to give over such power that move beyond forms of inclusion.

> to speak
> Ō Sí:yám
> to speak, in everyday ways
> over and over
> Ō Sí:yám
> The necessary steps to return,
> for restitution,
> involve more
> involve more
> Ō Sí:yám

EVENT SCORE TO ACT

You are called in
    to act:
      give   over   space for doing
      give   over   possibility
      give   up   the overdetermination of necessary action
      give   up   your excuse, your worry, the seeming impracticality
      give   up   oversight
lead, not leading

CONCLUSION

The current climate of reconciliation and a national ideology of official multiculturalism are predisposed toward—if not entirely predicated on—processes of dialogue and relationship building between Indigenous and settler Canadians. While developing such relationships on the level of the individual and within larger nation-to-nation negotiation does play a role in decolonization, the rhetoric of friendship and universalism that underpins such dialogues of reconciliation, as discussed in chapter 5, has its own hegemony that tends toward the elision of sovereignty, "together-apart" formats, and gatherings that are necessarily exclusive because of Indigenous protocol. Conversely, we cannot assume that spaces of reconciliation and multicultural gatherings are necessarily democratic and offer the possibility to forge politically efficacious cross-cultural solidarities simply through their existence. Garneau's concept of irreconcilable spaces of Aboriginality here acts as a corrective to such assertions that decolonization must necessarily proceed through multicultural and intersectional dialogue. According to Garneau, such irreconcilable spaces of Aboriginality are built from the premise that, "while decolonization and Indigenization is collective work, it sometimes requires occasions of separation—moments where Indigenous people take space and time to work things out among themselves, and parallel moments when allies ought to do the same" (Garneau 2016, 23). These spaces are necessary in part, Garneau argues, because "when Indigenous folks (anyone, really) know they are being surveyed by non-members, the nature of their ways of being and becoming alters. Whether the onlookers are conscious agents of colonization or not, their shaping gaze can trigger a Reserve-response, an inhibition or a conformation to settler expectations" (27). Finally, Garneau asserts that spaces of reconciliation are often spaces where the scopophilic drive enacts similar forms of hunger to those illustrated in this book:

> The colonial attitude is characterized not only by scopophilia, a drive to look, but also by an urge to penetrate, to traverse, to know, to translate, to own and exploit. The attitude assumes that everything should be accessible to those with the means and will to access them; everything is ultimately comprehensible, a potential commodity, resource, or salvage. The academic branch of the enterprise collects and analyzes the experiences and things of others; it transforms story into text and objects-in-relation into artifacts to be catalogued and stored or displayed. (23)

In contrast, *Hungry Listening* has considered several instances where irreconcilable spaces spatialize sovereignty in ways that hold the potential to enervate extractivist desire and divert hungry listening. These have included Jordan Wilson's curatorial intervention against the objectification of Indigenous belongings discussed in chapter 1, the "temporary longhouse" work of the Keane Tait, Michael Dangeli, and Mique'l Dangeli discussed in chapter 4, the section following the Introduction that settler readers are asked to not read, and the spaces described in the decolonial event score for Louie's *Take the Dog Sled* that follows chapter 4. While these irreconcilable spaces are "unwelcome" to non-Indigenous desire—ones that operate otherwise to the colonial desire to know and extract—they serve a more important function than to exclude for its own sake. They are necessary in order to provide space without a predetermined program for the "working out" of ideas, challenges, and futures *by* and *for* Indigenous folks. Diverting the gaze of institutional scopophilia, these spaces are necessarily defined through exclusions that are both partial and total. Building upon Garneau's work, David Gaertner, a settler scholar of Indigenous media, notes that,

> If new participants are invited into Indigenous groups that I feel welcome in, I must be ready to accept that my presence may, from one moment to the next, be unwanted or restricting for new members. When this moment arises, I must be willing to graciously remove myself or be open to the suggestion that I take my leave, at least until a later date. As anyone who has guests that visit regularly knows, part of being a respectful guest is knowing when to exit. . . . Exclusion is not an emotionally tranquil event, . . . [but] building on the idea of recog-

nizing the necessity of exclusion, I would further suggest that in order for Garneau's theory to fully function as a decolonial (or non-colonial) methodology, practitioners need to imagine the possibility of their own suspension from irreconcilable spaces of Aboriginality because these spaces are intersectional, which is to say that race, gender, class, sexuality, and ability interact on multiple and simultaneous levels within these spaces. In this sense, it may be necessary for Indigenous men to remove themselves from communities considering Indigenous women's issues, or for straight contributors to extract themselves from spaces concerned with queer or two-spirit issues. This is not to say that men or straight people have nothing to add to these conversations, but that their presence, well-intended though it might be, inflects the content and direction of the conversation therein. (Gaertner 2016, 151–53.)

Gaertner here describes an awareness of changing contexts that demonstrates how an inclusion or exclusion at one moment does not mean that this will hold true for another moment. As such, shifting contexts of inclusion and exclusion are Indigenous modes of being in relation that are not predicated on an epistemology of relationship as a static state. Resurgence and decolonization do not exist as completed work but instead as ongoing processes in flux. Along similar lines, chapter 4 described Indigenous conceptions of treaty, protocol, and Elders' sharing of songs with ethnographers for future generations of Indigenous people all as living structures guided by dynamic and context-specific forms of relationship. That is, these structures are not understood as final documents and unchanging objects but as living knowledge that is in motion and changing as our communities continue to change.[1]

This has particular import for the corelative of irreconcilable spaces of Aboriginality: spaces and processes of "radical inclusion." The concept of radical inclusion, as I understand it from media artist/songwriter Cheryl L'Hirondelle, does not mean unlimited access for all but instead extends participation toward nonhuman relations, including ancestors and forms of life around us. L'Hirondelle explains how "because of the animacy of nêhiyawin (Cree worldview) the term 'kiyânaw' (all of us together) includes not only everyone (hence not excluding any people or animals), but also includes all the animate 'things' present as well" (L'Hirondelle 2015, 50). Radical inclusion is a call to reconsider colonization's impact on how we conceptualize kinship, and from this reconsideration offer space to those who may not fit within settler colonial frameworks of relationship. As part of her long-term project "Why the Caged Bird Sings," L'Hirondelle has worked with incarcerated Indigenous women, men, and youth to compose freedom songs. For L'Hirondelle, radical inclusion through these songwriting processes has extended to prison guards when they have shown interest to take part. The choice to include guards emerged from L'Hirondelle's recognition that "the program staff and guards were to some degree, 'caged birds' themselves since they had been there day after day, year after year" (51). As L'Hirondelle notes, "as a generative approach to radical inclusivity, my project started out to be about women, then I realized the prison program staff were 'lifers' and needed to be included, and then youth, and then men."[2] L'Hirondelle's radical inclusivity also extends to communication, as she and the Indigenous women and men she works with write the majority of their songs in English, with other lyrics in Indigenous languages interspersed:

> To write a song in English is also ironically and contentiously to be radically inclusive—since it could be construed that to write lyrics only in one specific Indigenous language could be excluding others [both Indigenous and settler]. To extend the thinking, the "inclusivity" of English in terms of sharing the song most widely applied not only within the core group of songwriters and collaborators but also by extension to other inmates at the correctional facility and/or others who might wish to sing the song in the future. To leave that inclusive legacy, it was ironically important to use the widely understood medium of the English language, despite the political connotations of using the "colonizer's tongue." (L'Hirondelle 2015, 51–52)

An important distinction in these choices is that they are decided upon by L'Hirondelle and the women and men with whom she works. Radical inclusion, then, is not a call for everyone to be included at all times and all places (a call that would contravene many Indigenous cultural traditions across different nations), but instead a call for openness toward including those who are not granted legitimacy or status within the systems of work we participate in. Here, the power dynamics between extending welcome when interest is shown and *requiring* inclusion when that inclusion is not welcome by Indigenous people must be distinguished from each other.

To co-activate Garneau's and L'Hirondelle's frameworks, the next section of the Conclusion offers a space for decolonial thinking by two settler scholars. While the section following the Introduction provided a written space of sovereignty conceived of solely for readers who are Indigenous, the following space for decolonial work follows Garneau's assertion that irreconcilable spaces of Aboriginality must run parallel with moments where settlers also "work things out among themselves." In the final phase of writing this book, I approached two scholar-friend-mentors with whom I have had ongoing discussions about inclusionary performance, Indigenous sovereignty, and listening, to ask if they would be willing to read and give feedback on the manuscript for this book before I submitted it to the Press for consideration. Both scholars—Deborah Wong and Ellen Waterman—graciously agreed to my invitation, and as they read the manuscript they also encountered (here, in the Conclusion, as they read) a more radically inclusive offer of space for their thoughts as part of the Conclusion. In essence, I was offering them part of this book to "work out amongst themselves" what decolonial listening might entail. I was interested to know how they—as settler ethnomusicologists who think in compelling and deeply ethical ways about musical practices of collaboration—might respond to the questions of responsibility and positionality of listening. Each scholar brings a distinct perspective to this dialogue, including the different settler states they work withing (U.S. for Deborah Wong, Canada for Ellen Waterman); different genres they participate in as musicians (Taiko for Wong, experimental music and improvisation for Waterman); and their different histories/positionalities as third-generation Chinese American and multiethnic *hapa haole* (Wong) and as a white settler Canadian from rural Manitoba (Waterman). Perhaps most importantly, I invited Waterman and Wong to participate in this conversation because of their sustained engagement—as scholars and performers—with processes of collaboration, listening, and with questions around embodiment in performance. My hope was that their conversation might activate and modify ideas from previous chapters and consider new forms for decolonial listening and musical action. Their contribution in the next section is intended to complement the Introduction's written space of Indigenous sovereignty with a dialogue that seeks to define what a critical politics of intersectional writing might look like. What follows thus remains in a format of "working it out," which is to say that it documents

240 Conclusion

an imagined space for Wong and Waterman's improvisatory process of online dialogue over a few weeks, and my entry into this space toward the end of their conversation.

An Improvisation on Decolonial Listening and Action

Ellen: Before entering what we might call a settler ally textual space—a welcome but somewhat unsettling gift Dylan has offered to us—I felt it was important to reconsider my own critical listening positionality. So I wrote an autoethnographic narrative, a perhaps all-too-typical Canadian story about growing up in ignorance of our national racial politics that I had never before articulated. The exercise left me feeling discomfited and more than a little ashamed. In the end I have chosen to delete those paragraphs because focusing on my settler-origin story seems like a deflection of Dylan's invitation to improvise on the theme of irreconcilable spaces of performance *now*.

As George Lewis reminds us, improvisation is not just a musical technique but a "social location" one chooses to inhabit (Lewis 1996, 110). Each participant brings their own subjectivity and history to the encounter, but the goal of group improvisation is to work with others to create something that exceeds, and at the same time honors, the individual participant's experience. Good improvisation isn't always about achieving group harmony or consensus; instead, it might productively be about contest or dissensus, or it may traverse a broad spectrum of human interactions. Crucially, to improvise well requires good listening skills, responsiveness, and adaptability. This written conversation is both an improvisation and—like all edited writing—a composition made up of riffs, loops, interjections, and erasures that took place over several weeks. Dylan, Deborah, and I have talked a lot about what an ethical engagement between Indigenous and non-Indigenous artists might entail, but what we've learned is that "working things out among ourselves" is a messy and reiterative process—one in which time does not neatly progress to an elegant solution or cadence.

Here's all you really need to know about me before we begin. Growing up white and middle class in 1970s rural Manitoba, I understood "native" people to be part of the fabric of my life, but not something that needed to be thought about or questioned critically or even properly acknowledged. As a teenager, I remember being outraged by the fact that the local Rotary Club still put on a blackface minstrel show each year—I knew *that* was racist because I had read *To Kill a Mockingbird* and seen *Roots,* and like many young Canadians, I tended to conflate American and Canadian histories. The endemic racism against Indigenous people that permeated my family, my town, and my society was shrouded in silence. Centennial-era Canada [the late 1960s] was a celebration of multiculturalism that completely elided the lived realities of Indigenous people in Canada. The TRC has disrupted this sedative national narrative, but how and to what effect remains to be seen.

Deborah: Even more than Ellen, my understanding of Native American culture, history, and experience is uneven and superficial, and now that I know a little more—thanks to sustained contact with colleagues in Indigenous studies—I'm even more aware of my own lack of awareness and lack of ac/knowledge/ment. In my initial responses here, I put a lot of critical energy into explaining my own history as a woman of color, and I got a bit lost in it . . . in precisely the ways that the affect-driven TRC model can get stuck in a remedy-driven belief that feeling guilty and ashamed is equivalent to holding oneself accountable. So, like Ellen, I've removed most of that writing.

What might it mean to be *woke* to Indigenous rights? I think I have finally begun to comprehend that Indigenous studies is not just another strand in the powerful paradigm of ethnic studies but rather sets the terms for critical ethnic studies. As Glen Coulthard writes, "the Indigenous lead" in coalition politics "is founded on indigenous articulations of what a noncolonial situation might look like and [is] grounded on very tangible recommendations on how we might achieve that" (See 2016, 146). I still have a long way to go and I might never get there; it may not be possible to get there. I am the product of Asian settler colonialism: when my Chinese grandfather, grandmother, and great-grandfather emigrated from Toishan to Buffalo, New York, their immigrant presence was wholly dependent on, complacent with, and another layer of the settler state, though they had their own struggles (Fujikane and Okamura 2008; Saranillio 2013). I am a hungry listener, despite my best efforts. I read this book with joy and commitment, wanting to learn how to do better, yet brought up short by my own hungry desire to read the end of your Introduction, off limits to me as a non-Indigenous reader.

242 Conclusion

Twice in November 2016, I participated in round dances at U.S.-based academic conferences. I write this at a historical moment when we are asked to stand with those at Standing Rock in defiance of the proposed Dakota Pipeline, and the round dances at the Society for Ethnomusicology and the American Studies Association were extraordinary moments of unity. In other ways, I wonder how fully we non-Indigenous dancers are able to *hear* how non-extraordinary and quotidian the proposed Dakota Access Pipeline is. The resistance we view as thrilling and historic is actually business as usual for many Indigenous communities. How ready and able are we to devalorize our hungry desire to be allies?

Ellen's antiphonal response: And is there a role for shame here? Reading about shame and guilt (feeling bad about oneself, feeling bad about one's actions), both seem so negative (and also "all about me"). But without acknowledging our collective guilt and without the capacity to feel shame for our actions, how is a society to move forward to redress those actions? For surely the whole point of an activist Indigenous scholarship is to work toward this awareness and redress.

Deborah responds: Ellen, I agree that shame and acknowledgment may be useful steps toward accountability, but again, that's the truth and reconciliation procedural model, right? Transitional justice models of reconciliation and redress posit remedies. It's the national friendship model, as Dylan put it. It doesn't map out the terms for a new or transformed relationship. I wonder whether you and I should take a moment to think, talk, and write aloud together, here, before we turn back to Dylan. Dylan activated David Garneau's idea of "irreconcilable spaces of Aboriginality" in his own text, and he suggested that moments of separation may be useful or even necessary for effective ally work. I agree it's too easy to simply claim or assert that one is an ally. It shouldn't be easy, nor should it be claimed; it should be granted, or given. You and I aren't the same kind of settlers, so we can't hope to be the same kind of settler allies, but I think we share some skills. I'll come back to that below. I think I need a protocol for the thing Dylan has invited us to do.

Ellen responds: You are right, this dialogue is unknown territory into which we enter as foreigners, all too likely to blunder. I am listening from a place of uncertainty, of caution—trying very hard to listen with respect, and uncomfortably distracted by the noise in my own head (as my earlier narrative writing showed). Indeed, one of the most potent things I took from our conversations together is the need for non-Indigenous people in Canada (and everywhere) to be quiet now and *listen* to Indigenous people, who must determine for themselves what their needs are. But how to listen?

Listening deeply, in openness and humility, is extremely hard because it requires that we still our learned behaviors of intellectual processing—analysis, reaction, interpretation—and just listen. Above all, it demands that we acknowledge and then set aside our fear of the unknown.

A Sonic Meditation: Still Your Hungry Listening[3]

Pause now and sit quietly for a moment.
Consider your roots and acknowledge your prejudices, your shame, your fear and longing.
Set them aside; still your hungry listening.
Listen.

[*Deborah tries it.*] That was . . . hard. Impossible, actually. I like the utopianism of the exercise, though in another way, I felt like a Theravada Buddhist monk contemplating a corpse as a form of meditation! I'm not being facetious: they do it (though I haven't) to create mindful awareness of how transitory life is, and how unimportant the external. So I tried it again, like this:

Stop. Sit silently.
   Stop. Feel the weight of history. Own it.
   Stop. Hold your prejudices, your shame, your fear and longing in your hands.
   Stop. Listen to what you hold.
   Stop. Listen to your hands.
   Stop. Keep stopping. Listen to yourself stopping.

Hmmm, that's not it, either. [*laughing*] Dylan still doesn't yet want to actually enter the room we're in, but I was trying to respond to some of his off-stage comments: he asked whether we could try to think beyond "settler time" and the assumption that processes have quick, clear beginnings and ends. It's so hard to think beyond a linear concept of history and a giver–taker concept of listening.

[*Pause for thought and other work*]

Ellen (writing on November 25, 2016): I write today in sorrow over the passing of composer/improviser, educator, and humanitarian Pauline Oliveros yesterday morning. Pauline was a dear friend and mentor, the best listener I have ever known. Grieving for her, I am called to reconsider the importance and the special quality of her concept of Deep Listening, and I am wondering if this might serve as a kind of protocol for our conversation. Deb, when we were reading Dylan's manuscript, you brought up the possibility of Deep Listening as a method for decolonizing listening. It seems appropriate to return to it here.

Pauline said that Deep Listening is the attempt to listen to everything, everywhere all the time. It is a meditative practice, but definitely not a kind of navel gazing—the ear stretches outward to listen at the edge of perception, and also inward to pay attention to the intimate and the internal, and back out to the global. For Pauline, the purpose of Deep Listening was to pay attention, to give respect, to embrace the full spectrum of human experience. To the extent that Deep Listening calls us to witness and embrace instead of shutting out or turning away from the world, it is a form of activism. In her last ten years, she used her big ears to listen to people with disabilities, and—this is important—to develop collaborative projects led by artists with disabilities.

Deborah's antiphonal response: Early in September 2016, you and I spent three focused days in Kingston, Ontario, talking at length with Dylan about this book manuscript; three days ago, on November 24, 2016, Pauline crossed over. Dylan's book unsettles settler listening, and Pauline taught us and many others how to listen differently. In the past few days, I revisited Pauline's book *Deep Listening: A Composer's Sound Practice,* in an effort to share space with her. I found her there, of course. I was also keen to see—I mean, hear—whether she posited a liberal humanist listener, i.e., the unitary subject so foundational to settler logics, and it's not clear. Certainly you *can* take in her Deep Listening exercises as if they were meant to be experienced by a unitary subject. But I'm certain they can be understood in other ways as well, and that Pauline's approach troubles the self/world distinction so central to settler ideologies. Dylan asks us as settler listeners to try to activate different kinds of listening, without engaging mimetically with the Indigenous but by intentionally exploring other settler subjectivities. I can't help but think of the electrifying opening paragraph in José Esteban Muñoz's *Cruising*

Utopia, where he writes, "Queerness is essentially about the rejection of a here and now and an insistence on potentiality or concrete possibility for another world" (Muñoz 2009, 1). At the risk of misrepresenting Pauline's intent, I would like to excerpt one of her exercises because I think it models alternatives to the settler self and its attendant logics, including subjectivity, intersubjective encounter, and the world. Did Pauline posit an ahistorical and a-cultural listener? Perhaps. Still, I think something important happens in her exercise "Environmental Dialogue," published in 1974 and revised in 1996:

> Each person finds a place to be, either near to or distant from the others, either indoors or out-of-doors. The meditation begins by each person observing his or her own breathing. As each person becomes aware of the field of sounds from the environment, each person individually and gradually begins to reinforce the pitch of any one of the sound sources that has attracted their attention. The sound source is reinforced vocally, mentally or with an instrument. If one loses touch with the sound source, then wait quietly for another. Reinforce means to strengthen or to sustain by merging one's own pitch with the sound source. If the pitch of the sound source is out of vocal or instrumental range, then it is to be reinforced mentally.
>
> The result of this meditation will probably produce a resonance of the environment. Some of the sounds will be too short to reinforce. Some will disappear as soon as the reinforcement begins. It is fine to wait and listen. (Oliveros 2005, 35)

Parsing Pauline's meditation helps me step up to Dylan's questions, without setting history aside or succumbing to despair over its violence. Pauline asks the listener to reinforce sounds, not to imitate them or to transform them. The listener is directed to wait and be quiet, not to search or seek. The listener strengthens or sustains what she hears. Yes, a merging might take place. But the listener reinforces the environment: she doesn't absorb it or transform it, nor does she chase after it. I think this meditation invites us *not* to listen hungrily.

Ellen remembers: Early in 2016, I attended a concert based on the ethnographer Marius Barbeau, who recorded all kinds of folk and traditional music across Canada in the early twentieth century. To many of us listening to an ensemble of fine musicians all working together with good intentions, the show was nevertheless a bit "cringey" in the way it interpreted Barbeau's engagement with Indigenous song. In particular, it was hard to listen to extractive field recordings of Indigenous song being interpreted live in *bel canto* vocal style. Some of my non-Indigenous arts colleagues took the opportunity to display their newfound outrage and pass judgment on (and during) the concert. This was not how we were supposed to be doing things in Canada now and they were eager to explain how we should be collaborating with Indigenous artists *properly*. They thought they knew the protocol. At least one of the creators of the piece felt humiliated and persecuted and misunderstood. Perhaps it was important that they be confronted in this way, but I felt like the atmosphere of judgment (whitesplaining?) was as unhealthy as the piece, and I didn't know what to do with that (also judgmental) feeling.

Deborah's antiphonal response: But I think you *do* know what to do with that. By naming it, you've called out the critical problem of white possessive investment, and it can be most fully on display when settlers claim the right to dislodge the problem—to claim authority, including the authority to assert they're no longer part of the problem.

Ellen wonders: What would an artistic collaboration between Indigenous and non-Indigenous artists founded in Deep Listening be like? What new kinds of sociability might such a collaboration engender? Could a commitment to such collaborations enact both an ethics and a politics? Model a society that refuses to be governed by fear? How to arrive at a collaboration based on Deep Listening? For sure, it wouldn't be an artist writing a strategic grant to take advantage of new Canada Council funding for Indigenous arts. I suspect that a truly ethical collaboration would have to start with an invitation from Indigenous artists and not the other way around.

Deborah, excited: Exactly: it's all about listening. I don't yet know how to do it, but I know I aspire to a radical willingness to claim *nothing*. To claim no knowledge, no authority, and maybe not even request collaboration: I wonder whether elevating collaboration as the ideal terms for encounter isn't another kind of hunger. Maybe the first step is to sit just outside the door, without any expectation that we might even be invited in. Dylan asked us to explore "some balance between writing sovereignty and writing a critical politics of intersectionality." Pauline wrote, "What will you hear in the near future?" (Oliveros 2005, 34). I'm right in between those questions and invitations. It feels like a good

Conclusion 247

place to be. Is this the right point to ask Dylan if he'd like to rejoin us?

Dylan enters: I spent some time reading your conversation after a long series of flights to where I currently live, as a newly diasporic xwélmexw on Haudenosaunee and Anishinaabe lands now known as Kingston. So, I jumped right into reading, with an excitement to know that I think kept me from an initial careful and thoughtful reading-listening to your voices. This reminds me: hungry listening is not just a "settler problem." Developing practices of Deep Listening and critical listening positionality requires us to adopt self-reflexive ethics about the appropriate conditions for listening: the right place, time, and frame of mind. That, in turn, requires a self-reflexiveness of positionality as other than mere identity category, and instead as an alertness to the intersection of perception and relationality. For myself, this might mean, as my friend Dave Gaertner notes, self-removals from certain spaces (for example in a gathering of Indigenous women or two-spirit folks, or in a space of Sḵwx̱wú7mesh-only discussion); or it might mean finding ways (as in Oliveros's work) to place oneself in new relationships with that which one listens to.

I don't have access to the same depth of experience that you both have from working as participants in Pauline Oliveros's Deep Listening practice. And so my thoughts here surely signal my lack of knowledge around Deep Listening. But in the few exercises I've participated in I've wondered about how my experience of their meditative opening up of listening through the body has also seemed to distance me from the particularity of listening positionality rather than increase my ability to "tune-in" to positionality. I'm invested in finding ways to help us hear the normative ways that we listen, that then lead to re-positioning. But that re-positioning doesn't mean that we seek to adopt Indigenous ways of listening, because I wonder—if Indigenous methodologies are located in a deeply embodied/experiential relationship to culture and place, what does it mean to "adopt" such methods without that lived experience? At its worst this might result in an auditory form of "going native." I'm more interested in decolonial forms that allow for self-unsettlement as listeners.

Ellen responds: I can't speak for Pauline, of course, but she developed her practice of listening out of her subject position as a queer woman who was trying to participate in a male-dominated world of electronic

248   Conclusion

music and composition more generally. Her *Sonic Meditations* [1974] (the text pieces you may have performed) were developed through a project with women in San Diego in the 1970s—out of an intense process of collaborative listening and creating during many months. That's kind of what I mean by Pauline's stance on listening as activism. It's not passive. To listen is to pay attention and to pay attention is to be poised to act.

Deborah interjects: I want to echo Ellen's point that Pauline's intervention was a positioned response that had *everything* to do with difference (and specifically queer femininity in heterosexist environments). I feel impatient when Deep Listening is sometimes leveraged as a universalist practice. The burden of creating an intervention is (1) having to continually reexplain it, and (2) not letting it be reabsorbed into powerful master narratives.

Ellen continues: One of the conditions of critical listening positionality is being pretty confident of your position. How are we to be open to possibilities as yet unknown if we always have our ears open for that critical position? How can we avoid, as you put it, "slipping into a listening essentialism"?

Dylan wonders: I'm thinking about this (over)confidence in and overdetermining of positionality generally—in the form of critical listening positionality I raised in our earlier conversation as "listening essentialism"—that needs to be unsettled. There is a certain amount of stability in the expression and experience of positionality, but these are also provisional and shift depending on the who, what, and where of the situations we find ourselves in. This is in fact the key difference for me between positionality and identity. Identity is a cohesive fact, while positionality is a "shifty" state. My understanding of protocol is similarly provisional and relational: my actions change based on whose lands I am a visitor on, my relationships and kinship ties there (or lack thereof), and my responsibilities there. Self-acknowledging my critical listening positionality means I reflect on where I come from and my history, what grounds my listening, so that I am aware of tendencies that might result in listening as a practice of reducing alterity to the same.

I think critical listening positionality has a lot to do with resisting the fixity of categorization and analogization. I'm reminded of Helmut Lachenmann (a strange person to make an appearance in this conversation!), who articulates his desire for a different phenomenology of listening that involves "observing an acoustic event from the perspective of 'What happened?'" (Lachenmann 2003, 10). What does it mean, asks Lachenmann, to listen to music as if listening to an event, for example of two cars crashing: "If I hear two cars crashing—each against the other—I hear maybe some rhythms or some frequencies, but I do not say 'Oh, what interesting sounds!' I say, 'What happened?'" (10). This kind of rethinking the ontology of listening interests me. But does rethinking *settler* ontologies of listening primarily mean finding ways to listen that leave us uncertain of what kind of event/crash we are attending to? I'm aware, as I wrote in chapter 1, that this may result in what Daughtry identifies as the impossibility of listening to everything at once (Daughtry 2013). Is it even possible to have one ear open to the unknown and another to one's positionality? To what extent does this simply result in a kind of "schizo-audition" that forecloses upon Deep Listening? To what extent, in practice, does critical listening positionality overemphasize listening subjectivity more than musical subjectivity?

Deborah wonders: Isn't this what displaced and aggrieved communities often do so well? I take your point about overemphasizing listening subjectivity. It immediately made me think of Du Bois's double consciousness as a key skill developed in precarious circumstances that contains the means for decolonization (Du Bois 2007, 8). After all, the paradigm of "having" subjectivity, and the right to "a" subjectivity, makes less audible the ability to code switch and to own a multifocal, multilingual, multiphonic consciousness as a skill and a strategy. As you put it in chapter 1, "the colonial imposition of settling listening seeks to compel sensory engagement through practices of focusing attention that are 'settled'—in the sense of coming to rest or becoming calm." If the sounds of a postcolonial, post-redress, postreconciliation historical moment are multiphonic, then I want a way to hear all the asymmetries.

Ellen: My ears are spinning. [*Deborah:* Mine are ringing.] Daughtry is probably right, but then listening is always active—in everyday life we are constantly receiving and processing sounds from all kinds of perspectives, and musicians know that we can shift that listening perception at will: we are constantly filtering and shifting perspective simply to survive. In that sense Deep Listening is an ideal, which is why it is a practice not an end goal. Could Danielle Goldman's riff on Foucault be useful here? Writing about improvisation as "practices of freedom" she describes it as "incessant preparation, grounded in the present while open to the next moment's possible actions and constraints" (Goldman 2010, 142). Perhaps the quality of critical listening positionality is alertness.

Listening and sounding responsively (responsibly) are coterminous processes. If we're doing both well, we are constantly being pulled off-center and then recentering to a new position, which entails being open to exploring new ideas. The problems occur when we think we can pre-hear the outcome; and I think that applies as much to listening in the audience as it does to composition or performance. It's not surprising. A postsecondary, classical music education is almost entirely designed to train students to predict certain kinds of outcomes and to control for them. Collaborative music-making (choir, band, orchestra) is usually done under the direction of a professional leader whose interpretation the musicians are expected to follow. Everyone rushes from lessons to rehearsals to performances at a hectic pace dictated by the exigencies of end-of-term performances. Music history and theory curricula are geared to imparting a canonic body of information plus a set of boutique courses in "other" musical subjects, depending on the available resources. A great deal of thoughtful, creative, caring work is done with students but there is little time for experimentation with alternative formats. Composition studios may well encourage wide exploration of musical styles, but the professionalization of the composer entails learning to be efficient, to be oriented toward product over process. Professional music careers reinforce this training. Despite examples of progressive curricula, it is hard to imagine a truly ethical intercultural music curriculum under the current postsecondary music education model. In Canada, with very few exceptions, our music schools are capable of hearing only a certain kind of prospective student, one who has usually already invested in years of Western classical music training, one who already knows what the outcome of a musical performance is supposed to be. We listen for excellence, or perhaps for improvement, but the terms of that listening are most certainly already "settled." We do not teach alertness to new possibilities, and we do not teach practices of freedom. What would it mean for musicians and music scholars to adopt conscious strategies for decolonizing listening?

Deborah: That's exactly what's needed. Again, we can learn useful strategies from communities of color. I immediately think of bell hooks writing about how black women exert an "oppositional gaze" that interrogates the white gaze *and* calls it out (hooks 1992, 116). As she puts it, "By courageously looking, we defiantly declared: 'Not only will I stare. I want my look to change reality'" (116). I've written about how my third-generation Chinese American cousins cheer for Kato and Tonto rather than the Green Hornet or the Lone Ranger. Aggrieved communities already have decolonizing strategies that not only imagine other ways of being but activate, enact, and embody them. Looking, reading, and listening "against" the grain is an essential tool for spiritual and political survival.

One of my takeaways from this book and our conversations is that I don't think I can any longer write about "listening" without adjectives in front of the word. Sound studies is such a dynamic transdisciplinary area right now, but the risk of hardening and universalizing its central concepts is real.[4] While reading your book, Dylan, I had a world-shifting moment when I realized that the word *listening* should really have the word *settler* in front of it much of the time, in much scholarship. Outsiders know that the unmarked categories are the ones of which we should be most wary. Early in this book, you called for apposite methodologies, and I wonder whether I could commit to a decolonial practice of never writing about "listening" without an adjective. I'm attending to your argument that writing has a "proximal" relationship with what we (think we) know about music. Gus Stadler has called out "the underlying whiteness of the field" of sound studies (2015)—actually, you directed me to his essay in our first conversation several years ago, and I want to be careful not to move toward theoretical understandings that float above difference.

You have offered a practice of radical inclusion by inviting my thoughts and Ellen's into these pages. You are "extending welcome when interest is shown," to quote L'Hirondelle's practice of radical inclusion referred to above. In this book, you have also established spaces of Indigenous sovereignty. The question is whether it's possible to "imagine otherwise" (Chuh 2003)—to imagine a politics that would allow us to reflect with you on your argument. It's one thing to sit on your back deck in Kingston, Ontario, and talk about your book manuscript; it's another thing entirely to take up space—to hold space—right here on your pages. You spatialized your argument, and we are learning to "write" through apposite methodology together, right here.

252   Conclusion

But Ellen and I now need to generate the settler listening protocol that your book demands. Our ethics of accountability led us to ask you to give it to us, but you (gently) turned it back. During our three-way collaborative writing process, you commented,

> What's at the heart of asking for a protocol from me for your conversation/thinking together? (I ask this sincerely). I respect and am inspired by your work and commitment to thinking through politically engaged practices of collaboration . . . and I do think it is necessary that non-Indigenous settler scholars test out and speculate intersectional settler protocol for decolonial listening and writing about music.

More than one protocol for decolonial listening is needed, though. When on the outskirts of Indigenous sonic space, the protocol seems pretty straightforward to me: wait until invited in, and then listen . . . and speak only if invited, and keep listening.

If Indigenous protocols are useful outside sovereign space—and I'm certain they are—then we are reaching toward decolonial practices. May I begin to think of protocols as interventions and strategies into spheres where hunger and ownership are assumed and valorized? The "methodologies of gathering" you survey and thoughts around "song cleansing" (chapter 4) you offer make both loss and connection audible. Your methodology of recontextualizing works of music with Indigenous pre/performance instructions is profoundly disruptive in profoundly generative ways: you don't accept the imprimatur of the autonomous musical work. The postperformance implications of such a practice are exciting because they're both utopian and practical. You astutely show, over and over again, how affect is not the same as efficacy (chapter 5), and I find particularly useful your strategy of moving meaning away from the work to the Indigenous audience, and only then to the shared space. But if I've understood it correctly, a protocol is a formal, public understanding of how encounters take place in sovereign spaces. So for a protocol to have decolonizing effects, we will need new measures for the "non-performativity" you identify in chapter 5.

Irreconcilable and Radically Inclusive Spaces of Art Music Creation

Wong and Waterman's dialogue provides a process-based account of devising decolonial listening scores and strategies. I have included this conversation here in its entirety and in its relatively unedited form in order to show the full progression of thought and action by two scholars with very different positionalities. Their conversation for me exemplifies Tahltan artist Peter Morin's iterational view of decolonial arts practice:

> The difficult task is finding actions to activate this space where Indigenous knowledge meets settler ways of being. They are bodies of knowledge that mingle and impact each other. And often their meeting requires yet another meeting. (Morin 2016, 71)

Of course, the limitations of time and the format of the book mean that long-process iterational practices are challenging to implement. In the ideal scenario, as Morin suggests, this work would be followed by another meeting, perhaps of two differently disciplined scholars of music and sound, who would bring different positionalites to bear on this work. This model of scholarly "working, testing, and teasing out" through conversation and conversational return bears some resemblance to the practices of visiting discussed in chapter 4. What Wong and Waterman's "visiting" through collaborative writing models here is the expansion and redirection of thought in motion. To expand this model into an iterative practice of return and revision would, moreover, be to acknowledge Indigenous epistemic values defined through situated and context-specific relationships to place, time, and kinship.

Wong and Waterman's testing out of processes and event scores for decolonial listening—combined with other event scores, poetics, and discussion of intersubjective encounter included throughout the book—ask us to expand aesthetic forms for perceptual decolonization. Through these different event scores, discussion of unsettling normative audience protocol, and engagement with listening positionalities, *Hungry Listening* has provided prompts for listening otherwise. Yet the myriad combinatory possibility within critical listening positionality means that conversation and collaboration here become essential in order for specific gendered, raced, and abled "bodies of knowledge" to come into relationship and reorient listening norms.

While decolonizing listening practice arises from collaboration and conversation, I am left with the question of how such collaboration and conversation between various settler, diasporic, immigrant or "arrivant" subjects might proceed without (or with reduced) demand on Indigenous people to expend the considerable emotional, intellectual, and

Conclusion

physical labor required through leading such processes. What compositional methodologies might settler and allied composers explore that do not require Indigenous people to shoulder the burden of decolonization and instead allow us to focus our energies toward resurgence with and for Indigenous communities? How, moreover, does this work proceed "together apart," and avoid recentring whiteness and privilege through a focus on settler colonial perception, or becoming a mode of positionality "confession"?[5] As detailed in the example of restaging Louie's *Take the Dog Sled* after chapter 4, non-Indigenous composers and music organizations have significant opportunity to envision decolonial forms for presentation, performance, and composition. Such work does not necessarily centralize Indigenous stories or music, but might instead turn a critical lens toward individual inheritances of (hetero)normative, ableist, colonial, and racializing formations for compositional and presentational practice, and deconstruct these structures through aesthetically marking what has been previously unmarked.

Models for deconstructing compositional and presentational norms are nearly nonexistent in new music composition and presentation, and so my thoughts turn to a number of settler artists whose practices focus on historical and ongoing structures of settler colonialism: Leah Decter, Hadley Howes, Michael Farnan, the Doublewide collective, and Korean-born, Vancouver-based artist Jin-Me Yoon's work of lateral exploration. Moving from an earlier examination of diasporic belonging in Canada, in 2008 Yoon's work began to shift toward a practice of moving across cities—Beppu, Japan (2008), and Seoul, Korea (2008), Mexico City (2009), Vancouver (2010, during the Winter Olympics)—through the action of crawling. In this work, Yoon moves across the ground on a low platform with wheels to aid her lateral explorations. Most significant for the context of this book's focus on perception, these lateral explorations were not simply a "work" or "performance" presented for the camera; instead, the work was a process through which Yoon worked to understand the city, and the relationships between bodies and cities, outside of the habitual pedestrian mobility.[6] As Yoon writes,

> The body, any body, walking through space has an associational
> field of meanings constituted through the relation of that body to its
> environment. These meanings, which include those of history, are
> considered to be stable or fixed. In response to this fixity, I have been

experimenting with displacing the vertical, bi-pedal way we typically move through the world by giving it a horizontal orientation.[7]

Kinaesthetic practices of thought have a long history from the Peripatetic school of philosophy in ancient Greece, to the modernist *deambulations* of the Dadaists and Situationist *dérives*. Since the late 1960s and early '70s, artists have created a diverse array of walking-based work, including Richard Long's *A Line Made by Walking* (1967), Vito Acconci's *Following Piece* (1969), Hamish Fulton's fifty-year career as a walking artist creating solo works and works for large groups of walkers, and La Monte Young's "Draw a Straight Line and Follow It." This history of walking practice has overwhelmingly been dominated by white male artists, as much as the writing on walking methodologies has been dominated by white male geographers (Edensor, Lorimer, Ingold). In this context, we can understand settler colonial modes of thought as not merely the product of interpellation by the state and educational institutions, but formed and maintained through the rhythms of everyday experience. If, as Rebecca Solnit notes, walking results in "rhythms of thinking" (Solnit 2000, 5), then the absence of critical positionality in the range of walking art practices and writing named above calls for a significant expansion of antiracist, queer, feminist, and decolonial proprioception that operates outside of the often teleological form of the

Figure 23. Jin-me Yoon, *The dreaming collective knows no history*, 2006. Video still, single channel video, runtime 18 min 8s. Courtesy of the artist.

Figure 24. Jin-me Yoon, *As It Is Becoming (Beppu, Japan): Atomic Treatment Centre, Onsen*, 2008. Video still, single channel video, runtime 10 min 33s. Courtesy of the artist.

walk, and colonial-exploratory modes of discovery enacted through the *dérive*. These forms are, however, not irrevocably compromised by their normative frameworks named here. Nor do they remain impervious to Indigenous agency. Tim Edensor cautions against "assumptions that managed normative rhythms possess an overarching force that compels individuals to march to their beat" (Edensor 2010, 72). Overdeterministic homologies between the infrastructure of modern cities and settler colonial forms of inhabiting the city elide the agency of individuals who make daily choices to move against the city's performative law. Indeed, desensitization to one's location generated by "the sterile, flattened surfaces—the smooth tactilities of urban paving—[that] ensure that the feet and legs are not enlivened by contact with the ground" (Edensor 2008, 131) effects settler colonial proprioceptive ignorance. This is compounded by urban design that covers over Indigenous lands, foreclosing on public engagement with the fact of the Indigenous "city before the city" (chapter 1).

It is here that Yoon's movement charts a path of most resistance through settler colonial, imperial, and "home" civic infrastructures by imposing an embodiment that returns her body back into relationship with place, through renewed negotiation with pedestrians, traffic, refuse, and storm-drain covers. Through lateral movement, by crawling around the city, its normative everyday features become obstacles, or better yet, what Lauren Berlant and Ann Cvetkovitch call "impasses" (Berlant 2011, 32; Cvetkovitch 2012, 13). Like blockades, impasses obstruct the progression of the body along the street designed in such a way to streamline forward momentum from one destination to the next. Intellectually, the impasse acts as "a holding station that doesn't hold but opens out into anxiety, that dog-paddling around a space whose contours remain obscure" (Berlant 2011, 199). Cvetkovitch describes Berlant's productive impasse as something that "slows us down, preventing easy recourse to critique or prescription for action, instead inviting us to see it as 'a singular place that's a cluster of noncoherent but proximate attachments that can only be approached awkwardly, described around, shifted'" (Cvetkovich, 20; quoting Berlant 2011, 434–35). Yoon's lateral exploration self-imposes the physical impasse in order to materialize thinking outside of the city's smooth space of destination teleology, to linger in thought, and consider anew her relations to—and belonging in—places where she has lived as long-term guest (Vancouver), where she has been a temporary visitor (Mexico City and Vienna), where she has attachments to ancestral histories of home (Korea), and disidentification with colonial power (Japan).

Yoon's movement also embodies an insurgent form of proprioception. Her horizontal movement is not simply crawling; it additionally references and embodies a militarized form of "advance." Crawling through the city, Yoon's body is marked by the black clothes she wears, and by the form of arm-over-arm "military crawl" she uses, with her hands bandaged in white. How does one experience the city when one embodies this kind of insurgent action, aligned with trying to strategically gain access to a site (perhaps even one's home) that is "enemy territory"? What does it mean to understand one's belonging to a place by placing oneself within the physicality of an "enemy," or within an agonistic context, what Mouffe would call an "adversary"? This movement enacts positionality through transit, by not embodying any essentializing physicality of the immigrant, arrivant, or diasporic settler, in favor of placing her body in question to the material fact of the city's racializing and colonizing infrastructure. By doing so, Yoon's practice has significant ramifications for reorienting how we understand our own and others' belonging to space and new critical positionalities of perception.

How then might one embody a critical positionality of guest movement, listening, and touch? Might this paradoxically take place, as in Yoon's lateral exploration, through a practice of imposing other forms of perceptual restriction, and listening impass? Might we envision settler virtual realities that, rather than expanding the possibilities for perception, radically limit it instead?

To begin this conversation on reparative perception,[8] *Hungry Listening* has offered several strategies not only for decolonizing and resurgent listening, but for decolonial and resurgent forms of writing that resist the epistemic violence of listening experience. These examples offer only a few formats of many for the decolonizing and resurgent work undertaken by composers, presenting organizations, ensembles, performers, and listeners. What lies ahead must expand and refine new protocol for this work to benefit future generations. Taken together, such an expansion of protocol might enable the kind of "cultural hearing aid" and "can openers for tin ears" called for by Walt Taylor in his response to the *Delgamukw v. Queen* trial. How settler subjects begin to hear beyond settler colonial predispositions, beyond the "white noise" of daily settlement, fixity, certainty, and other principles that guide the perceptual logic of settler colonialism, can only continue not just through the increase of decolonial methodology but from acts and actions that restructure these logics. In tandem, Indigenous frameworks of resurgence must continue to seek reconnections of kinship between Indigenous peoples and the life of our songs through ongoing actions of doing sovereignty.

ACKNOWLEDGMENTS

éy kws hákw'elestset te s'í:wes te siyolexwálh: it is good to remember the teachings of our ancestors. This statement, offered by xwélmexw (Stó:lō people) at the opening of gatherings, encapsulates the deep gratitude I feel toward those Indigenous artists, scholars, sí:yá:m / respected leaders and ancestors who have come before and have fought for—and succeeded in making—space for Indigenous artists, scholars, and leaders in my generation. I hope this book and my work here might contribute in some small way to opening space for future generations to challenge normative and settler colonial paradigms of perception and to affirm resurgent forms of attention.

Despite its potential to give thanks and gratitude, the word *acknowledgment* is increasingly awkward to use at the current juncture of reconciliation, given its bureaucratization and instrumentalization by institutions. The sense of obligation and formality that the word "acknowledgment" has come to hold for institutions across Canada does not characterize the ways in which we, as Indigenous people, affirm sovereignty and give thanks. I struggle to find words that are adequate to express my feelings of being humbled by the time, knowledge, meals, laughter, friendship, and challenge that have been offered by so many over the course of the many years the ideas for this book germinated and grew.

Hungry Listening is very much a record that traces changes in my thinking across a ten-year research trajectory. From the project's original focus on the appropriation of Indigenous song in contemporary classical music, it then expanded to include a focus on shxwelítemelh/ hungry, decolonial. and resurgent forms of listening. The book similarly charts the development of my writing from musicological analysis through to a reconsideration of the epistemic violence and accountability of writing, and reparative modes of writing otherwise. At the heart of this transformation of research focus, methodology, and writing are those friendships, mentorships, and conversations with individual colleagues that have pushed this work into challenging and new areas I would not have been able to reach on my own. The book speaks alongside the changing conversations and communities I have had the opportunity to learn from over the same ten years that this writing has taken place.

Commencing with a postdoctoral fellowship in the Faculty of Music at the University of Toronto, this research first found its focus with the support of Robin Elliott, Chalmers Chair of Canadian Music, who provided space, support, and guidance that was essential to the germination of the project. While in Toronto I had the great fortune of meeting Patrick Nickleson and Jeremy Strachan, with whom I have continued to work on various projects focused on collaboration between Indigenous people and art / new music ensembles. Their friendship, our conversations through the years, and their reading and re-reading of the entire manuscript at its different stages have strengthened this work immeasurably. I am inspired by their work as settler scholars who are deeply engaged with decolonial work needed in musicology. In a similar way, Anna Höstman and David Cecchetto have been there in friendship, laughter, and intensely playful / playfully intense conversation about art and music. The structural foundation for my thinking on apposite methodologies was only possible through years of work with David and Anna on installations for thinking about music, not to mention covering over Russian palace theatres, music school rehearsal rooms, and Mexican courtyards in copious amounts of paper. The first case studies for the book—what is now chapter 3—were first tested in the Interdisciplinary Perspectives on Music in Canada (IPMC) meetings that I co-organized with Mary Ingraham, who has always accepted the challenge of collaborating on interdisciplinary projects that have greatly enriched my thinking about this work. My thanks to scholars and friends who joined multiple iterations of IPMC gatherings to hear and give feedback on my initial musings: Beverley Diamond, David Gramit, Andra McCartney, Kip Pegley, Colleen Renihan, Jeremy Strachan, and Ellen Waterman in particular.

Acknowledgments

A second phase of the book's development—one that took place roughly during the same time as the Truth and Reconciliation Commission on the Indian Residential Schools and the 2010 Vancouver Winter Olympics—saw the work expand in relationship with these two very different contexts that centralized Indigenous histories and culture in very different ways. During this time the book's focus changed dramatically while I worked alongside colleagues who were part of the SSHRC-funded Aesthetics of Reconciliation project, led by myself and Keavy Martin. The conversations I took part in with scholars and artists on this project indelibly marked my thinking around reconciliation, conciliation, and redress. I offer my thanks for this time spent learning from Naomi Angel, Beverley Diamond, Byron Dueck, David Garneau, Elizabeth Kalbfleisch, Keavy Marin, Sam McKegney, Peter Morin, Jill Scott, Niigaan Sinclair, and Pauline Wakeham, as we listened to all that was shared with us at the Truth and Reconciliation Commission on the Indian Residential Schools. After witnessing numerous days of survivors' and intergenerational survivors' testimony, the long and often meandering walks and emotional processing with Peter, Elizabeth, and Naomi were particularly important. Also during this time, I began to work with Tahltan artist Peter Morin, whose incisive performances continue to challenge my thinking on nonhuman relationality and kinship. It has been a gift to continue working and laughing with Peter, and I am grateful for the generosity with which he lends his ear-heart-mind along the twists and turns on our path through ideas and creative action. Financial support for this research during these years was provided both through the Social Sciences and Humanities Research Council of Canada (SSHRC) and through a postdoctoral fellowship with the Indigeneity in the Contemporary World project based at Royal Holloway, University of London. While based in (almost) London, working far from home in the center of colonial power, I re-met Carlo Cenciarelli. Many fledgling thoughts and unfurlings of ideas took place in Twickenham while walking along the Thames with Carlo and my wife, Keren. Having this space for thinking together was a profound gift. Carlo, your daily presence kept me focused and inspired, especially during the fraught final days and months living in the United Kingdom.

This book is as much about the Indigenous resurgence of imagination as anything else. This aspect of the work truly came into focus after a return home to lhqʼaːlets / Vancouver for a Banting Postdoctoral Fellowship in the University of British Columbia's First Nations and Indigenous Studies program. This was the first time in fourteen years of study I was able to receive mentorship from an Indigenous scholar, Daniel Heath Justice, a Canada Research Chair in Indigenous Literature and Expressive Culture, Cherokee scholar, and maker of luminous writing. I have always been inspired by Daniel's writing that "imagined otherwise" to challenge myself similarly to "write otherwise." I was also incredibly fortunate upon moving back to Vancouver to meet tel iwestéleq qas siyám siyáye Lumlamelut Wee Lay Laq by enrolling in my first Halqʼeméylem language course at the University of the Fraser Valley held at the Stóːlō Resource Centre. I am so thankful for your friendship and for your continued time and mentorship over the years; it has given me the foundation to increasingly build Halqʼemélem and shxwélméxwelh sqwálewel into the infrastructure of my writing and daily life. yúːwqwlhate sqwáːltset! Conversations with many other colleagues and friends while I was based at UBC provided the inspiration for the ways this book attempts to merge resurgent imagination with scholarly writing. Co-conspirators David Gaertner and Kelsey Wrightson offered much feedback on the work through reading chapters and helping me work out the practice and subsequent fallout from the implementation of models for irreconcilable Indigenous space. Their support continues to be felt from afar and in those rare moments when our locations align. While in Vancouver I met Bracken Hanuse Corlett, whose public artwork *Giants Among Us* inspired me in its focus on engaging youth and our children. I am incredibly honored that Bracken agreed to have his artwork grace the cover of this book. Also while in Vancouver I was inspired daily by Miqueʼl Dangeli and tel qʼoltheteq Mike Dangeli. I am so glad for your enduring friendship, in addition to having the opportunity to learn from Miqueʼlʼs incisive thinking around "dancing sovereignty" and from your leadership of the dance group Git Hayetsk Dancers. Our conversations have sustained me and provided a space to think about resurgence of Indigenous legal orders. I am grateful for all you have shared with me through the years, and for your words that affirm sovereignty throughout the book. My friendship and long-term collaboration with Candice Hopkins also began while in Vancouver. I count myself incredibly lucky to have had such opportunity to collaborate with you,

Acknowledgments 263

Candice, over the past years on different projects including the Soundings exhibition and the *Sensate Sovereignty: Indigenous Public Art* project. You have challenged me in all the best ways to think spatially and curatorially about Indigenous art and sound.

The most recent phase of this book's development coincided with my appointment as Canada Research Chair in Indigenous Arts at Queen's University, where I have been grateful for the support of a fantastic group of scholars, curators, and artists, including Jan Allen, Alicia Boutilier, Laura Cameron, Heather Castleden, Lisa Guenther, Kanonhsyonne Jan Hill, Sammi King, Julien Lefort-Favreau and Anne-Renée Caillé (and Mischa), Susan Lord, Heather MacFarlane, Jeff Masuda, Katherine McKittrick, Scott Morgensen, Laura Murray, Ali Na and Eric Chalfant (and of course Mayhem and Ebey), Dorit Naaman, Kip Pegley, Colleen Renihan, Matt Rogalsky, Armand Ruffo, Julie Salverson, Jill Scott, Gordon Smith, and Margaret Walker. The final submission of the book manuscript was strengthened immensely by feedback from Ellen Waterman and Deborah Wong, who so generously accepted an invitation to workshop the complete manuscript and even more generously accepted my "sneaky" invitation to have a dialogue that would comprise a significant section of the conclusion. Thank you, Ellen and Deborah, for saying yes to "figuring it out" and then sharing many other spaces for figuring together. Your critical engagement has been so central to the book not just through the workshop that summer in Kingston but across the many years I have known you and meals we've shared together from bad conference hotel lounges to back porches to the gastronomic adventures that St. John's and Ottawa had to offer. From one windy Newfoundland coast to another in California, I am so grateful for the spaces we have shared in listening together and reverberant response.

The chapters of this book have also benefitted from many close readings by graduate students I have had the pleasure of working with in the Cultural Studies Graduate Program at Queen's University. I am particularly appreciative of the careful feedback provided by Camille Georgeson-Usher and Sebastien De Line on the Indigenous Space for Writing. Anthony Lomax's fast response time to copyediting was unsurpassed, while Laura Phillips's exceptional gift for finding "image needles" in archival haystacks has been incredibly helpful. While I single out the specific attention to detail in reading and research assistance provided by these students, the many conversations with graduate students I have had the pleasure of supervising in Cultural Studies have also allowed theoretical and creative speculation to emerge through discussion of their own work. It is one of the most enjoyable aspects of my job to be able to work with graduate students in this program, many of whom are artists and curators. I learn so much from your work on a daily basis. In addition to those students named above, my conversations with Leah Decter, Lara Fullenwieder, Marshall Hill, Geraldine King, Cheryl L'Hirondelle, Tanya Lukin Linklater, Carina Magazzeni, Lisa C. Ravensbergen, Sarah Garton Stanley, Erin Sutherland, and Ellyn Walker have had been impactful. To the most recent readers of this work, including Olivia Bloechl, Tamara Levitz, and an anonymous external reader, I express my sincere and heartfelt thanks for your generous feedback; it has been invaluable in strengthening the work, and has given me the confidence to amplify the volume on certain ideas.

Several workshops and invited talks have allowed me to receive feedback on most aspects of the book. While it is impossible to name all here, presentations of particular importance to the development of the book have included the travel to University of California, Riverside, arranged and fantastically hosted by Michelle Raheja; a Society for Ethnomusicology Presidential Plenary in 2015 organized by then SEM president Beverley Diamond; a workshop at University of California, San Diego, in 2017 organized by Roshy Kheshti, Julie Burelle, and Katie Walkiewicz; the John Hooker Distinguished Visiting Professorship at McMaster University and an Orion Visiting Guest in Indigenous Art at the University of Victoria, both in 2018; the Arctic Media, Indigeneity, and Social Justice in the 21st Century gathering at University of California, Davis, organized by Jessica Bissett Perea in 2015; and a visiting lecture at the University of Michigan in 2019 coordinated by Bethany Hughes. In between these visits, I am a beneficiary of the conversation, wit, and creativity of an inspiring community of scholars and artists, including Parmela Attariwala, Lorna Brown, Raven Chacon, Selena Couture, Ian Cusson, Michael Di Risio, Jeremy Dutcher, David Garneau, Mimi Gellman, Tasha Hubbard, Rachel Iwaasa, Lisa Jackson, Roshy Kheshti, Carey Newman, Marion Newman, Jeneen Frei Njootli, Beth Piatote, Karyn Recollet, Trevor Reed, and Tania Willard, among many others.

Acknowledgments 265

This book would not exist without the initial interest and ongoing support of Robert Warrior within the Indigenous Americas Series, and Jason Weidemann at the University of Minnesota Press. I extend my thanks to you and the editorial staff. I have appreciated your questions, guidance, and editorial finesse that have brought clarity to the book's ideas and presentation over its development.

Finally, to my family: Mom and Dad, you persisted in telling me through years of trial and training that anything I dreamt was possible, even when it felt impossible. This has been a guiding light for me not just in terms of persistence but in nurturing the creativity of dreaming itself. Keren—you have witnessed this work emerge from its (and our) very beginnings and change as extensively as our travels together across the globe. This book would have been impossible to start or to complete without your support and love. I am overwhelmed by your unwavering encouragement, and sacrifice of your own time, over and again, that allowed for my thinking to zigzag along its course toward becoming a real book. Through the years your writing has provided me with vital theoretical tools and inspiration to think about reception and spectatorship, while its craft has always modeled a clarity that I continue to aspire to. Becoming a father as this book neared its completion has attuned my listening in a very different way. To Chloe, your little songs, delight at the world, and knack for storytelling reminds me every day of sensate life around us.

NOTES

Introduction

1. For a thorough bibliography of works by Canadian composers who have resourced First Nations and Inuit song and story in their compositions, see Strachan (2005). While this guide lists nearly three hundred compositions held in the collection of the Canadian Music Centre, since its publication the number has steadily increased. For a comparative list, including works by Canadian composers not represented by the Canadian Music Centre, see the appendix to Keillor (1995).

2. The word Stó:lō identifies intercommunity kinships across a number of nations and bands along the Fraser River within S'ólh Témexw. While it has become an identity marker and remains useful to designate political solidarity between our people, it is a term we use less frequently to identify ourselves. Individual bands/nations are used within formal and informal introduction, while "xwélmexw" is the word used both as the plural form to indicate "the people" or singular form to indicate "Indian."

3. In 2017, to coincide with Canada's one hundred and fiftieth anniversary of confederation, the Canada Council for the Arts overhauled its funding models with a significant focus on diversity. For a comprehensive overview of the effects of the Canadian Multiculturalism Act (1988) on arts funding councils (particularly Canada's largest federal funding organization, the Canada Council for the Arts and the Toronto Arts Council) see Attariwala (2013).

4. For further work in this area see Everett (2004), Utz (2005), and Winzenburg (2013).

5. The Official Multiculturalism Act of 1988 set guidelines for institutions receiving federal funding to "promote policies, programs and practices that enhance the understanding of and respect for the diversity of the members of Canadian society" and to "carry on their activities in a manner that is sensitive

and responsive to the multicultural reality of Canada" (Government of Canada 1988). As Parmela Attariwala writes, "by spelling out the responsibility of the Government of Canada and its institutions to uphold multiculturalism in the second part of the 1988 Multicultural Policy, the government placed its own institutions (including Crown Corporations such as the CBC, the Canada Council, and the National Film Board) at the heart of structural change, effectively imposing a kind of affirmative action. As a result, the federal arts funder, the Canada Council, had no choice but to change its internal policies for hiring, granting programs, and funding priorities in order to comply with the Multiculturalism Act. The council's Music Section had to fundamentally alter its aesthetic and artistic priorities, until then firmly oriented around Western classical music" (Attariwala 2013, 143).

6. Although important arguments against recognition-based forms of reconciliation have been advanced by Coulthard, Garneau, and L. Simpson, among others, these critiques also risk undercutting the agency of Indigenous participants as co-opted victims rather than as actors who have considered the political implications of their participation. Like the lack of nuance around the categories of "Indigenous" and "settler" this binary between victim and agent needs further refinement in the post–Truth and Reconciliation Commission on Indian Residential Schools (TRC) context of [re]conciliation in Canada. As a xwélmexw scholar cognizant of the need to develop a critical discourse around the work that Indigenous artists, musicians, and composers take part in, I seek for *Hungry Listening* to offer critique of settler composers, ensembles, and arts organizations and engage in a discussion of accountability with the Indigenous artistic and scholarly communities I consider myself part of. It is my hope that my calling forth of accountability is done in as respectful a way as possible, and is understood as a challenge toward strengthening artistic practices and forms of scholarship that benefit Indigenous artists, musicians, and performers.

7. The difference between ontologies of Indigenous and Western song, as I describe throughout the book—and particularly in chapter 1—is here important to note. This difference means that there is a distinction between a Western notion of songs that more simply promote healing, or refer to history and law, and songs that are the equivalent of law, Western medicine, and primary historical documentation (books).

8. In reading conference programs from the American Musicological Society, Society for Ethnomusicology, Society for American Music, and other music gatherings, I am repeatedly struck by the formulation "race/indigeneity topic in x piece of music," as if the premise for music scholarship on race and Indigeneity is to locate race *in* works. Scholarship on musical representations of race has a long history, while there has been far less of a focus on how music is a tool of

Notes to "Writing Indigenous Space" **269**

racialization or how methodologies in musicology, music theory, and ethnomusicology are subtended by normative, settler colonial, patriarchal forms of thought.

9. The category of "settler" is not used to exclusively or even primarily designate the "original settlers" of the nation-states of Canada and the United States, but to any who have come to stay in Indigenous lands. For further discussion of settler positionality, see chapter 1.

10. Pratt's use of this concept builds upon the work of Cuban anthropologist Fernando Ortiz.

11. On the colonial histories of academic disciplines and scholarly associations, see Levitz 2018. See also Tuck and Guishard 2013.

12. The hyperbolic tone of this critique is exemplified in Elaine Barkin's review of McClary's *Feminine Endings* (1991): "Were I, were concert-goers to take literally her post-neo-Freudian, 'gender-encoded' explanations of what's really—or what's also—going on down in Western 'absolute' music, we'd all be sitting in those high-backed seats [of the concert hall], one hand between our (or another's) legs, actively groping, stifling (auto)erotic cries of ecstasy, during an otherwise prim and proper reception of any seventeenth-century-through-Corelli trio sonata (in which 'two equal voices rub up against each other, pressing into dissonances . . . reaching satiety only at conclusions')" (Barkin 1992, 214).

13. The important work of musicologist Tamara Levitz has been unflinching in its critical investigation of the history of the Society for American Music and "the early history of the American Musicological Society as an institution of white supremacy with the goal of providing the understanding necessary to dismantle that system in the present" (Levitz 2016).

Writing Indigenous Space

1. Rice writes, "Much as 2017 marks the 150th anniversary of Canadian Confederation, 1992 was the year in which America celebrated the 500th anniversary of Christopher Columbus's 'discovery of the New World.' Festivities across the Americas were planned and executed. Just as many Onkwehón:we in Canada are unenthusiastic about the country's sesquicentennial, Onkwehón:we across the Americas felt there was no cause for celebration in 1992. . . . [yet] 1992 ended soon enough, and Onkwehón:we artists and curators were faced with the question 'What happens next?' It soon became apparent that the 'celebratory' funds for exhibitions, exchanges, and residencies were gone. The party was over. . . . the mood was one of a lingering hangover, a time to reflect" (R. Rice 2017, 47).

2. It is important for me to note that the group discussion held after *The*

270   Notes to "Writing Indigenous Space"

Magic Flute was also a space of sovereignty, and I would like to believe that our discussion there was qualitatively different than it might have been in the company of non-Indigenous participants. At the very least I can say it felt this way for me.

3. I am attendant to the way in which this statement could be conflated with an understanding of drag as being "artificial" and as such effecting a heteronormative view of drag. This is far from my own intention or that of Reder.

4. The intercommunity kinship represented in the potlatch scene of *The Magic Flute* does not of course only reference historical travel between First Peoples across the Northwest coast, our families continue to travel across great distances to attend potlatches and other longhouse work today. Moreover, Tribal Canoe Journeys continues this practice of long-distance travel between Indigenous communities along the Northwest coast, as a form of intergenerational and intercommunity teaching significantly oriented toward cultural resurgence for our youth.

5. And yet, following Richard Rath (2014), who warns against analogizing wampum as a kind of written document or financial currency, it is important to remember that these figures are also entirely unlike immigration officials, in order that we continue the ontological specificity of the thing/action itself.

6. The word "belongings" is itself an important choice made by Wilson and the Musqueam community that both refuses the word "artifact" and its location of First Peoples' culture as part of history rather than the present. "Belongings" also names the fact that these belongings (also sometimes considered beings and ancestors) continue to belong to Musqueam people despite their location in the museum.

7. There is also a need to problematize the necessity for Indigenous writing always to demonstrate an essential orality, or representational authority for the community and nation the writer comes from. As an Indigenous scholar, artist, and language learner, I am already speaking in an "authentic voice." It is the voice I use every day in English with a smattering of Halq'eméylem, sometimes using what some consider academic jargon, and adopting a more polemic timbre. "Speaking freely" does not need to be conflated with high oratory or "plain speech."

8. I recognize this will be disappointing to any settler readers who decided to read this section against my explicit request not to. Because nothing shared here is sacred knowledge, I am happy for other Indigenous writers to paraphrase their understandings of the ideas I present in this section for other publication (accessible to non-Indigenous readers) in relation with their own cultural knowledge and teachings, and would rather this take place instead of direct citation.

Notes to Chapter 1

1. Hungry Listening

1. Stadler's account prefigures the arrival of several books that engage with listening and race, notably Roshanak Khesthi (2015), Ashon Crawley (2016), and Jennifer Stoever (2016). Fred Moten (2003) and Ana María Ochoa Gauthier (2014) should also be noted as significant contributions to the area of listening and race. In the rapid development of the field of sound studies over in the early twenty-first century, the paucity of research represented by these four books supports Stadler's assessment of this aporia.

2. Elsewhere I argue that while returning Indigenous lands is essential in the process of state reparation, we might also consider other conceptions of ground including "core curricula"—the core history, the theory, the artistic practices of the departments in which we teach. "If we think of our curricula as the 'the ground,' we might then also consider core curriculum as the educational equivalent of land. It might then follow that in order for decolonization not to merely be a metaphor (Tuck and Yang 2012), curriculum might need to be one of the things 'given back,' where curriculum is the ground that we provide through the courses, the texts, and the performances we teach. Substantive forms of redress that Indigenous people call for are not reducible to the singularity of 'the land,' but include other foundations, other ground" (Robinson 2019a, 21).

3. In particular, I do not account for listening from diasporic, immigrant, and what Jodi Byrd has described as "arrivant" subjectivities, and how these might have their attendant forms of listening, themselves multiple and contingent on their relationships with and negotiations between national identities and histories of displacement and migration. This work is imperative if we are to think through the diversity and range of listening positionalities that are employed by individuals.

4. Such encounters are brought together and analyzed cogently by musicologist Olivia Bloechl (2008; 2013).

5. Although Justice McEachern ruled that the song was inadmissible as evidence, it could be argued that this inclusion sets precedent in the realm of Indigenous legal orders in Canada.

6. Often referred to as a dirge song, within the Delgamuukw court proceedings Gitxsan elder Martha Brown, Xhliimlaxha, noted that "whenever a Chief dies they use the limx'ooy in many different ways. . . . it's a crying song, or a mourning song. That's all" (British Columbia Supreme Court 1985, 7).

7. Val Napoleon describes the adaawk as that which "links each House to its territories and establishes ownership of the land and resources. The adaawk tell of the origins and migrations of groups to their current territories, explorations, covenants established with the land, and songs, crests, and names that result from the spiritual connection between people and their land" (Napoleon 2001, 7).

Notes to Chapter 1

8. Important work on the range of settler subjectivity is reflected in the literature on settler heteropatriarchy and queer settler subjectivity (Morgenson 2011) and Asian diasporic forms of settler subjectivity (Fujikane and Okamura 2008; Day 2016). On intersectional forms of settler subjectivity, see Snelgrove, Dhamoon, and Corntassel (2014) and Dhamoon (2015). Although I begin to move toward a consideration of these intersectional forms of listening in the book's Conclusion, more nuanced work needs to be done in this area. Intersectional forms of settler subjectivity need also to be accounted for alongside nuanced intersectional and nation-specific forms of perception that orient how we see, listen, and feel.

9. I use xwélmexw here and elsewhere in the book as the Halq'eméylem term used to refer to Stó:lō people in the plural for "the people" or individually for "person." The word Stó:lō in fact means "river," and so it is appropriate at least in the sense that our daily lives, histories, and communities are all oriented toward the river.

10. This appropriation has often been coded as "significant influence" by writers attempting to demonstrate the greatness of modernist Canadian painters.

11. Of course other forms of "listening for" are key in survival and sustenance. Beverley Diamond notes that "Hunters, to name one obvious example, certainly listen for the location of game or the birds they seek. This is indeed a form of 'hungry listening'—literally" (e-mail message to author, March 1, 2017).

12. sqwálewel is the Halq'eméylem word used for thoughts or feelings. Its literal translation is "talk or speech on insides."

13. There are numerous classical music concerts that include the addition of video or set as a "backdrop" (while keeping every other concert ritual the same). While adopting a visual component may certainly be of use in promoting decolonial listening, less attention has been given to new formations of presentation and audience location, new sites of presentation, and ways that fundamentally reorient the ways in which we give attention to the aural. There are models of this outside of the concert music realm, notably in the outdoor settings of work by R. Murray Schafer, in the reorientations of concert music through Fluxus event scores, and by sound artists such as Janet Cardiff. Yet despite these models, more flexible and explicitly decolonial strategies for art music presentation and listening have been slow to advance.

14. An excellent overview of this work is given by Michelle Raheja (2015).

15. I use "work" here not in the sense of a discrete artwork, but in the same way we refer to the work done within the longhouse, at potlatches, and at winter dances. The "work" is thus not an object but a process.

16. hənq̓əminəm̓—spoken downriver by xʷməθkʷəy̓əm people—and Halq̓eméylem—spoken upriver by Stó:lō—are sometimes considered dialects;

Notes to Chapter 2   273

nevertheless, it is important not to conflate the significant differences between them. Charting such differences and similarities is demonstrated with great care by Brent Galloway (2009).

2. Writing about Musical Intersubjectivity

1. I read Sontag here against her prioritizing of purely formalist analysis, while emphasizing her engagement with the appearance and sensory qualities of the work. Indeed, in advocating sensory-formalist analysis, this chapter seeks to revise Sontag's closing line: "in place of a hermeneutics we need an erotics of art" (10) to "we need a hermeneutic erotics of art."

2. Many, if not the majority, of the writings I refer to in this chapter do not explicitly adopt the phrase "performative writing" as the genre the work falls within. Despite this, the works I consider share the essential feature identified by Peggy Phelan (1997) and Della Pollock (1998) in their definitions of performative writing, including poetic address, a textual engagement with materiality and the senses including embodied and haptic approaches, a foregrounding of the writer-subject, and a questioning of normative forms of writing.

3. For a detailed discussion of non-representational theory's challenge to the subject–object divide, see Robinson and Ingraham's "Introduction: Toward Non-Exceptionalist Experiences of Music in Canada," in *Intensities: Toward Non-Exceptionalist Experience of Music in Canada*.

4. In a more related blog post "Disciplinarity and Gatekeeping," Bellman notes, "Say what *you* have to say, but don't lard it with 'brilliance and dash'— simply play *your* game, as the sports announcers say and I never tire of repeating. *Your* game. In the vast landscape of American academia, the 'searing' written idiom has receded, as has cultural criticism itself to a certain extent, and I have to wonder if it was the bitter tone that eventually wore everyone out" (Bellman 2015). What Bellman fails to note here is that quite possibly one's game might need to involve "brilliance and dash" or "bitter tone" (later he calls these "vinegary critiques") when that is the language necessary to convey knowledge of specific musical experiences of bitterness (or injustice) or of brilliance (exaltation).

5. Other important examples of performative writing in music scholarship can be found in the work of music theorists James Randall and Benjamin Boretz (2003) and in the ethnomusicologial scholarship of Tomie Hahn (2007), Deborah Wong (2004; 2008), and Martin Daughtry (2013).

6. Admittedly, there is some irony here in my application of the term "apposite" to a methodology intended to undercut the unmarked heteronormative, patriarchal, and colonizing forms of writing. "Apposite," commonly used as a synonym for "appropriate," might bring to mind the very opposite approach of

274 Notes to Chapter 2

the decolonial, queer, and antinormative. "Apposite" might similarly seem to suggest that music scholars pursue strikingly *appropriate* ways of writing about music, in comparison with other supposedly *inappropriate* methodologies. This, however, is not the valence of the word "apposite" I wish to emphasize.

7. Ironically, this is in a sense what Levin himself argues for in operatic stagings as artistic "readings" of opera, as I discuss later in the chapter. There is some contradiction here in Levin's lack of recognition that the prose forms of performative writing engaged by Koestenbaum (1993) might be another mode of the model he suggests in operatic staging. Koestenbaum's writing, as much as it engages in an examination of the material circumstances of opera's (domestic, recorded) expression, is not recognized as demonstrating an analysis of the operatic work, and for this reason violates the unspoken hierarchy of musicology to privilege the work over the event.

8. Morin here does not take for granted that the ancestor knows the history of residential schools, given that it has been held (incarcerated) in the collection without having a chance to hear from an Indigenous relation for somewhere between eighty and a hundred years.

9. Lawrence Kramer, in "Odradek Analysis: Reflections on Musical Ontology," turns to Kafka's figure Odradek, half subject, half object that "is not silent. It, or he, will even talk to you, even laugh. But 'it is only the kind of laughter that has no lungs behind it. It sounds rather like the rustling of fallen leaves'" (Kramer 2004b, 287). While Kramer remains focused on the ontological condition of music as a kind of Odradek, his analysis also points toward the life of the house itself and the way Odradek inhabits it with its laugh: "The laughter both belongs to your house and unsettles it. It is a house well stocked with familiar forms, some common and comfortable (a chord in the foyer, a cadence in the hall) and some more recherché (a *Kopfton* on the stairs, a collection of pitch-class sets in the attic)" (288; italics in the original). Also of note here is Georgina Born's essay "On Nonhuman Sound—Sound as Relation."

10. In *The Ignorant Schoolmaster,* Rancière writes, "Explication is not necessary to remedy an incapacity to understand. On the contrary, that very incapacity provides the structuring fiction of the explicative conception of the world. It is the explicator who needs the incapable and not the other way around; it is he who constitutes the incapable as such. To explain something to someone is first of all to show him he cannot understand it by himself. Before being the act of the pedagogue, explication is the myth of pedagogy, the parable of a world divided into knowing minds and ignorant ones, ripe minds and immature ones, the capable and the incapable, the intelligent and the stupid. The explicator's special trick consists of this double inaugural gesture. On the one hand he decrees the absolute beginning: it is only now that the act of learning will begin. On the other,

Notes to "xwélalà:m, Raven Chacon's *Report*"   275

having thrown a veil of ignorance over everything that is to be learned, he appoints himself to the task of lifting it" (Rancière 1991, 6–7; see also Fricker 2009).

11. In *Red on Red: Native American Literary Separatism* (1999), Creek-Cherokee scholar Craig Womack asserts "that it is valuable to look toward Creek authors and their works to understand Creek writing. My argument is not that this is the *only* way to understand Creek writing but an important one given that literatures bear some kind of relationship to communities, both writing communities and community of the primary culture, from which they originate" (Womack 1999, 4). Similarly, Leanne Simpson in *Dancing on Our Turtle's Back* notes, "We need to rebuild our culturally inherent philosophical contexts for governance, education, healthcare, and economy. We need to be able to articulate in a clear manner our visions for the future, for living as *Indigenous Peoples* in contemporary times. To do so, we need to engage in *Indigenous* processes, since according to our traditions, the processes of engagement highly influence the outcome of the engagement itself. We need to do this on our own terms, without the sanction, permission or engagement of the state, western theory or the opinions of Canadians" (L. Simpson 2011, 17). Such views have also been predominant in Native Nationalist literary criticism (Warrior 1994; Justice 2004), and in political theory (Alfred 1999; 2005; Coulthard 2014b). While both Womack and Simpson are interested in sovereign forms of Indigenous writing and scholarship, Womack's statement is situated against exclusivity, while Simpson's more explicitly rejects non-Indigenous theory. I have been in several gatherings where Indigenous advocates for resurgence and "grounded normativity" understand these practices as ones where Indigenous scholars and writers should only draw upon the work of other Indigenous scholars and writers. While this has the important effect of centering Indigenous thought and fostering the growth of Indigenous theories and methodologies, it also has the effect of censoring Indigenous writers who gain inspiration, and develop strategies for Indigenous creative, intellectual, and political flourishment through intersectional relationships. My work here aligns more with the approach articulated by Simpson and Smith, that "intellectual sovereignty requires not isolationism but theoretical promiscuity" (A. Simpson and Smith 2014, 9).

xwélalà:m, Raven Chacon's *Report*

1. "The very emergence of noise pollution as a topic of public concern testifies to the fact that modern man is at last becoming concerned to clean the sludge out of his ears and regain talent for clairaudience—clean hearing" (Schafer 1994, 11). My thanks to Laura Phillips for this citation.

2. Naxaxalhts'i (Sonny McHalsie), quoted in Wilcock 2011, 234.

3. Contemporary Encounters between Indigenous and Early Music

1. The term "early music" is here as nebulous to define as "First Nations and Inuit cultural practices," as generalizable categories that speak more to a broad category relating to the musical examples discussed in this chapter. These categories are nonetheless employed throughout this chapter to refer to the encounter between two different sound worlds.

2. Although established on June 2, 2008, the resignation of the chair of the commission, Justice Harry S. Laforme of the Ontario Court of Appeal in October 2008, and followed in January 2009 by the resignation of the other two commissioners Claudette Dumont-Smith and Jane Brewin Morley, caused the commission's work to stall. The re-commencement of the TRC took place in June 2009, following the appointment of new commissioners including Justice Murray Sinclair, Marie Wilson, and Chief Wilton Littlechild.

3. In the Royal Commission on Aboriginal People (a precursor to the TRC) the emphasis placed upon "Aboriginal nations in most circumstances welcome[ing] the first newcomers in friendship" (Dussault et al. 1996, 12) derives from this myth of historical friendship and good relations.

4. For numerous examples, see Robinson and Martin 2016.

5. This narrative of contribution is not just prevalent in the settler imaginary but also structured the guiding framework of the popular Canadian Broadcasting Corporation show *8TH Fire,* hosted by Wab Kinew, in which the aim was largely to demonstrate how Indigenous people across Canada are contributors to the economic stability of the state.

6. An earlier iteration of this chapter, written for the collection *Aboriginal Music in Contemporary Canada: Echoes and Exchanges,* edited by Anna Hoefnagels and Beverley Diamond, included an overview of two other works: *Medieval Inuit* and *Thunderbird.* Camerata Nova's *Medieval Inuit* concert alternated between Nordic folksong and Inuit throat singing or drum songs. In the program notes, Cree composer Andrew Balfour describes the premise for the concert: "to explore musically the mystery of the first contact between the Vikings or Norse and the indigenous people of Canada's Arctic. . . . Although there is no firm evidence that these early Norse encountered the indigenous people of the region, this concert and composition, in an abstract, musical way, imagine this happening. I also realize that, if the Norse did encounter indigenous people, they would have been from the now-extinct Dorset culture, rather than the Inuit. I hope people will forgive my license" (*Medieval Inuit* concert program, 2010). Marion Newman's collaboration with Aradia, in contrast, presents Kwagiulth stories and dances performed by members of her family—George Taylor (singer-drummer) and Jason Taylor (dancer), both from the Le La La Dancers—and using masks carved by Newman's father, Victor Newman.

Both *Thunderbird* and *Medieval Inuit* invert inclusion through changing the sense of Indigenous presence within their respective performance spaces. In *Medieval Inuit* this is achieved by projecting large photographs on a scrim of thirty by forty feet of Inuit men, women, and children taken between 1910 and 1930 by Henry Thomas Ford. These photos documented early encounters between Inuit from Qamani'tuaq / Baker Lake and settlers who arrived for trading posts and as missionaries. Equally transformative of the space was the ceremonial lighting of the *qulliq* by elder Lavinia Brown at the beginning of the concert. While *Thunderbird* opens more conventionally, with the Aradia Baroque Ensemble arriving from backstage to the customary welcome of audience applause, this is subverted shortly thereafter by the Kwagiulth performers entering from behind the audience and between the aisles. Their movement and song—the characteristically moderate pace of their drums and low pitch of their voices—immediately deepened the sense of space around the audience members. Their song moved toward us and beside us, enveloping and physically transforming the space through the sound of still cedar forest; the dampened sound of depth.

7. A previous version of this chapter, in fact, did the opposite: leaving my individual reception unspoken, and in doing so implicitly claiming the analysis of the work as generalizable to other audience members. That the practice of musicology is still based upon this model of analysis that denies individual and idiosyncratic reception speaks to the anxiety of "merely" individual reception that operates as a binary to supposed fact.

8. Audiences are often described by organizers, composers, performers, and audience members themselves as semi-cohesive communities with shared values, often in relation with genre: the opera audience, the country music audience, the Cree fiddling audience. In larger cities such distinctions are even further nuanced. In Toronto, for example, one might encounter people talking about micro-communities of new music including "the Esprit Orchestra audience," "the Soundstreams audience," or "the Array Music audience." These audiences identify with the aesthetic values and cultural capital (or subcultural "anticapital") that ensembles and arts institutions take up as their focus.

9. The category "early music" is often understood as encompassing repertoire from early Middle Ages to the end of the seventeenth century.

10. Reviewers were also quick to note that they "conspicuously avoid[ed] a dissonant 'modern classical' sound" (Eatock 2010).

11. Given that *Giiwedin* was presented in 2010, during the early stages of the Truth and Reconciliation Commission on the Indian Residential Schools where public consciousness of Canada's genocidal policies against Indigenous people was still emergent, the opera might be understood as an instance of public education for members of the settler Canadian public.

278   Notes to Chapter 3

12. For an excellent examination of the rise in *barococo* easy listening in the 1950s, see Fink (2005, particularly chapter 4). *Barococo* as a term was first coined by musicologist H. C. Robbins-Landon, who used it dismissively to describe "easy listening" to Baroque music.

13. The term *organum* refers to plainchant melody on which early heterophonic and polyphonic vocal music was composed in the Middle Ages. Pérotin's organum is central to the history of medieval polyphony, not to mention in the core curriculum of music programs and music history surveys.

14. Qimmiijaqtauniq translates to "many dogs (or dog teams) being taken away or killed."

15. Given Canada's history of best intentions that produced the residential school system, the sixties and seventies scoop, the disproportionate number of incarcerated Indigenous people in prisons, and murdered and missing Indigenous women and girls, it should go without saying that best intentions do not preclude harm and injustice. Despite this knowledge of best intentions going awry, a significant number of settler Canadians assume that being a good person means that one cannot at the same time espouse racist views, or benefit from, participate in, and act as *active* bystanders in the ongoing injustices that Indigenous peoples face. I have elsewhere named this position of good-intentioned bystanderism "intergenerational perpetration" (Robinson 2016).

16. The documentary contains the first and final movements of *Winter,* both of which are analyzed here.

4. Ethnographic Redress, Compositional Responsibility

1. See Trevor Reed (2016) and Robin Gray (2015).

2. The terminology used to refer to those who collected songs is as diverse as the situations that enabled the collection of Indigenous songs. From work supported by the Canadian Museum of Civilization (now Canadian Museum of History) to unfunded work by amateur folklorists, the terms "ethnographer," "anthropologist," "folklorist," and "ethnomusicologist" are often used to describe individuals engaged in documenting Indigenous material culture and intangible cultural heritage. I use the term "ethnographer" here as a general placeholder to refer to those engaged in Indigenous song collection.

3. The sixties scoop is the term given to "series of policies enacted by provincial child welfare authorities starting in the mid-1950s, which saw thousands of Indigenous children taken from their homes and families, placed in foster homes, and eventually adopted out to white families from across Canada and the United States. These children lost their names, their languages, and a connection to their heritage. Sadly, many were also abused and made to feel ashamed of who they were" (Dart 2017).

Notes to Chapter 4

4. This ascription of Indigenous identity is all the more notable given that the Group of Seven did not explicitly name such influence.

5. In the liner notes to the 1967 Folkways Records recording *Indian Music of the Pacific Northwest Coast,* Halpern states, "When reproached by other chiefs for having given away his songs he said 'I was a sick man when starting to sing for her. Now after the year's singing I sang myself to health and am well again'" (Halpern 1967, 4).

6. Kenneth Chen notes that Halpern was criticized by some for not presenting detailed notes on the singers in the liner notes for the recordings. Refuting this criticism, Chen refers back to Halpern's writing to demonstrate how she "endeavoured in her liner-notes to foreground her 'native experts' as the primary and proper authorities of their own cultures. She kept '[f]or authenticity's sake the words [and logic] of the informants in the explanations . . . as close as possible to their way of expressing themselves [in English],' further clarifying in her 1967 but not 1974 liner-notes that what came 'directly from [them] . . . were the explanations of songs and meanings.' This was her understanding and personal practice of an 'Emic approach,' which she defined as 'research directly from Native Indians'" (Chen 1995, 54).

7. The gathering at UBC was coorganized by musicologist Sherry Lee and Klisala Harrison, and featured a wide range of scholars including Chief Justice of Canada Beverley McLachlin and Jean Teillet, noted lawyer and Louis Riel's great-grandniece, among other notable scholars and performers. In a 2017 symposium called *Hearing Riel* that coincided with the Canadian Opera Company and National Arts Centre's remount of the opera, also coorganized by Lee, no participants focused upon this appropriation, with the exception of Peter Hinton, the director for the 2017 remount. Hinton was one of a few people present at *Hearing Riel* and a gathering I organized that was explicitly aimed at redressing the appropriation of the Nisga'a limx oo'y. Hinton's presentation at *Hearing Riel* focused on sharing in knowledge from the meeting I organized. I detail this history of musicological gathering to illustrate how the consciousness raising orientation of musicological symposia do not often engage applications of the knowledge gained—in this case redress and reparation.

8. For a more extensive discussion of Morin's *Cultural Graffiti,* see Robinson (2019).

9. For more information, see https://cargocollective.com/makerbros/Apology-Dice.

10. In October 2015, as part of the SSHRC-funded Insight Grant project *Sensate Sovereignty: Indigenous Public Art,* Hopkins and I organized a gathering on the U.S.–Mexico border to coincide with the Indigenous arts collective Postcommodity's work *Repellent Fence.* Called "De-socializing Social Art Practices, Views from Borderzones," this gathering focused on refining ideas around

280 Notes to Chapter 4

de-socializing and intersections between social practice and border politics from Indigenous perspectives. Our questions focused on how artistic practices engaging with strategies of de-socialization might provide sites of temporary sovereignty, from which the increasing militarization and politicization of the border are being addressed. We asked how social space is created as well as how living in border zones socializes Indigenous people.

11. For example, see Peter Morin (2016).

12. A notable exception is the volume *Improvisation and Social Aesthetics,* edited by Georgina Born, Eric Lewis, and Will Straw (2017).

13. As Owen Hulatt writes, according to Adorno, "Art does not merely present or resemble the world external to it; it is capable of interceding in that world by providing a critical expression of the rational structures which govern that world. . . . Adorno has a radical conception of artistic and aesthetic autonomy, in which the creation and reception of art is purely governed by means of aesthetic properties, with no room for the intercession of other kinds of norms (e.g. moral or political norms). . . . he understands the process of creating 'authentic' art to be entirely governed by formal demands and problematics. As a consequence, he claims, the artwork is 'blind' and incapable of intentionally mirroring or criticizing anything external to these autonomous aesthetic formal problematics" (Hulatt 2013, 171).

14. The exception is Patrick Carrabré's *Inuit Games,* which not only scores laughter for the throat singers at the ending of the composition, but for the orchestra as well. Notwithstanding Carrabré's important choice to centralize laughter in the work, it must also be noted that this laughter follows the temporality set out by the composer rather than that of a throat game itself.

15. This fact exists in sharp contrast with the vast resources expended to bring the performance to northern locations. For the first tour of *Take the Dog Sled* from September 11 to 15, 2008, the Orchestre Symphonie du Montreal (OSM) was able to fly approximately thirty people, including Maestro Kent Nagano; seven instrumentalists from the OSM; composer Alexina Louie; narrator Jobie Weetaluktuk, and singers Evie Mark and Taqralik Partridge to the Nunavik communities of Inukjuak, Kangiqsujuaq, and Kuujjuaq. From September 9 to 19, 2018, the OSM gave performances in the Inuit villages of Kuujjuaq, Salluit, and Kuujjuarapik, in the Cree community of Oujé-Bougoumou, and the Innu communities of Mashteuiatsh and Uashat mak Mani-Utenam.

Event Score for Responsibility

1. While the first part of the title "qimmit katajjaq" is Inuktitut for "dog throat songs," the second part "sqwélqwel tl' sqwmá:y" translates as "dogs' sto-

ries" in Halq'eméylem. I consider this title entirely provisional, open to revision by the youth whom I call the presenting organizations to involve in realizing the second set of pre-performance instructions. My reasoning behind including dual languages in the title of the piece is to acknowledge my own positionality and to resist the conflation of my knowledge/approach with that which another Inuit artist may deem necessary.

2. This recording of Alexina Louie's voice is taken from a podcast of a preconcert talk at the National Arts Centre. See Louie 2013, *NACOcast: Paul Wells Interviews Alexina Louie.*

3. All quotations below by Alexina Louie are drawn from a preconcert interview between her and Paul Wells at the National Arts Centre. See Louie 2013, *NACOcast: Paul Wells Interviews Alexina Louie.*

4. An Inuit Story, http://www.thecanadianencyclopedia.ca/en/article/inuit -myth-and-legend/.

5. Feeling Reconciliation

1. Bruce Ruddell, interview with the author, September 1, 2012.

2. An increasing number of studies have taken up the transformative potential of performance, including Erika Fischer-Lichte (2008), James Thompson (2009), and Jill Dolan (2005).

3. In the numerous performances I have attended, audience responses of tears and ecstatic support are unnervingly consistent. For contemporary art music performances where standing ovations are more the exception than the norm, this behavior is even more noteworthy. In addition to the performances addressed in the book, I have witnessed this response at the Victoria Symphony's concert, "Legends of the First Nations," featuring Barbara Croall's *Stories from Coyote* and *Midawewe'igan (Sound of the Drum)* as well as Colin Doroschuk's *Heaven* featuring Esquimalt First Nations Master Singer August Thomas and the South Island Dancers on February 13, 2009; Derek Charke's *Tundra Songs* for the Kronos Quartet and Tanya Tagaq on January 30, 2010 at the Chan Centre in Vancouver; *Thunderbird*; the *Oscana Symphony* by Cree composer Andrew Balfour, September 3, 2010, at the Conexus Arts Centre, Regina; and *Tree People* and *Seven* by Barbara Croall presented by the Victoria Symphony Orchestra on October 15, 2011.

4. Robert Fink's work on recombinant teleological structures of popular music and minimalist art music provide a useful extension of teleological theories of tonality and affect in Classical and Romantic music developed by Susan McClary and other feminist musicologists. Musical teleology, "this feeling that the work as a whole 'is going somewhere' (and that it makes you, the listener,

want to go there too)" (Fink 2005, 31) has often been defined in relation to the (male) drive to orgasm, particularly in feminist and queer musicology examining Classical and Romantic art music with its extended harmonic procedures that entail the delaying of a single climax. Popular music as well as minimalist art music, in contrast, have been considered anti-teleological, or unconcerned with the drive of teleology in their emphasis on repetition. Fink argues, however, that the drive toward resolution *is* present in repetitive popular musics (disco and electronic dance music in particular) and minimalist art music genres, albeit as a form of "recombinant teleology." Recombinant teleology is here a form of prorogating desire, where the music is structured around the repetition of short four-bar climaxes that circle back on themselves.

5. Works that center traumatic residential school narratives will not be the focus of this chapter. Examples of art music works that treat residential school narratives include *Fatty Legs,* performed at the Atlantic Truth and Reconciliation national event in Halifax (2011), and Barbara Croall's *Bigiiwe* (2007). *Fatty Legs* is a staged version of residential school survivor Margaret Pokiak-Fenton's experience created by the Camerata Xara Young Women's Choir and includes the choral work *Snowforms* by R. Murray Schafer and other Western art music for choir. Odawa composer Barbara Croall's song cycle *Bigiiwe* is based on her mother's experience at residential school. For a comprehensive list of Indigenous music presented at the Truth and Reconciliation Commission, see Diamond (2016).

6. This chapter focuses on the material qualities of reconciliation in music, while acknowledging that the auditory is merely one sensory vector among many that compose reconciliation's non-representational life. For a more detailed analysis of reconciliation and the senses, see Robinson (2016).

7. It should be acknowledged that not all music performances, including those performed in contexts of reconciliation, entail such flow experiences. However, we might also understand such flow experiences as operating on a continuum wherein audiences experience similar micro-moments of flow, or ebbing and intensification of sensation. For an overview of "flow experience," see Turino (2008, 4–5).

8. Félix Guattari, Sara Ahmed, and Brian Massumi have each written about the sticky quality of affect. While Guattari notes how "affect sticks to subjectivity, it is a glischroid matter" (Guattari 1996, 158), Massumi characterizes affect as "the invisible glue that holds the world together" (Massumi 2002, 217). Ahmed, in turn, describes affect as agglutinating in the way it sticks to objects, or imbues them with affective value: "emotions work by sticking figures together (adherence), a sticking that creates the very effect of a collective (coherence) . . ." (Ahmed 2004, 119). My own work draws on this concern with affect's stickiness,

but also on the idea that music's perceived transcendence (its liminal quality) allows the meanings ascribed to it to stick. Indeed, perhaps it is the "beyond" or inarticulate qualities of affect and music that allow them to stick to things.

9. As Eva Mackey notes, "Announced by then Canadian Prime Minister Pierre Trudeau on October 8, 1971, Multiculturalism within a Bilingual Framework . . . asserted that . . . 'there is no official culture, nor does any ethnic group take precedence over any other'" (Mackey 2002, 64). Mackey has criticized this policy as a form of "difference management," with the explicit aim of undercutting Quebec's and First Nations' struggles for sovereignty (Mackey 2002, 50–70). In her case studies of festivals, including Canada 125 and Canada Day celebrations, Mackey argues that settler Canadian festival participants often understand multiculturalism within a framework of exceptionalism. Through a series of interviews with festival participants at national celebrations, Mackey shows how many of her interlocutors understand multiculturalism in Canada as that which essentially and uniquely constitutes Canadian identity (often as opposed and superior to cultural pluralism and race relations in the United States). This celebratory exceptionalism of multiculturalism, Mackey notes, deploys a rhetoric wherein an unmarked Canadian-Canadian "we" "possess 'our' ethnic groups, which 'we' (Canadians) 'recognise and appreciate.' . . . [This] provides Canadians with the necessary differentiating characteristics that draw a distinction from the USA and construct national identity" (Mackey 2002, 115). While Mackey's case studies are focused on events during the summer of 1992, Canadian multicultural exceptionalism continues to influence the reception of a wide range of intercultural music performance styles. As Casey Mecija, the former lead singer of Ohbijou, wrote on the band's blog in August 2013, "I am frustrated by the ways that my Asian-ness and my sexuality have been at times hidden and at times showcased to support notions of an 'inclusive' Canadian multiculturalism. . . . There have been many moments where our band has been sutured to notions of multiculturalism. The media has often referred to Ohbijou as 'multicultural.' In an article written for a college weekly the author describes us as: 'multicultural in both influence and membership.' . . . Attendant to this proclamation is often a conflation between our bodies and the sound of our music: our music becomes a multicultural sound, or is referenced to as 'world music,' which is a slippage of reading raced bodies" (Mecija 2013).

10. With its goal of "contributing to the search for peaceful and diplomatic solutions to the conflicts around the world" (International Olympic Committee 2009), the International Olympic Committee (IOC) upholds the ideals of "the Olympic Truce." Established in Greece in the ninth century BCE, this truce enabled "athletes, artists, and their families" to "travel in total safety to participate in or attend the Olympic Games and return afterwards to their respective

countries" (IOC 2009.). In present-day terms, this and other principles of peace are translated in the various symbols employed by the IOC, like the different colors of the interlocking rings on the Olympic flag, or the Olympic Truce symbol. Explained by the IOC, this symbol depicts how "the Olympic flame has brought warm friendship to all the people of the world through sharing and global togetherness. In the symbol, the flame is made up of colourful effervescent elements—reminiscent of festivities experienced in the celebration of the human spirit. These elements represent people of all races coming together for the observance of the Truce" (International Olympic Committee, n.d.). The ideal of the Olympic Truce, as told through the symbol's various visual components, both represents a state of temporary reconciliation and also reinforces those qualities of reconciliation previously mentioned: warm friendship and togetherness.

11. These statements, both live and online, take as a given that reconciliation is the thing that should matter "to us" over other concerns about restitution, redress, or perhaps even truth. However, while the "It" of "It Matters to Me" is meant to refer to reconciliation, it also allows for polysemic slippage.

12. Attending the Victoria Truth and Reconciliation regional event, I would estimate that roughly 80 percent of attendees at "It Matters to Me" were settler Canadian. This was reflected in the higher-than-expected non-Indigenous attendance rate at the event itself. As an indication of the demographic of participants at the Victoria regional event, we can turn to Rogers's dumbfounding statement made at the first session: "I know there are people here who may never have been in the company of Aboriginal people." In contrast, at the Montreal TRC event, the MC for "It Matters to Me" often curtailed some of the more "angry" responses that focused on the challenges faced by Indigenous people in the region, instead reminding the audience that he was primarily interested in examples of successful moments of reconciliation.

13. Bruce Buchan, in "Traffick of Empire: Trade, Treaty, and *Terra Nullius* in Australia and North America, 1750–1800," describes the early history of *res nullius* particularly well: "Samuel Purchas . . . claimed that Native Americans did not make proper use of the soil, and had thereby 'lost their owne Naturall, and given us [colonisers] another Nationall right' to subdue them and take possession of the new land. John Locke invoked the same principle in more philosophical form in his Two Treatises. Property, as Locke famously defined it, existed in those things (including land) that a person 'hath mixed his Labour with, and joyned to it something that is his own.' Just as Locke believed that at 'the beginning' of time, 'all the world was America'—unowned, vacant and waste—so 'Labour, in the Beginning, gave a Right to Property.' The native inhabitants of

North America had no title of ownership to their land, he argued, because they had not cultivated it efficiently" (Buchan 2007, 389).

14. My thanks to an anonymous external reader for these comments on pow-wow dance movement, and the suggestion that their lack of "taking up space" might be read as a discomfort with the model of movement being imposed on them.

15. The music used here was "The Weasley Stomp" from the soundtrack to *Harry Potter and the Half-Blood Prince,* which has a marked similarity to Aaron Copland's "Hoedown" from the ballet score *Rodeo.*

16. In addition to performing at the Abbotsford Torch Relay Ceremony *Hannah and the Inukshuks* were also stationed outside of Olympic venues where spectators were invited to have their photos taken while cuddling up to the *Ilanaaq.*

17. Prime Minister Harper's apology presented on June 8, 2011, in the House of Commons varies slightly from the official written version. This above quotation is drawn from Harper's presentation; see Indigenous and Northern Affairs Canada (2015).

18. The salvage paradigm is reflected in early ethnographic views that Indigenous peoples were dying and their material and expressive culture was in need of being preserved in museums. As ethnographer Marius Barbeau notes in *Indian Days in the Canadian Rockies,* "It is clear that the Indian, with his inability to preserve his own culture or to assimilate ours, is bound to disappear as a race . . . His passing is one of the great tragedies of the American continent" (Barbeau 1923, 7–8). Ethnographers like Barbeau narrate the end of Indigenous culture as an inevitable fact, a fact that granted them the authority to salvage what they could in the ways they saw fit.

19. Such contextual information is given in the program notes for the musical's second run in Calgary.

20. See Duffek and Townsend-Gault (2004) for further examination and critique of the trope of the Haida Renaissance.

21. For a more detailed examination of the intergenerational reconciliation taking place within families, see Robinson (2016).

22. Despite these restrictions, survivors have not been content to limit their testimony to past residential school experience; they have used the TRC to voice their opposition to natural-resource development, to address the urgent need to improve substandard living conditions for Aboriginal Peoples on and off reserve, and to call for greater support for education and language revitalization. Notably, survivors have often refused the narrative of reconciliation with the nation-state altogether and have instead asked forgiveness of their children for the abuse they carried over into their own parenting.

286   Notes to Chapter 5

23. Beverley Diamond's "Resisting Containment," in *Arts of Engagement* (2016) provides a particularly nuanced account of the role that music has played at the TRC national events.

24. Susan Aglukark, e-mail to author, January 16, 2013.

Conclusion

1. Eva Mackey's (2016) discussion of settler fixations on certainty illustrates how ownership, history, relationship are oriented toward the mutual exclusion of simultaneous knowledge and practice.

2. Cheryl L'Hirondelle, e-mail correspondence with author, January 25, 2016.

3. This text score is a result of our collective writing. It is an homage to Pauline Oliveros (1932–2016), whose *Sonic Meditations* (1974) comprise twenty-five listening-based text pieces intended for "group work over a long period of time with regular meetings" (Oliveros 1974, "Introduction I"). *Sonic Meditations* are intended to promote "a tuning of mind and body" with music being a "welcome by-product" (Oliveros 1974, "Introduction I").

4. Tom Rice writes that "listening is understood to involve a deliberate channeling of attention toward a sound" (Rice 2015, 99), yet the concept actually represents multiple theoretical genealogies, or as he puts it, "these taxonomies of listening have also created what can feel like infinite regress, where modes of listening continually proliferate without necessarily interlinking or building on one another in productive ways" (104).

5. One of the book's external reviewers noted that the opening of the conversation "left me wondering how settler allies of Indigenous communities (or any allies) can contribute in non-confessional ways—that is, in ways that try to avoid reflective introspection that consolidates a good ally self . . . What does disclosing this (or another) settler subjectivity do for this decolonial work?" In particular, the reviewer is here referring to positionality statements that do in many instances take up space through admissions to ignorance. While there is often vulnerability and honesty in making such statements, and while such statements may seem to run parallel with opening statements by Indigenous people that situate our relationships to the territory we are in, or are from, the vulnerability in naming positionality/history can paradoxically take up the space of moving toward substantive commitment and action. While making oneself vulnerable is often hard affective work, that labor of vulnerability itself does not articulate accountability and action.

6. In a similar vein, black artist William Pope.L has organized more than thirty group and solo crawls over the last four decades. Yoon's work differs sig-

nificantly here as a process undertaken by the artist alone, and by the representation of this process on film.

7. Jin-Me Yoon, e-mail to author, January 15, 2017.

8. I use *reparative* here in a similar way to Eve Sedgewick, whose focus on moving beyond the paranoid principle of critique toward forms of active possibility was discussed in chapter 2.

BIBLIOGRAPHY

Abbate, Carolyn. 2004. "Music—Drastic or Gnostic?" *Critical Inquiry* 30, no. 3 (Spring): 505–36.

Abel, Samuel D. 1996. *Opera in the Flesh: Sexuality in Operatic Performance.* Boulder, Colo.: Westview Press.

Ahmed, Sara. 2004a. "Affective Economies." *Social Text* 79, vol. 22, no. 2 (Summer): 117–39.

Ahmed, Sara. 2004b. "Declarations of Whiteness: The Non-performativity of Anti-racism." In *borderlands e-journal* 3, no. 2.

Ahmed, Sara. 2012. *On Being Included: Racism and Diversity in Institutional Life.* Durham, N.C.: Duke University Press.

Alfred, Taiaike. 1999. *Peace, Power, Righteousness: An Indigenous Manifesto.* Oxford: Oxford University Press.

Alfred, Taiaike. 2005. *Wasáse: Indigenous Pathways of Action and Freedom.* Toronto: University of Toronto Press.

Alfred, Taiaike. 2009. "Restitution Is the Real Pathway to Justice for Indigenous Peoples." In *Response, Responsibility, and Renewal: Canada's Truth and Reconciliation Journey,* ed. Gregory Younging, Jonathan Dewar, and Mike DeGagné, 181–87. Ottawa: Aboriginal Healing Foundation.

Alpers, Svetlana. 1983. *The Art of Describing: Dutch Art in the Seventeenth Century.* Chicago: University of Chicago Press.

Althusser, Louis. 2014. *On the Reproduction of Capitalism: Ideology and Ideological State Apparatuses,* trans G. M. Goshgarian. New York: Verso.

Amtmann, Willy. 1975. *Music in Canada 1600–1800.* Cambridge, Ont.: Habitex Books.

Andrew-Gee, Eric. 2017. "The Making of Joseph Boyden." *The Globe and Mail.* https://www.theglobeandmail.com/arts/books-and-media/joseph-boyden/article35881215/. Last modified November 12, 2017.

Archibald, Jo-ann. 2008. *Indigenous Storywork: Educating the Heart, Mind, Body, and Spirit.* Vancouver.: University of British Columbia Press.

Bibliography

Attariwala, Pamela. 2013. "Eh 440: Tuning into the Effects of Multiculturalism on Publicly Funded Canadian Music." PhD diss., University of Toronto.

Austin, J. L. 1975. *How to Do Things with Words.* 2nd ed. Cambridge, Mass.: Harvard University Press.

Barbeau, Marius. 1923. *Indian Days in the Canadian Rockies.* Toronto: Macmillan.

Barbeau, Marius. 1933. "Songs of the Northwest." *Musical Quarterly* 19, no. 1 (January): 101–11.

Barbeau, Marius. 1951. "Tsimshian Songs." In *The Tsimshian: Their Arts and Music,* ed. Marian W. Smith, 97–109. New York: J. J. Augustin.

Barbeau, Marius, and James Sibley Watson, dirs. 2001. *Nass River Indians.* Reconstruction by Lynda Jessup. Montreal: Associated Screen News. 35 mm film, 23 min.

Barkin, Elaine. 1992. "Either/Other." *Perspectives of New Music* 30, no. 2 (Summer): 206–33.

Barthes, Roland. 1975. *The Pleasure of the Text.* Translated by Richard Miller. Oxford: Blackwell.

Barthes, Roland. 1977. "The Grain of the Voice." In *Image, Music, Text,* ed. and trans. Stephen Heath, 179–89. London: Fontana Press.

Barthes, Roland. 1985. *The Responsibility of Forms.* Trans. Richard Howard. Berkeley: University of California Press.

Beaglehole, John Cawte, ed. 1967. *The Journals of Captain James Cook on His Voyages of Discovery: The Voyage of the Resolution and Discovery 1776–1780,* vol. 3, part 2: 1361–1455. Hakluyt Society Extra Series XXXVI. Cambridge: Cambridge University Press.

Bellman, Jonathan. 2000. *A Short Guide to Writing about Music.* London: Longman.

Bellman, Jonathan. 2015. "Disciplinarity and Gatekeeping." *Dial "M" for Musicology: Music, Musicology, and Related Matters* (blog). July 4, 2015. https://dialmformusicology.com/2015/07/04/disciplinarity-and-gatekeeping/.

Benjamin, Walter. 1968. *Illuminations: Essays and Reflections.* New York: Harcourt, Brace & World.

Benjamin, Walter. 1996. *Selected Writings,* vol. 1, *1913–1926,* ed. Marcus Bullock and Michael W. Jennings; trans. Rodney Livingstone. Cambridge, Mass.: Harvard University Press.

Berlant, Lauren. 2011. *Cruel Optimism.* Durham, N.C.: Duke University Press.

Bishop, Claire. 2004. "Antagonism and Relational Aesthetics." *October,* no. 110 (Fall): 51–69.

Bishop, Claire, ed. 2006. *Participation.* Cambridge, Mass.: MIT Press.

Bishop, Claire. 2012. *Artificial Hells: Participatory Art and the Politics of Spectatorship.* New York: Verso.

Bloechl, Olivia. 2005. "The Pedagogy of Polyphony in Gabriel Sagard's Histoire du Canada." *The Journal of Musicology* 22, no. 3 (Summer): 365–411.

Bloechl, Olivia. 2008. *Native American Song at the Frontiers of Early Modern Music.* Cambridge: Cambridge University Press.

Bloechl, Olivia. 2013. "On Not Being Alone: Rousseauean Thoughts on a Relational Ethics of Music." *Journal of the American Musicological Society* 66, no. 1 (Spring): 261–66.

Bonds, Mark Evan. 2014. *Absolute Music: The History of an Idea.* New York: Oxford University Press.

Born, Georgina. 2019. "On Nonhuman Sound—Sound as Relation." In *Sound Objects,* ed., James A. Steintrager and Rey Chow, 185–210. Durham, N.C.: Duke University Press.

Born, Georgina, Eric Lewis, and Will Straw, eds. 2017. *Improvisation and Social Aesthetics.* Durham, N.C.: Duke University Press.

Bourriaud, Nicholas. 2002. *Relational Aesthetics.* Paris: Presses du Réel,

Brennan, Teresa. 2004. *The Transmission of Affect.* New York: Cornell University Press.

British Columbia Supreme Court. 1985. "[Commission Evidence of Martha Brown Vol. 2]." T. Delgamuukw Transcripts. Vancouver: United Reporting Service Ltd. September 19. https://doi.org/10.14288/1.0018292.

brownamsavenger. 2017. "#AMSSOWHITE." *LiveJournal* (blog). https://brownamsavenger.livejournal.com/612.html?page=2. Accessed November 6, 2018.

Buchan, Bruce. 2007. "Traffick of Empire: Trade, Treaty, and *Terra Nullius* in Australia and North America, 1750–1800." *History Compass* 5, no. 2 (March): 386–405.

Byrd, Jodi. 2011. *The Transit of Empire: Indigenous Critiques of Colonialism.* Minneapolis: University of Minnesota Press.

Byrd, Jodi A., and Michael Rothberg. 2011. "Between Subalternity and Indigeneity." Special Issue of *Interventions* 13, no. 1: 1–12.

Canadian Broadcasting Corporation. n.d. "8TH Fire: Aboriginal People, Canada & the Way Forward." *8th Fire.* https://www.cbc.ca/8thfire/. Accessed May 12, 2013.

Carlson, Keith Thor. 2010. *The Power of Place, the Problem of Time: Aboriginal Identity and Historical Consciousness in the Cauldron of Colonialism.* Toronto: University of Toronto Press.

Charke, Derek. 2005. *Cercle du Nord II.* Musical composition.

Cheater, Dan. 2018. "I Am the River, and the River Is Me: Legal Personhood and Emerging Rights of Nature." *West Coast Environmental Law.* https://www.wcel.org/blog/i-am-river-and-river-me-legal-personhood-and-emerging-rights-nature.

Chen, Kenneth. 1995. "Ida Halpern: A Post-Colonial Portrait of a Canadian Pioneer Ethnomusicologist." *Canadian University Music Review* 16, no. 1: 41–59.

Cherney, Brian. 1975. *Harry Somers.* Toronto: University of Toronto Press.

Chuh, Kandice. 2003. *Imagine Otherwise: On Asian Americanist Critique.* Durham, N.C.: Duke University Press.

Cixous, Hélène. 1976. "The Laugh of the Medusa." Trans. Keith Cohen and Paula Cohen. *Signs* 1, no. 4 (Summer): 875–93.

Cizmic, Maria. 2011. *Performing Pain: Music and Trauma in Eastern Europe.* Oxford: Oxford University Press.

Clarke, Eric. 2013. "Music, Space, and Subjectivity." In *Music, Sound, and Space: Transformations of Public and Private Experience,* ed. Georgina Born, 90–110. New York: Cambridge University Press.

Cloutier, Sylvia, Aruna Narayan, Wen Zhao, Jeanne Lamon, and Taflemusik Baroque Orchestra. 2005. *The Four Seasons Mosaic,* DVD. Toronto: Media Headquarters Film & Television.

Coleman, Elizabeth Byers, Rosemary J. Coombe, and Fiona MacArailt. 2009. "A Broken Record: Subjecting 'Music' to Cultural Rights." In *The Ethics of Cultural Appropriation,* ed. James O. Young and Conrad G. Brunk, 173–210. Chichester, U.K.: Wiley-Blackwell.

Cook, Nicholas. 2014. *Beyond the Score: Music as Performance.* New York: Oxford University Press.

Cornellier, Bruno. 2016. "Extracting Inuit: The *of the North* Controversy and the White Possessive." *American Indian Culture and Research Journal* 40, no. 4: 23–48.

Cornfield, Eitan. 2006. "Harry Somers Documentary." *Canadian Composers Portraits: Harry Somers.* Centrediscs CD 1.

Corntassel, Jeff, Chaw-win-is, and T'lakwadzi. 2009. "Indigenous Storytelling, Truth-Telling, and Community Approaches to Reconciliation." *ESC: English Studies in Canada* 35, no. 1 (March): 1–23.

Coulthard, Glen Sean. 2011. "Recognition, Reconciliation, and Resentment in Indigenous Politics." Lecture presented as part of Simon Fraser University Woodward's Office of Community Engagement series of public talks and accessible education opportunities, Vancouver, B.C., November 16.

Coulthard, Glen Sean. 2014a. "#IdleNoMore in Historical Context." In *The Winter We Danced: Voices from the Past, the Future, and the Idle No More Movement,* ed. Kino-nda-niimi Collective, 32–36. Winnipeg: Arbeiter Ring Press.

Coulthard, Glen Sean. 2014b. *Red Skin, White Masks: Rejecting the Colonial Politics of Recognition.* Minneapolis: University of Minnesota Press.

Coulthard, Glen, and Leanne Betasamosake Simpson. 2016. "Grounded Normativity / Place-Based Solidarity." *American Quarterly* 68, no. 2 (June): 249–55.

Bibliography   293

Crawley, Ashon. 2016. *Blackpentecostal Breath: The Aesthetics of Possibility.* New York: Fordham Unviersity Press.

Crosby, Marcia. 1991. "Construction of the Imaginary Indian." In *Academic Reading: Reading and Writing across the Disciplines,* 2d ed., ed. Janey Giltrow, 488–92. Peterborough, Ont.: Broadview Press.

Cruikshank, Julie. 2005. *Do Glaciers Listen? Local Knowledge, Colonial Encounters, and Social Imagination.* Seattle: University of Washington Press.

Cusick, Suzanne G. 1994. "On a Lesbian Relationship with Music: A Serious Effort Not to Think Straight." In *Queering the Pitch: The New Gay and Lesbian Musicology,* ed. Philip Brett, Elizabeth Wood, and Gary C. Thomas, 67–83. New York: Routledge.

Cvetkovich, Ann. 2012. *Depression: A Public Feeling.* Durham, N.C.: Duke University Press.

Dangeli, Mique'l. 2015. "Dancing Sovereignty: Protocol and Politics in Northwest Coast First Nations Dance." PhD diss., University of British Columbia.

Dangeli, Michael, and Mique'l Dangeli. 2015. Personal conversation, Institute of American Indian Arts, Santa Fe. October 2.

Daughtry, J. Martin. 2013. "Acoustic Palimpsests and the Politics of Listening." *Music and Politics* 7, no. 1 (Winter): 1–34.

Dawn, Leslie. 2006. *National Visions, National Blindness: Canadian Art and Identities in the 1920s.* Vancouver: University of British Columbia Press.

Day, Iyko. 2016. *Alien Capital: Asian Racialization and the Logic of Settler Colonial Capitalism.* Durham, N.C.: Duke University Press.

DeNora, Tia. 2000. *Music in Everyday Life.* Cambridge: Cambridge University Press.

Derrida, Jacques. 1986. *Glas.* Trans. John P. Leavey Jr. and Richard Rand. Lincoln: University of Nebraska Press.

Dhamoon, Rita. 2015. "A Feminist Approach to Decolonizing Anti-Racism: Rethinking Transnationalism, Intersectionality, and Settler Colonialism." *Feral Feminisms,* no. 4: 20–37. https://feralfeminisms.com/wp-content/uploads/2015/12/ff_A-Feminist-Approach-to-Decolonizing-Anti-Racism_issue4.pdf.

Diamond, Beverley. 1994. "Introduction." In *Canadian Music: Issues of Hegemony and Identity,* ed. Beverley Diamond and Robert Witmer, 1–21. Toronto: Canadian Scholars' Press.

Diamond, Beverley. 2016. "Resisting Containment: The Long Reach of Song at the Truth and Reconciliation Commission on Indian Residential Schools." In *Arts of Engagement: Taking Aesthetic Action in and beyond Canada's Truth and Reconciliation Commission,* ed. Dylan Robinson and Keavy Martin, 239–66. Waterloo, Ont.: Wilfrid Laurier University Press.

Dolan, Jill. 2005. *Utopia in Performance: Finding Hope at the Theatre*. Ann Arbor: University of Michigan Press.

Du Bois, W. E. B. 2007. *The Souls of Black Folk*. Oxford: Oxford University Press.

Duffek, Karen, and Charlotte Townsend-Gault, eds. 2004. *Bill Reid and Beyond: Expanding on Modern Native Art*. Vancouver: Douglas and McIntyre.

Dunsby, Jonathan. 2009. "Roland Barthes and the Grain of Panzéra's Voice." *Journal of the Royal Musical Association* 134, no. 1: 113–32.

Dussault, René, Georges Erasmus, Paul L. A. H. Chartrand, J. Peter Meekison, Viola Robinson, Mary Sillett, and Bertha Wilson. 1996. *Looking Forward, Looking Back*. Vol. 1 of *Royal Commission on Aboriginal Peoples*. http://data2.archives.ca/e/e448/e011188230–01.pdf. Accessed November 4, 2018.

Dyer, Richard. 2002. *Only Entertainment*. 2d ed. London: Routledge.

Eales, Lindsay. 2016. "Loose Leaf." *Canadian Journal of Disability Studies* 5, no. 3 (October): 58–76.

Eatock, Colin. 2010. "A New Opera Gets a Bit Lost in the Woods." *The Globe and Mail*. April 10. https://www.theglobeandmail.com/arts/music/a-new-opera-gets-a-bit-lost-in-the-woods/article4314275/.

Edensor, Tim. 2008. "Walking through Ruins." In *Ways of Walking: Ethnography and Practice on Foot,* ed. Tim Ingold and Jo Lee Vergunst, 123–42. Farnham, UK: Ashgate Publishing.

Edensor, Tim. 2010. "Walking in Rhythms: Places, Regulation, Style, and the Flow of Experience." *Visual Studies* 25, no. 1 (April): 69–79.

Eisenberg, Andrew J. 2015. "Space." In *Keywords in Sound,* ed. David Novak and Matt Sakakeeny, 193–207. Durham, N.C.: Duke University Press.

Episkenew, Jo-Ann. 2009. *Taking Back Our Spirits: Indigenous Literature, Public Policy, and Healing*. Winnipeg: University of Manitoba Press.

Esprit Orchestra. 2009. "Take the Dog Sled." https://www.musiccentre.ca/sites/www.musiccentre.ca/files/resources/pdfmedia/60187_dogsled_837_louie_prog.pdf. Accessed November 8, 2018.

Everett, Yayoi Uno. 2004. "Intercultural Synthesis in Postwar Western Art Music: Historical Contexts, Perspectives, and Taxonomy." In *Locating East Asia in Western Art Music,* ed. Yayoi Uno Everett and Frederick Lau, 1–21. Middletown, Ct.: Wesleyan University Press.

Fink, Robert. 2005. *Repeating Ourselves: American Minimal Music as Cultural Practice*. Berkeley: University of California Press.

First Story. 2001. Episode 422. Aired March 23, 2001, on CTV.

Fischer-Lichte, Erika. 2008. *The Transformative Power of Performance: A New Aesthetics*. New York: Routledge.

Forfa, Agnieszka. 2016. "invite in. go steady crazy." *Canadian Journal of Disability Studies* 5, no. 3 (October): 12–17.

Fricker, Miranda. 2009. *Epistemic Injustice: Power and the Ethics of Knowing.* Oxford: Oxford University Press.

Fujikane, Candace, and Jonathan Y. Okamura, eds. 2008. *Asian Settler Colonialism: From Local Governance to the Habits of Everyday Life in Hawaii.* Honolulu: University of Hawai'i Press.

Gaertner, David. 2016. "'Aboriginal Principles of Witnessing' and the Truth and Reconciliation Commission of Canada." In *Arts of Engagement: Taking Aesthetic Action in and beyond Canada's Truth and Reconciliation Commission,* ed. Dylan Robinson and Keavy Martin, 135–55. Waterloo, Ont.: Wilfrid Laurier University Press.

Gallop, Jane. 2002. *Anecdotal Theory.* Durham, N.C.: Duke University Press.

Galloway, Brent D. 2009. *Dictionary of Upriver Halkomelem.* Oakland: University of California Press.

Garneau, David. 2016. "Imaginary Spaces of Conciliation and Reconciliation: Art, Curation, and Healing." In *Arts of Engagement: Taking Aesthetic Action in and beyond Canada's Truth and Reconciliation Commission,* ed. Dylan Robinson and Keavy Martin, 21–42. Waterloo, Ont.: Wilfrid Laurier University Press.

Goldman, Danielle. 2010. *I Want to Be Ready: Improvised Dance as a Practice of Freedom.* Ann Arbor: University of Michigan Press.

Gordon, Gwendolyn J. 2018. "Environmental Personhood." *Columbia Journal of Environmental Law* 43, no. 1 (January): 49–92.

Government of Canada. 1988. "Canadian Multiculturalism Act (R.S.C., 1985, c.24(4th Supp.))." http://laws-lois.justice.gc.ca/eng/acts/C-18.7/page-1.html. Accessed September 26, 2018.

Government of Canada. 2013. "Canadian Museum of History Act: S.C. 2013, c. 38." *Justice Laws Website.* https://laws-lois.justice.gc.ca/eng/annualstatutes /2013_38/FullText.html. Accessed November 8, 2018.

Government of New Zealand. 2017. "Te Awa Tupua (Whanganui River) Claims Settlement Bill 2017. Government Bill 129-2, cl 14." *New Zealand Legislation Website.* Accessed November 2, 2019.

Gray, Robin. 2015. "Ts'msyen Revolution: Poetics and Politics of Reclaiming." PhD diss., University of Massachusetts Amherst. https://scholarworks.umass .edu/cgi/viewcontent.cgi?article=1448&context=dissertations_2. Accessed November 8, 2018.

Guattari, Félix. 1996. *The Guattari Reader.* Ed. Gary Genosko. London: Blackwell.

Hage, Ghassan. 2010. "The Affective Politics of Racial Mis-interpellation." *Theory, Culture & Society* 27, no. 7–8: 112–29.

Hahn, Tomie. 2007. *Sensational Knowledge: Embodying Culture through Japanese Dance.* Lebanon, N.H.: University Press of New England.

Halliwell, Michael. 2014. "'Voices within the Voice': Conceiving Voice in Contemporary Opera." *Musicology Australia* 36, no. 2: 254–72.

Halpern, Ida. 1967. *Indian Music of the Pacific Northwest Coast.* Liner Notes. Folkways Ethnic Library FE 4523, CD.

Halpin, Marjorie. 1986. *Jack Shadbolt and the Coastal Indian Image.* Vancouver: University of British Columbia Press.

Harvie, Jen. 2013. *Fair Play: Art, Performance, and Neoliberalism.* New York: Palgrave Macmillan.

Hatzis, Christos. 1998. "Footprints in New Snow: Postmodernism or Cultural Appropriation?" Lecture presented at Sound Symposium, St. John's Newfoundland, July 14, 1998. http://homes.chass.utoronto.ca/~chatzis/footpaper.htm.

Hatzis, Christos. n.d. "Viderunt Omnes." Christos Hatzis. http://homes.chass .utoronto.ca/~chatzis/Viderunt.htm. Accessed November 6, 2016.

Heble, Ajay, Donna Palmateer Pennee, and J. R. Struthers, eds. 1997. *New Contexts of Canadian Criticism.* Peterborough, Ont.: Broadview Press.

Henderson, Jennifer, and Pauline Wakeham. 2013. "Introduction." In *Reconciling Canada: Critical Perspectives on the Culture of Redress,* ed. Jennifer Henderson and Pauline Wakeham, 3–27. Toronto: University of Toronto Press.

Hinge, Gail. 1985. "Indian Acts and Amendments, 1868–1975." Vol. 2 of *Consolidation of Indian Legislation.* Ottawa: Department of Indian and Northern Affairs. http://publications.gc.ca/collections/collection_2017/aanc-inac/R5 -158-2-1978-eng.pdf. Accessed November 8, 2018.

Hisama, Ellie M. 2007. "John Zorn and the Postmodern Condition." In *Locating East Asia in Western Art Music,* ed. Yayoi Uno Everett and Frederick Lau, 72–84. Middletown, Ct.: Wesleyan University Press.

hooks, bell. 1992. *Black Looks: Race and Representation.* Boston: South End Press.

Hopkins, Candice, Jolene Rickard, and Maria Thereza Alves. 2016. "Fair Trade Heads, a Conversation on Repatriation and Indigenous Peoples." *South Magazine* online (guest edited by documenta 14). https://www.documenta 14.de/en/south/.

Horton, Jessica L., and Janet Catherine Berlo. 2013. "Beyond the Mirror: Indigenous Ecologies and 'New Materialisms' in Contemporary Art." *Third Text* 27, no. 1 (January): 17–28.

Hulatt, Owen. 2013. "Critique through Autonomy: On Monads and Mediation in Adorno's Aesthetic Theory." In *Aesthetic and Artistic Autonomy*, ed. Owen Hulatt, 171–96. London: Bloomsbury.

Indigenous and Northern Affairs Canada. 2015. "The Day of Apology." https://www.aadnc-aandc.gc.ca/eng/1100100015657/1100100015675. Accessed October 24, 2018.

International Olympic Committee. 2009. "Olympic Movement Promotes Peace Worldwide." https://www.olympic.org/news/olympic-movement-promotes-peace-worldwide. Accessed April 15, 2013.

International Olympic Committee. n.d. "Olympic Truce." https://www.olympic.org/olympic-truce. Accessed January 2, 2014.

Jackson, Shannon. 2011. *Social Works: Performing Art, Supporting Publics*. New York: Routledge.

Jameson, Anna. 1852. *Sketches in Canada, and Rambles among the Red Men*. London: Longman, Brown, Green, and Longmans.

Jankélévitch, Vladimir. 2003. *Music and the Ineffable*. Trans. Carolyn Abbate. Princeton, N.J.: Princeton University Press.

Justice, Daniel Heath. 2004. *Our Fire Survives the Storm: A Cherokee Literary History*. Minneapolis: University of Minnesota Press.

Kallman, Helmut. 1960. *A History of Music in Canada, 1534–1914*. Toronto: University of Toronto Press.

Keillor, Elaine. 1995. "Indigenous Music as a Compositional Source: Parallels and Contrasts in Canadian and American Music." In *Taking a Stand: Essays in Honour of John Beckwith*, ed. Timothy McGee, 185–218. Toronto: University of Toronto Press.

Kester, Grant H. 2013. *Conversation Pieces: Community and Communication in Modern Art*. Berkeley: University of California Press.

Keyes, Sarah. 2009. "'Like a Roaring Lion': The Overland Trail as a Sonic Conquest." *The Journal of American History* 96, no. 1 (June): 19–43.

Khesthi, Roshanak. 2015. *Modernity's Ear: Listening to Race and Gender in World Music*. New York: New York University Press.

King, Thomas. 2003. *The Truth about Stories: A Native Narrative*. Minneapolis: University of Minnesota Press.

Kisynska, Sylwia. 2016. "The Elders Say We Don't Visit Anymore." *Gallery Gachet* (blog). June 7. http://gachet.org/2016/06/07/the-elders-say-we-dont-visit-anymore/.

Knowles, Ric. 2010. *Theatre and Interculturalism*. London: Palgrave Macmillan.

Koestenbaum, Wayne. 1993. *The Queen's Throat: Opera, Homosexuality, and the Mystery of Desire*. New York: Poseidon Press.

Kopelson, Kevin. 1996. *Beethoven's Kiss: Pianism, Perversion, and the Mastery of Desire*. Stanford, Calif.: Stanford University Press.

Kopelson, Kevin. 2002. "Critical Virtuosity." *The Iowa Review* 32, no. 1 (Spring): 90–100.

Kramer, Lawrence. 2002. *Musical Meaning: Toward a Critical History*. Berkeley: University of California Press.

Kramer, Lawrence. 2004a. "Music, Metaphor, and Metaphysics." *The Musical Times* 145, no. 1888 (Autumn): 5–18.

Kramer, Lawrence. 2004b. "Odradek Analysis: Reflections on Musical Ontology." *Music Analysis* 23, no. 2–3 (July–October): 287–309.

LaBelle, Brandon. 2010. *Acoustic Territories: Sound Culture and Everyday Life*. New York: Bloomsbury.

Lachenmann, Helmut. 2003. "Interview with Helmut Lachenmann—Toronto, 2003." Interview by Paul Steenhuisen. *Contemporary Music Review* 23, no. 3/4 (September/December): 9–14.

Leroux, Darryl. 2019. *Distorted Descent: White Claims to Indigenous Identity*. Winnipeg: University of Manitoba Press.

Levin, David. 2007. *Unsettling Opera: Staging Mozart, Verdi, Wagner, and Zemlinsky*. Chicago: University of Chicago Press.

Levin, David. 2012. "Is There a Text in This Libido? *Diva* and the Rhetoric of Contemporary Opera Criticism." In *Between Opera and Cinema*, ed. Jeongwon Joe and Rose Theresa, 121–33. New York: Routledge Press.

Levinas, Emmanuel. 1998. *Otherwise than Being, or Beyond Essence*. Trans. Alphonso Lingis. Pittsburgh: Duquesne University Press.

Levitz, Tamara. 2016. "Tamara Levitz presents Decolonizing the American Musicological Society." *NYU Department of Music*. Facebook, February 18, 2016. https://www.facebook.com/events/1500123930295790/.

Levitz, Tamara. 2018. "Decolonizing the Society for American Music." *The Bulletin of the Society for American Music* 43, no. 3 (Fall): 1–13. http://www.american-music.org/publications/bulletin/2017/VolXLIII3-Fall2017.php. Accessed September 27, 2018.

Lewis, George. 1996. "Improvised Music after 1950: Afrological and Eurological Perspectives." *Black Music Research Journal* 16, no. 1 (Spring): 91–112.

L'Hirondelle, Cheryl. 2015. "Why the Caged Bird Sings: Radical Inclusivity, Sonic Survivance, and the Collective Ownership." Masters thesis, OCAD University, 2015. http://openresearch.ocadu.ca/id/eprint/287/1/L%27Hirondelle_Cheryl_2015_MDes_INCD_THESIS.pdf.

Lorde, Audre. 1981. "The Uses of Anger: Women Responding to Racism." *Women's Studies Quarterly* 9, no. 3 (Fall): 7–10.

Lott, Eric. 1993. *Love and Theft: Blackface Minstrelsy and the American Working Class*. Oxford: Oxford University Press.

Bibliography

Louie, Alexina. 2008. *Take the Dog Sled*. Toronto: Esprit Orchestra.

Louie, Alexina. 2013. "NACOcast: Paul Wells Interviews Alexina Louie." http://nac-cna.ca/en/podcasts/episode/paul-wells-interviews-alexina-louie. Accessed November 6, 2016.

Louie, Alexina. n.d. "Catalogue." Alexina Louie. www.alexinalouie.ca/catalogue. Accessed November 6, 2016.

Mackey, Eva. 2002. *The House of Difference: Cultural Politics and National Identity in Canada*. Toronto: University of Toronto Press.

Mackey, Eva. 2016. *Unsettled Expectations: Uncertainty, Land, and Settler Decolonization*. Winnipeg and Halifax: Fernwood Press.

Maracle, Lee. 2015. *Talking to the Diaspora*. Winnipeg: ARP Books.

Marks, Laura. 2002. *Touch: Sensuous Theory and Multisensory Media*. Minneapolis: University of Minnesota Press.

Massumi, Brian. 2002. *Parables for the Virtual: Movement, Affect, Sensation*. Durham, N.C.: Duke University Press.

McClary, Susan. 1991. *Feminine Endings: Music, Gender, and Sexuality*. Minneapolis: University of Minnesota Press.

McHugh, Susan. 2013. "'A Flash Point in Inuit Memories': Endangered Knowledges in the Mountie Sled Dog Massacre." *ESC: English Studies in Canada* 39, no. 1 (March): 149–75.

McQueen, Robert, Tracey Herbert, Marion Newman, Dylan Robinson, Lorna Williams, and Cathy Charles Wherry. 2011. "Vancouver Opera's Coast Salish-inspired *Magic Flute*: A Conversation with Robert McQueen, with responses by Lorna Williams, Cathy Charles Wherry, Tracey Herbert, and Marion Newman." In *Opera Indigene: Re/presenting First Nations and Indigenous Cultures*, ed. Pamela Karantonis and Dylan Robinson, 309–24. New York: Routledge.

Mecija, Casey. 2013. "Goodbye Obijou: Notes on Music, Labour, and the Impossibilities of Satisfying Multicultural Ideals in Canada." *Ohbijou* (blog). August 16. http://ohbijouband-blog-blog.tumblr.com/post/58425133293/goodbye-ohbijou-notes-on-music-labour-and-the. Accessed January 30, 2014.

Mills, Antonia. 1994. *Eagle Down Is Our Law: Witsuwit'en Law, Feasts, and Land Claims*. Vancouver: University of British Columbia Press.

Minh-ha, Trinh T. 1989. *Woman, Native, Other: Writing Postcoloniality and Feminism*. Bloomington: Indiana University Press.

mishi45. 2008. "Susan Aglukark—O Siem." August 23, 2008. YouTube Video, 3:14. https://www.youtube.com/watch?v=RcrQjHygy5o.

Mitchell, W. J. T. 2005. *What Do Pictures Want? The Lives and Loves of Images*. Chicago: University of Chicago Press.

Monet, Don (Niis Biins), and Skanu'u (Ardythe Wilson). 1992. *Colonialism on Trial, Indigenous Land Rights and the Gitksan and Wet'suwet'en Sovereignty Case*. Gabriola Island, B.C., and Philadelphia: New Society Publishers.

Monson, Ingrid. 2008. "Hearing, Seeing, and Perceptual Agency." Supplement, *Critical Inquiry* 34, no. S2 (Winter): S36–38.

Moray, Gerta. 2001. "Emily Carr and the Traffic in Native Images." In *Antimodernism and Artistic Experience: Policing the Boundaries of Modernity*, ed. Lynda Jessup, 67–92. Toronto: University of Toronto Press.

Moreton-Robinson, Aileen. 2015. *The White Possessive: Property, Power, and Indigenous Sovereignty*. Minneapolis: University of Minnesota Press.

Morgenson, Scott Lauria. 2011. *Spaces between Us: Queer Settler Colonialism and Indigenous Decolonization*. Minneapolis: University of Minnesota Press.

Morin, Peter. 2016. "This Is What Happens When We Perform the Memory of the Land." In *Arts of Engagement: Taking Aesthetic Action in and beyond Canada's Truth and Reconciliation Commission*, ed. Dylan Robinson and Keavy Martin, 67–92. Waterloo, Ont.: Wilfrid Laurier University Press.

Morin, Peter, and Dylan Robinson. 2013. Interview. Royal Holloway, University of London, May 23.

Moten, Fred. 2003. *In the Break: The Aesthetics of the Black Radical Tradition*. Minneapolis: University of Minnesota Press.

Mouffe, Chantal. 2000. *Deliberative Democracy or Agonistic Pluralism*. Vienna: Institut für Höhere Studien.

Muñoz, José Esteban. 2009. *Cruising Utopia: The Then and There of Queer Futurity*. New York: New York University Press.

Napoleon, Val. 2001. "Ayook: Gitksan Legal Order, Law, and Legal Theory." PhD diss., University of Victoria. http://dspace.library.uvic.ca:8080/bitstream/handle/1828/1392/napoleon%20dissertation%20April%2026–09.pdf?sequence=1.

Napoleon, Val. 2005. "*Delgamuukw*: A Legal Straightjacket for Oral Histories?" *Canadian Journal of Law and Society* 20, no. 2 (August): 123–55.

National Post. 2017. "How Contemporary Composers Are Revitalizing—and Reinventing—Classical Music." March 8. https://nationalpost.com/entertainment/music/how-contemporary-composers-are-revitalizing-and-reinventing-classical-music.

Ochoa Gautier, Ana María. 2014. *Aurality: Listening and Knowledge in Nineteenth-Century Colombia*. Durham, N.C.: Duke University Press.

Oliveros, Pauline. 1974. *Sonic Meditations*. Baltimore: Smith Publications.

Oliveros, Pauline. 2005. *Deep Listening: A Composer's Sound Practice*. Bloomington, Ind.: iUniverse, Inc.

Panagia, Davide. 2009. *The Political Life of Sensation*. Durham, N.C.: Duke University Press.

Bibliography

301

Phelan, Peggy. 1997. *Mourning Sex: Performing Public Memories*. New York: Routledge.

Pilzer, Joshua D. 2012. *Hearts of Pine: Songs in the Lives of Three Korean Survivors of the Japanese "Comfort Women."* Oxford: Oxford University Press.

Pollock, Della. 1998. "Performative Writing." In *The Ends of Performance*, ed. Peggy Phelan and Jill Lane, 73–103. New York: New York University Press.

Polzonetti, Pierpaolo. 2016. "Don Giovanni Goes to Prison: Teaching Opera behind Bars." *Musicology Now* (blog). http://musicologynow.ams-net .org/2016/02/don-giovanni-goes-to-prison-teaching_16.html. Accessed November 6, 2016.

Pratt, Mary Louise. 2008. *Imperial Eyes: Travel Writing and Transculturation*. New York: Routledge.

Qikiqtani Inuit Association. 2010. "QTC Final Report: Achieving Saimaqatigiingniq." http://qtcommission.ca/sites/default/files/public/thematic_reports/ thematic_reports_english_final_report.pdf. Accessed November 14, 2018.

Qikiqtani Truth Commission (QTC). https://www.qtcommission.ca/en. Accessed November 7, 2019.

Radhakrishnan, Rajagopalan. 2012. *A Said Dictionary*. Chichester, UK: Wiley-Blackwell.

Raheja, Michelle H. 2015. "Visual Sovereignty." In *Native Studies Keywords*, ed. Stephanie Nohelani Teves, Andrea Smith, and Michelle H. Raheja, 25–34. Tucson: University of Arizona Press.

Raibmon, Paige. 2005. *Authentic Indians: Episodes of Encounter from the Late-Nineteenth-Century Northwest Coast*. Durham, N.C.: Duke University Press.

Rancière, Jacques. 1991. *The Ignorant Schoolmaster: Five Lessons in Intellectual Emancipation*. Stanford, Calif.: Stanford University Press.

Rancière, Jacques. 2010. *Dissensus: On Politics and Aesthetics*. Ed. and trans. Steven Corcoran. New York: Continuum International Publishing Group.

Randall, J. K., and Benjamin Boretz. 2003. *Being about Music: Textworks 1960–2003*. Red Hook, N.Y.: Open Space Publications.

Rath, Richard Cullen. 2014. "Hearing Wampum: The Senses, Meditation, and the Limits of Analogy." In *Colonial Mediascapes: Sensory Worlds of the Early Americas*, ed. Matt Cohen and Jeffry Glover, 290–324. Lincoln: University of Nebraska Press.

Reed, Trevor. 2016. "Who Owns Our Ancestors' Voices? Tribal Claims to Pre-1972 Sound Recordings." *Columbia Journal of Law and the Arts* 275: 275–310.

Regan, Paulette. 2010. *Unsettling the Settler Within: Indian Residential Schools, Truth Telling, and Reconciliation in Canada*. Vancouver: University of British Columbia Press.

Renihan, Colleen L. "The Politics of Genre: Exposing Historical Tensions in Harry Somers's Louis Riel." In *Opera Indigene: Re/presenting First Nations and Indigenous Cultures,* ed. Pamela Karantonis and Dylan Robinson, 259–76. New York: Routledge. Originally published with Ashgate Press.

Rice, Ryan. 2017. "Presence and Absence Redux: Indian Art in the 1990s." *RACAR: revue d'art canadienne / Canadian Art Review* 42, no. 2, special issue on Continuities between Eras: Indigenous Art Histories: 42–53.

Rice, Tom. 2015. "Listening." In *Keywords in Sound,* ed. David Novak and Matt Sakakeeny, 99–111. Durham, N.C.: Duke University Press.

Rickard, Jolene. 2011. "Visualizing Sovereignty in the Time of Biometric Sensors." *South Atlantic Quarterly* 110, no. 2 (Spring): 465–86.

Robinson, Dylan. 2012. "Intercultural Art Music and the Sensory Veracity of Reconciliation: Brent Michael Davids' Powwow Symphony on the Dakota Music Tour." *MUSICultures* 39, no. 1: 111–28.

Robinson, Dylan. 2016. "Intergenerational Sense, Intergenerational Responsibility." In *Arts of Engagement: Taking Aesthetic Action in and beyond Canada's Truth and Reconciliation Commission,* ed. Dylan Robinson and Keavy Martin, 43–66. Waterloo, Ont.: Wilfrid Laurier University Press.

Robinson, Dylan. 2017. "Enchantment's Irreconcilable Connection: Listening to Anger, Being Idle No More." In *Performance Studies in Canada,* ed. Laura Levin and Marlis Schweitzer, 211–35. Montreal and Kingston: McGill-Queen's University Press.

Robinson, Dylan. 2019a. "Rethinking the Practice and Performance of Indigenous Land Acknowledgement." *Canadian Theatre Review* 177 (Winter): 20–23.

Robinson, Dylan. 2019b. "Speaking to Water, Singing to Stone: Peter Morin, Rebecca Belmore, and the Ontologies of Indigenous Modernity." In *Music and Modernity among Indigenous Peoples of North America,* ed. Victoria Lindsay Levine and Dylan Robinson, 220–39. Middletown, Conn.: Wesleyan University Press.

Robinson, Dylan, and Mary Ingraham. Forthcoming. "Introduction: Intersensory Approaches to Music and Sound in Canada." In *Intensities: Toward Non-exceptionalist Experience of Music in Canada,* ed. Dylan Robinson and Mary Ingraham. Waterloo, Ont.: Wilfrid Laurier University Press.

Robinson, Dylan, and Keavy Martin. 2016. *Arts of Engagement: Taking Aesthetic Action in and beyond Canada's Truth and Reconciliation Commission.* Waterloo, Ont.: Wilfrid Laurier University Press.

Robinson, Dylan, and Keavy Martin. 2016. "Introduction: 'The Body Is a Resonant Chamber.'" In *Arts of Engagement: Taking Aesthetic Action in and beyond Canada's Truth and Reconciliation Commission,* ed. Dylan Robinson and Keavy Martin, 1–20. Waterloo, Ont.: Wilfrid Laurier University Press.

Ruddell, Bruce, and Bill Henderson. 2011. "Beyond Eden." Workshop draft of score.

Saranillio, Dean Itsuji. 2013. "Why Asian Settler Colonialism Matters: A Thought Piece on Critiques, Debates, and Indigenous Difference." *Settler Colonial Studies* 3, no. 3–4: 280–94.

Sarris, Greg. 1993. *Keeping Slug Woman Alive: A Holistic Approach to American Indian Texts.* Berkeley: University of California Press.

Saul, John Ralston. 2008. *A Fair Country: Telling Truths about Canada.* Toronto: Viking Canada.

Schafer, R. Murray. 1961. "On the Limits of Nationalism in Canadian Music." *Tamarack Review* 18 (Winter): 71–78.

Schafer, R. Murray. 1971. *Miniwanka, or The Moments of Water.* New York: Universal Edition.

Schafer, R. Murray. 1994. *The Soundscape: Our Sonic Environment and the Tuning of the World.* Rochester, Vt.: Destiny Books.

Schafer, R. Murray. 2012. "The Soundscape." In *The Sound Studies Reader,* ed. Jonathan Sterne, 95–103. New York: Routledge Press.

Schwebel, Paula L. 2012. "Walter Benjamin's Monadology." PhD diss., University of Toronto. https://tspace.library.utoronto.ca/bitstream/1807/44082/6/Schwebel_Paula_L_201203_PhD_thesis.pdf.

Scott, Jill. 2010. *A Poetics of Forgiveness: Cultural Responses to Loss and Wrongdoing.* Basingstoke, UK: Palgrave Macmillan.

Sedgewick, Eve Kosofsky. 2003. *Touching Feeling: Affect, Pedagogy, Performativity.* Durham, N.C.: Duke University Press.

See, Sarita Echavez. 2016. "Critical Contradictions: A Conversation among Glen Coulthard, Dylan Rodríguez, and Sarita Echavez See." In *Critical Ethnic Studies: A Reader,* ed. The Critical Ethnic Studies Editorial Collective, 138–58. Durham, N.C.: Duke University Press.

Simpson, Audra. 2014. *Mohawk Interruptus: Political Life across the Borders of Settler States.* Durham, N.C.: Duke University Press.

Simpson, Audra, and Andrea Smith. 2014. "Introduction." In *Theorizing Native Studies,* ed. Audra Simpson and Andrea Smith, 1–30. Durham, N.C.: Duke University Press.

Simpson, Leanne Betasamosake. 2011. *Dancing on Our Turtle's Back: Stories of Nishnaabeg Re-Creation, Resurgence, and a New Emergence.* Winnipeg: Arbeiter Ring Press.

Simpson, Leanne Betasamosake, and Naomi Klein. 2013. "Dancing the World into Being: A Conversation with Idle No More's Leanne Simpson." *Yes! Magazine,* March 5, 2013. https://www.yesmagazine.org/peace-justice/dancing-the-world-into-being-a-conversation-with-idle-no-more-leanne-simpson.

Small, Christopher. 1998. *Musicking: The Meanings of Performing and Listening.* Hanover, N.H.: University Press of New England.

Smith, Gordon. 1989. "Ernest Gagnon on Nationalism and Canadian Music: Folk and Native Sources." *MusicCULTURES* 17: 32–39.

Smith, Gordon, Lynda Jessup, and Andrew Nurse, eds. 2008. *Around and about Marius Barbeau: Modelling Twentieth-Century Culture.* Ottawa: Canadian Museum of Civilization.

Smith, Mark M. 2007. *Sensing the Past: Seeing, Hearing, Smelling, Tasting, and Touching in History.* Berkeley: University of California Press.

Snelgrove, Corey, Rita Kaur Dhamoon, and Jeff Corntassel. 2014. "Unsettling Settler Colonialism: The Discourse and Politics of Settlers, and Solidarity with Indigenous Nations." *Decolonization: Indigeneity, Education & Society* 3, no. 2: 1–32.

So, Joseph K. 2010. "*Giiwedin*: Aboriginal Voices in Opera." *The Music Scene,* Spring, 4–5.

Solnit, Rebecca. 2000. *Wanderlust: A History of Walking.* New York: Viking.

Sontag, Susan. 1966. "Against Interpretation." In *Against Interpretation and Other Essays,* 1–10. New York: Farrar, Straus & Giroux.

Stadler, Gustavus. 2015. "On Whiteness and Sound Studies." *Sounding Out!* (blog). http://soundstudiesblog.com/2015/07/06/on-whiteness-and-sound -studies/. Accessed November 6, 2016.

Stanyek, Jason. 2004. "Diasporic Improvisation and the Articulation of Intercultural Music." PhD diss., University of California. ProQuest/UMI.

Steblin, Rita. 1994. "Shubert à la Mode." *The New York Review of Books.* October 20, 1994. https://www.nybooks.com/articles/1994/10/20/schubert-a-la -mode/.

Steenhuisen, Paul. "The Resocialization of Concert Music." Interview with Marc Couroux. http://pages.infinit.net/kore/writings.html (site discontinued). Accessed August 10, 2008.

Sterne, Jonathan. 2012. "Quebec's #casseroles: On Participation, Percussion, and Protest." Supplement, *Theory & Event* 15, no. 3. http://muse.jhu.edu.ezproxy .library.yorku.ca/article/484454. Accessed November 14, 2018.

Stoever, Jennifer Lynn. 2016. *The Sonic Color Line: Race and the Cultural Politics of Listening.* New York: New York University Press.

Strachan, Jeremy. 2005. "Music Inspired by Aboriginal Sources at the Canadian Music Centre." *Canadian Music Centre.* http://old.musiccentre.ca/media/ downloads/en/CMC_Rep_Guide_Aboriginal.pdf. Accessed November 6, 2016.

Strachan, Jeremy. 2012. "Sounding Empire: Coloniality and Environment in Canadian Art Music," Paper presented at Ecomusics/Ecomusicologies, Tulane University, New Orleans, October 30, 2012.

Strunk Jr., William, and E. B. White. 1999. *The Elements of Style*, 4th ed. Boston: Allyn & Bacon.

Such, Peter. 1972. *Soundprints: Contemporary Composers*. Toronto: Clarke, Irwin & Co.

Symonds, Dominic. 2007. "The Corporeality of Musical Expression: The Grain of the Voice and The Actor-Musician." *Studies in Musical Theatre* 1, no. 2 (August): 167–81.

Szekely, Michael David. 2006. "Gesture, Pulsion, Grain: Barthes' Musical Semiology." *Contemporary Aesthetics* 4. https://contempaesthetics.org/newvolume/pages/article.php?articleID=409. Accessed November 6, 2016.

Tafelmusik. 2007. "Press release." October. http://www.tafelmusik.org/media/presspdfs/Tafelmusik_CD_L'estro_armoinco.pdf (site discontinued). Accessed June 28, 2011.

Tafelmusik. n.d. "Celebrating the Cycle of the Seasons with Music from Baroque Italy, China, India, and the Canadian North." http://www.tafelmusik.org/flash/learningcentre/PDF/TheFourSeasons.pdf. Accessed December 3, 2016.

Tan, Marcus Cheng Chye. 2012. *Acoustic Interculturalism: Listening to Performance*. Basingstoke, UK: Palgrave Macmillan.

Taylor, Charles. 1992. *Multiculturalism and the Politics of Recognition*. Princeton, N.J.: Princeton University Press.

Thompson, James. 2009. *Performance Affects: Applied Theatre and the End of Effect*. London: Palgrave Macmillan.

Thrift, Nigel. 2008. *Non-representational Theory: Space | Politics | Affect*. New York: Routledge.

Todd, Jane Marie. 1986. "Autobiography and the Case of the Signature: Reading Derrida's *Glas*." *Comparative Literature* 38, no. 1 (Winter): 1–19.

Todd, Loretta. 1990. "Notes on Appropriation." *Parallelogramme* 16, no. 1: 24–33.

Todd, Zoe. 2016. "An Indigenous Feminist's Take on the Ontological Turn: 'Ontology' Is Just Another Word for Colonialism." *Journal of Historical Sociology* 29, no. 1 (March): 4–22.

Toronto Consort. 2016. "Kanatha/Canada: First Encounters." https://torontoconsort.org/concerts-tickets/2016–17-season/kanathacanada-first-encounters/. Accessed April 1, 2017.

Truth and Reconciliation Commission of Canada. 2015. *Canada's Residential Schools: The History, Part 1 Origins to 1939*. Vol. 1 of *The Final Report of the*

Truth and Reconciliation Commission of Canada. Montreal and Kingston: McGill-Queen's University Press.

Truth and Reconciliation Commission of Canada. n.d. "Reconciliation . . . Towards a New Relationship." http://www.myrobust.com/websites/reconcil iation/index.php?p=649. Accessed January 15, 2017.

Tuck, Eve. 2009. "Suspending Damage: A Letter to Communities." *Harvard Educational Review* 79, no. 3 (Fall): 409–27.

Tuck, Eve. 2018. "Biting the University That Feeds Us." In *Dissident Knowledge in Higher Education,* ed. Marc Spooner and James McNinch, 149–67. Regina: University of Regina Press.

Tuck, Eve, and Monique Guishard. 2013. "Uncollapsing Ethics: Racialized Sciencism, Settler Coloniality, and an Ethical Framework of Decolonial Participatory Action Research." In *Challenging Status Quo Retrenchment: New Directions in Critical Qualitative Research,* ed. T. M. Kress, C. S. Malott, and B. J. Portfilio, 3–27. Charlotte, N.C.: Information Age Publishing.

Tuck, Eve, and K. Wayne Yang. 2012. "Decolonization Is Not a Metaphor." *Decolonization: Indigeneity, Education & Society* 1, no. 1: 1–40.

Turino, Thomas. 2008. *Music as Social Life: The Politics of Participation.* Chicago: University of Chicago Press.

UCLA. 2015. "'Imagining the New World' UCLA Early Music Ensemble." *UCLA Library.* http://www.library.ucla.edu/events/imagining-new-world -ucla-early-music-ensemble. Accessed April 1, 2017.

Utz, Christian. 2005. "Beyond Cultural Representation: Recent Works for the Asian Mouth Organs Shō and Sheng by Western Composers." *The World of Music* 47, no. 3: 113–34.

van den Toorn, Pieter C. 1991. "Politics, Feminism, and Contemporary Music Theory." *The Journal of Musicology* 9, no. 3 (Summer): 275–99.

van den Toorn, Pieter C. 1995. *Music, Politics, and the Academy.* Berkeley: University of California Press.

Vannini, Phillip. 2015. "Non-representational Research Methodologies: An Introduction." In *Non-representational Methodologies: Re-envisioning Research,* ed. Phillip Vannini, 1–18. New York: Routledge Press.

Warrior, Robert. 1994. *Tribal Secrets: Recovering American Indian Traditions.* Minneapolis: University of Minnesota Press.

Warrior, Robert. 2009. "Native American Scholarship and the Transnational Turn." *Cultural Studies Review* 15, no. 2 (September): 119–30.

Wickwire, Wendy. 2006. "'They Wanted . . . Me to Help Them': James Teit and the Challenge of Ethnography in the Boasian Era." In *With Good Intentions: Euro-Canadian and Aboriginal Relations in Colonial Canada,* ed. Celia Haig-Brown and David Nock, 297–320. Vancouver: University of British Columbia Press.

Bibliography

Wilcock, Deidre Ann. 2011. "Living Landscapes: 'Ethnogeomorphology' as an Ethical Frame of Communication in Environmental Decision-Making," PhD diss., York University.

Williams, Linda. 1989. *Hard Core: Power, Pleasure, and the Frenzy of the Visible.* Berkeley: University of California Press.

Wilson, Jordan. 2015. "sq̓əq̓ip—GATHERED TOGETHER." Master's thesis, University of British Columbia.

Wilson, Jordan. 2016. "Gathered Together: Listening to Musqueam Lived Experiences." *Biography* 39, no. 3 (Summer): 469–94.

Winzenburg, John. 2013. "Heteroglossia and Traditional Vocal Genres in Chinese-Western Fusion Concertos." *Perspectives of New Music* 51, no. 2 (Summer): 101–40.

WochenKlausur. n.d. "From the Object to the Concrete Intervention." http://www.wochenklausur.at/kunst.php?lang=en. Accessed November 8, 2018.

Wolfe, Patrick. 1999. *Settler Colonialism and the Transformation of Anthropology.* London: Bloomsbury Press.

Womack, Craig. 1999. *Red on Red: Native American Literary Separatism.* Minneapolis: University of Minnesota Press.

Wong, Deborah. 2004. *Speak It Louder: Asian Americans Making Music.* New York: Routledge.

Wong, Deborah. 2008. "Moving: From Performance to Performative Ethnography and Back Again." In *Shadows in the Field: New Perspectives for Fieldwork in Ethnomusicology,* 2d ed., ed. Gregory Barz and Timothy Cooley, 76–89. New York: Oxford University Press.

Younging, Greg, Jonathan Dewar, and Mike DeGagné, eds. 2009. *Response, Responsibility, and Renewal: Canada's Truth and Reconciliation Journey.* Ottawa: Aboriginal Healing Foundation.

Yúdice, George. 2003. *The Expediency of Culture: Uses of Culture in the Global Era.* Durham, N.C.: Duke University Press.

INDEX

Page numbers in *italics* refer to illustrations.

Abbate, Carolyn, 83

Abel, Sam, 92

accessibility in music, 125–27, 215, 219

accommodation policies. *See* recognition and accommodation

adaawk, 41, 273n7. *See also* oral history and documentation

Adams, John, 85

Adorno, Theodor W., 180, 280n13

affect, shared, 202–5, 217–18, 226, 252, 281n3; as *communitas,* 202, 204–5, 215; scholars on "sticky" quality of, 282n8

agglutination, 205, 282n8

Aglukark, Susan: "O Siem" and, 202, 203, 226–29, 231

Ahmed, Sara, 39, 229–30, 282n8

Alpers, Svetlana, 85

Alvarez, Steven, 143

American Musicological Society, 9–10, 268n8, 269n13

Amtmann, Willy, 12

ancestors, relationships with, 86–92, 237

"Apology Dice" (Garneau and Yeh), 171–72, *173*

apposite methodology, 81–84, 100–102, 273n6

appropriation, 5, 13, 49, 51, 150, 159–61; earliest example of, 118–19; Hatzis and, 130–31; as "significant influence," 272n10

Archibald, Jo-ann, 51

Assu, Billy, 156

Atagootak, Angela, 113, 128, 132

Attariwala, Parmela, 268n5

attention, Indigenous forms of, 51–52, 54–56, 72. *See also* xwélala:m

audience–performer relationship, 15–16, 18, 58, 81, 88, 123–26, 177–79, 205, 213–14; communities in, 277n8; "flow experiences" in, 205, 282n7; settings for, 61, 272n13. *See also* affect, shared; utopianism

Austin, J. L., 39, 45, 166, 217

Avery, Dawn, 3, 123, 143–45, 214

awareness raising, 17–18, 39, 152, 180–81

Bach, Johann Sebastian, 143

Baird, Thomas, 134

310 Index

Baker, Bob (S7aplek), 134
Baker, Geoffrey, 117
Balfour, Andrew, 3, 276n6, 281n3
Barbeau, Marius, 149, 151, *153,* 154, 155–56, 158, 159, 161–62, 245–46; salvage paradigm and, 285n18
Barenboim, Daniel, 144
Barkin, Elaine, 269n12
Baroque music, contemporary reception of, 127, 278n12
Barthes, Roland, 77–80, 102
Bellman, Jonathan, 80, 273n4
Benjamin, Walter, 102
Bennett, Jane, 98
Berio, Luciano, 130
Berlant, Lauren, 257
Berlo, Janet, 79
Beyond Eden (rock musical), 201–4, 206, 217–23
bhangra dancing, 202, 203, 209–13
Bloechl, Olivia, 16, 118–19
Bolton, Frank, *153*
Bolton, Laura, 215
Bonds, Mark Evan, 84
Boretz, Benjamin, 273n5
Borges, Jorge Luis, 59
Born, Georgina, 83
Boyden, Joseph, 49
Brecht, Bertolt: *verfremdungseffekt* of, 23, 73, 199
Brown, Martha, 271n6
Buchan, Bruce, 284n13
Bunn-Marcuse, Kathryn, 149
Butler, Judith, 229
Byrd, Jodi, 271n3

Cage, John, 177
camp, 85
Canada Council for the Arts, 4, 117, 246, 267n3, 268n5

Canadian Museum of History, 150, 156, 278n2
Canadian national identity, 64, 121, 122, 129, 154–55, 161, 283n9
Cardiff, Janet, 272n13
Carlick, Beal, 90
Carlick, Johnny S., 90
Carlson, Keith, 48–49
Carr, Emily, 49
Carrabré, Patrick, 280n14
Cartier, Jacques, 116
cəsnaʔəm, the city before the city (exhibition), 69–71, *71,* 171, 172
Chacon, Raven, 3, 4, 128, 174; *Report, 106,* 107–10, *111*
Charke, Derek, 188, 281n3
Chartrand, Yvonne, 160–61
Chassé, Charles, 155–56
Chen, Kenneth, 279n6
Chilcott, Barbara, 159
Child, Musgamdzi Kalerb, 149
Child, Nasgamkala, 150
Child, Yakawilas Corrine, 149
Churchill, Winston, 1, 182
citational practices, 11, 22, 103, 104, 130, 229
"clairaudience," 107, 275n1
Cloutier, Sylvia, 4, 129–30, 138–43
Coleman, Elizabeth Byers, et al., 157, 161
collaborations. *See* inclusion and inclusionary performances
colonialism/colonization, 14, 22–23, 24, 47, 99, 121, 138, 168, 175, 177, 225, 230, 235, 254; settler colonialism, 10, 14, 67–68, 132, 224, 254, 258
compositional ethics and responsibility, 150–51, 152; formal vs. ethical music choices, 132–33

Index

consciousness raising. *See* awareness raising

Conversations in Indigenous Arts series, 89

Cook, James, 116, 119, 122, 134

Cook, Nicholas, 83

Copland, Aaron, 203, 285n15

copyright, 131, 156, 161, 163

Cornellier, Bruno, 18

Corntassel, Jeff, 47

Coulthard, Glen, 7, 21, 22, 23–24, 122, 225, 241, 268n6

counterpoint, 134, 144

Cram, Robert, 159

Crawley, Ashon, 271n1

critical-affective writing, 15–21

critical listening positionality. *See* positionality

critical race studies, 18, 20, 37

Croall, Barbara, 3, 281n3, 282n5

Crosby, Marcia, 49

Cruikshank, Julie, 93, 96–97

Cusick, Suzanne, 81, 83, 93, 94–96

Cusson, Ian, 3

Cvetkovitch, Ann, 257

Dadaism, 255

Dangeli, Mike, 15, 87, 89–92, 151, 161–66, 170, 173, 236; print by, 163, *165*

Dangeli, Mique'l, 63, 87, 89–92, 135, 151, 161–62, 163, 168, 173, 236

Danna, Mychael, 137–40, 185

Daughtry, Martin, 58–62, 249, 273n5

Davids, Brent Michael, 3, 4

decolonial listening, 11, 37, 72, 181, 258, 272n13; Wong and Waterman on, 239–53. *See also* positionality

decolonization, 23, 39, 181, 225, 235, 237, 254

Decter, Leah, 254

Deep Listening, 244–49

Deer, Beatrice, 142–43

Delgamuukw v. the Queen, 37, 41–46, *42–43,* 53, 98, 258, 271nn5–6

Dénommé-Welch, Spy, 124, 125–26

DeNora, Tia, 230–31

Derksen, Cris, 3, 203, 209, 211

de-socialization, 172, 279n10

Destrubé, Marc, 134

Diamond, Beverley, 272n11, 286n23

Different Drum (Olympic performance), 202, 203, 209–14, *210,* 215–16; abundance and, 213–14

dogsled travel, representations of, 152, 182, 183–88. *See also* qimmiijaqtauniq

Dolan, Jill, 217, 227, 230

Doing Sovereignties gathering, 162–66, 173–75

Doroschuk, Colin, 281n3

Doublewide collective, 254

Du Bois, W. E. B., 249

Duff, Wilson, 219, 221

Dutcher, Jeremy, 3, 152, 168, 173–79

Dutt, Hank, *5*

Dyer, Richard, 213

Dynasty (TV series), 85

early music and Indigenous music, 113–21, 122–45, 276n1; early encounters, 118–22; taxonomy of, 122–23; timeline of recent collaborations, 114–16

Edenshaw, Gwaai, 222

Edensor, Tim, 256

8TH Fire, The (miniseries), 211, 276n5

Eisenberg, Andrew, 96

"encounter" term, 117

Index

environmental activism, 14, 98, 180, 189, 242

environmental personhood, 98–99

Episkenew, Jo-Ann, 225–26

epistemic violence, 10, 11–12, 16, 21, 23, 46, 83, 101, 104, 137, 144, 258, 260

ethnography. *See* Indigenous song: ethnographic collection of

event scores, 75–76, 99–100, 147, 152, 191–99, 233, 236, 253

Evergreen Club Contemporary Gamelan, 4

exclusion, 236–37

"experimental" designation, 124, 128

extraction and "extractivism," 14, 49, 119, 121, 130

Fanon, Frantz, 7

Farnan, Michael, 254

Fatty Legs (choral adaptation), 282n5

Fink, Robert, 19; and recombinant teleology, 203, 281n4

First Story (Pacific Baroque Orchestra/ Spakwus Slolem collaboration), 133–36

Fleming, Robert, 215

Fluxus, 191, 272n13

Foucault, Michel, 249

Four Seasons, The (Tafelmusik concert and documentary), 114, 123, 129, 137–43, 145, 185

Fox, Aaron, 149

Fraser, Simon, 116

Fraser Canyon Gold Rush, 2, 48–49, *48*

friendship, rhetoric of, 17, 206–7, 231, 235, 242, 276n3; at Olympics, 208, 214, 284n10

Frobisher, Martin, 65, 142

Fulton, Hamish, 255

Gaertner, David, 236, 247

Gagnon, Ernest, 12, 154–55, 156

Garneau, David, 21–24, 171–72, 268n6; on "irreconcilable spaces of Aboriginality," 24, 235–39, 242

generalizability, 124, 276n1

Gettin' Higher Choir, 202, 203, 226–27, *228*

Gibal, 162

Giiwedin (Dénommé-Welch and Magowan), 115, 123–28, 277nn10–11

glaciers, sentience of, 96–97

Goldberg, Theo, 157

Goldman, Danielle, 249–50

Gould, Glenn, 144

governmental funding, 4, 6, 246, 267n3, 267n5

Grant, Howard E., 71

Gray, Robin, 149

Grey Owl (Archibald Stansfeld Belaney), 155

Grimes, Linda, 207

"grounded normativity," 22, 275n11

Group of Seven, 155, 279n4

Guattari, Félix, 282n8

Hage, Ghassan, 226–27

Hahn, Tomie, 273n5

Haida people, 219–22

Halpern, Ida, 156–58, 279nn5–6

Hannah and the Inukshuks (Olympic performance), 202, 203, 214–16, *216*, 222, 285n16

haptic visuality and writing, 78, 93–94

Harper, Stephen, 17, 215, 285n17

Harrison, Klisala, 279n7

Hatzis, Christos, 113, 128–33, 140

Heath, Stephen, 78

Index

Heble, Ajay, 144
Hinton, Peter, 279n7
Hisama, Ellie, 20
Hoffmann, E. T. A., 84
hooks, bell, 250–51
Hopkins, Candice, 99, 162, 173, 279n10
Horton, Jessica, 79
Howes, Hadley, 254
Hulatt, Owen, 280n13
human and nonhuman relations, 22, 79, 92–93, 98–100, 189, 237
"hungry listening," 13, 50–51, 53, 73, 88, 118, 123, 126, 145, 236, 247; etymology of, 2–3; range of appetites for, 216, 272n11; resisting, 243, 245. *See also* scopophilia; settler hunger and consumption
hymns, 48, 54, 55, 140

Igloliorte, Jim, 184
impasses, 72, 257, 258
improvisation, 137, 140, 184, 240, 250
inclusion and inclusionary performances, 5–10, 46, 49, 58, 60–62, 117–18, 122–23, 132, 136–37, 140, 181, 184, 239, 246; inversion of, 277n6; "radical inclusion," 237–38, 239, 251; reconciliation and, 202–32
Indian Act, 3, 38, 156; "Potlatch Ban" of, 55–56, 150, 151
indigenization, 235
Indigenous belongings, 69, 86–90, 167, 236
Indigenous logics of performance, 8, 105, 137
Indigenous mobility, 54–56
"Indigenous+art music," 9, 46, 51, 58, 123, 143, 161, 181, 186

Indigenous song: cleansing of ("bringing to life"), 167–68, 252; communal nature of, 177–78; ethnographic collection of, 149–51, 153–62, 245–46, 278n2; functions and ontologies of, 8, 41, 44–47, 50, 51, 68, 131, 152, 161, 167, 268n7; as resources, 12–13, 58, 107, 130–31, 132, 150, 154–58, 161; transcription of, 149, 150
Indigenous Story Keepers, 171
Indigenous studies, 18, 21, 103, 104, 241; exclusivity in, 275n11
Inga, Doug, 87
intersectionality, 23, 104–5, 237, 239
intersubjectivity, 16, 79, 81, 83, 102, 179, 245; haptic, 93–94; nonhuman, 93, 97–100, 189; spatial, 96–100. *See also* ancestors, relationships with
Inuit culture, 128–30, 182–83, 189
Inuit throat singing: in *The Four Seasons*, 138–43; improvisation in, 184; in *Inuit Games,* 280n14; in *Medieval Inuit,* 276n6; Schafer's description of, 1, 182; in *Take the Dog Sled,* 182, 184–87, 193; in *Viderunt Omnes,* 113, 128, 131–32

Jameson, Anna, 54, 141
Jankélévitch, Vladimir, 83
Johnson, Mary, 37, 41–45, 46
Johnston, Charlotte, 54

Kafka, Franz, 274n9
Kallman, Helmut, 12
Keillor, Elaine, 13, 49
Kelly, Dara, 170
Kester, Grant, 181
Keyes, Sara, 57

Index

Khesthi, Roshanak, 271n1
King, James, 119–20
Klein, Naomi, 14
Knockwood, Isabelle, 57
Knowles, Ric, 5
Koestenbaum, Wayne, 81, 84–85, 274n7
Kopelson, Kevin, 81, 86, 93
Kramer, Lawrence, 83, 205, 274n9
Kronos Quartet, 4, 281n3
ksi-giikw, 164, 166
Kwidzinski, Lee, 209, 211–12
Kyak, Pauline, 113, 128, 132

Lachenmann, Helmut, 248–49
Lamon, Jean, 140–41, 142–43
Laozi, 189
Latour, Bruno, 93
LaVallee, Michelle, 171
law: Indigenous vs. Western, 41–46, 98–99, 271n5
Lee, Sherry, 279n7
Lescarbot, Marc, 118–19
Levin, David, 80, 83–85, 93, 100, 274n7
Levinas, Emmanuel, 15, 179
Levitz, Tamara, 269n13
Lewis, George, 240
L'Hirondelle, Cheryl, 164, 172, 237–38, 251
limx oo'y (dirge), 41–45, 52, 53, 151, 161, 271n6, 279n7
Linklater, Duane, 4
listening. *See* decolonial listening; Deep Listening; "hungry listening"; positionality; xwélala:m
Liu Fang, 4
Long, Richard, 255
Lorde, Audre, 17
Louie, Alexina, 152, 181–82, 183–89,

193, 195–96, 198, 280n15, 281nn2–3
Louis Riel (opera and conferences), 151, 159–61, *160,* 279n7
Lukin Linklater, Tanya, 4, 105; *Accompaniment,* 87–88

Ma, Yo-Yo, 4
Mackenzie, Alexander, 116
Mackey, Eva, 8, 129, 136, 283n9, 286n1
MacMillan, Ernest, 15, 149, *153,* 159, 161; *Three Songs of the West Coast,* 162–63, 166
Magowan, Catherine, 124, 125–26
Maracle, Lee, 77
Mark, Evie, 182, 185, 186, 193, 198, 280n15
Marks, Laura, 78, 93–95
Martin, Mungo, 156, 169
Martínez, Esteban José, 116
Massumi, Brian, 282n8
McClary, Susan, 47, 72, 203, 269n12, 281n4
McEachern, Allan, 37, 41–45, 53, 161, 271n5
McHugh, Susan, 183
McIvor, Melody, 3
McLachlin, Beverley, 279n7
McMurray, William, 54
Mechling, William H., 152, 156, 177
Mecija, Casey, 283n9
Medieval Inuit (Camerata Nova concert), 276n6
Menuhin, Yehudi, 4
Métis people, 159–60
métissage, 118; Canada as "Métis nation," 121–22, 128
Mi'kmaq people, 118–19, 176
Miner, Dylan, 172

missionaries/missionization, 40, 54–55, 130, 132, 138

Mitchell, W. J. T., 93

modernity, 149, 153, 226

Monet, Don: cartoons by, *42–43,* 45

Monkman, Kent, 4

Monson, Ingrid, 95

Morin, Peter, 4, 70, 87, 152, 174, 177, 253; *Cultural Graffiti* series, 88, 168–70, *170,* 172; Isabel Bader Centre performance, 89–92, *91,* 274n8; museum performances, 88, *89*; Saint Olave's performance, 65–68; TRC performance, 178–79

Morrison, James, 44, 51, 52, 53, 72

Morton, Wendy, 207

Moten, Fred, 271n1

Mouffe, Chantal, 145, 257

Mountie Sled Dog Massacre. *See* qimmiijaqtauniq

multiculturalism: Canadian exceptionalism and, 283n9; extractivist, 122; "official," 6, 37, 64–65, 136, 145, 205, 213–14, 222, 229–30, 235, 241, 267n5, 283n9

Multiculturalism Act, 4–5, 267n5

Muñoz, José Esteban, 244–45

museums and galleries, 69–70, 86–88, 91–92, 150, 154, 158, 167, 171

music education, 50, 250

musicology, 12–13, 15–17, 77–80, 100–103, 268n8; Barthes on, 77–78; norms in, 81–83, 101, 277n7; resistance to critical-affective scholarship, 18–20, 80, 83, 101, 103; "stylistic excess" in, 80, 83–84. *See also* performative writing; queer musicology; race and sound studies; whiteness

Nancy, Jean-Luc, 83

Napoleon, Val, 271n7

Narayan, Aruna, 4, 138, 139

narratocracy, 39–40, 105; defined, 204

Nass River Indians (film), 153

National Film Board films, 215

National Museum of Canada, 154, 177

Native American Composer Apprentice Project, 4

Native Earth Performing Arts, 115, 125, 126

Newman, Marion, 4; *Thunderbird,* 276n6

new materialism theory, 16, 79, 93, 189

Nisga'a people: songs of, 15, 151, 159–64

nonhuman kinship. *See* human and nonhuman relations

non-representational theory, 79, 83, 84, 85, 180, 189, 203–4, 206, 213, 217, 230

Northern Cree Singers, 4

Nuu-chah-nulth people, 116, 118, 119–21, *120,* 122, 134

Ochoa Gauthier, Ana Maria, 271n1

Oliveros, Pauline, 244–48, 286n3

Olympic Games. *See* Vancouver Winter Olympics

Olympic Truce, 207–8, 214, 283n10; symbols of, *208,* 284n10

"On My Own" (*Les Misérables*), 219

Ono, Yoko, 191

oral history and documentation, 41, 55–56, 67, 151, 172

Ortiz, Fernando, 269n10

Ortman, Laura, 87–88

Oswald, John, 130

Index

Pacific Baroque Orchestra, 123, 133–35

palimpsest metaphor, 58–62, 86

Panagia, Davide, 204

Paukk, Alex, 157

performative and non-performative utterances, 39, 217; non-performative diversity discourse, 229–30, 252

performative writing, 16, 23, 77–86, 92–96, 99–105, 199, 203, 273n2; "critical virtuosity" and, 86, 93; definitions of, 79, 81; "indisciplinarity" of, 83–84. *See also* queer musicology

Pérotin, 113, 128, 131, 278n13

Phelan, Peggy, 81, 273n2

pipeline development, 14, 189; Dakota Access Pipeline, 242

Pocahontas, 169–70, *170*

Pollock, Della, 273n2

Polzonetti, Pierpaolo, 9–10, 18–19

Pope, William L., 288n6

positionality, 1, 3, 20, 37–73, 81, 247–48; critical listening positionality, 2, 10–11, 51, 53, 60, 62, 240, 247–50, 253; on movement, 257–58; oscillation and, 60–61, 62; settler listening positionality, 10, 11, 38, 40, 45, 50–51, 72, 98, 244, 251

potlatches, 54, 67, 134, 162–63; banning of, 55–56, 132, 150, 151

powwow music and dancing, 202, 209–13, 285n14

Pratt, Mary Louise, 11

proprioception, 11, 24, 55, 78, 96, 255–57

protocols: 13, 21, 68, 134–36, 150–52, 158, 161–62, 166–69, 172–76, 235, 246, 248, 252, 258; "protocops" on, 174–75

Qikiqtani Truth Commission (QTC), 129, 152, 182–84, 194

qimmiijaqtauniq, 129, 152, 182–83, 188, 194; defined, 278n14

queer issues, 39, 51, 60, 92, 237; Muñoz on, 245; Oliveros and, 247–48

queer musicology, 18, 82, 83–84, 94–96, 282n4

race and sound studies, 9–10, 18–20, 103–4

"racial mis-interpellation," 226–27

Radhakrishnan, Rajagopalan, 144

Raheja, Michelle, 63

Raibmon, Paige, 55

Raminsh, Imant, 157

Rancière, Jacques, 68, 102, 104, 117, 214, 274n10

Randall, James, 273n5

Rath, Richard, 64–65

recognition and accommodation, 5, 7, 144, 268n6

reconciliation, 17, 116–17, 235; etymology of, 204, 205–6; musical works of, 116, 136, 202–32; non-representational forms of, 204–7, 213–14, 217; representational politics and, 121–22

redress and reparation: artistic, 152, 166; disciplinary, 11–15, 16–17, 152–53, 271n2; ethnographic, 149–50; for hungry listening, 58–62; of land, 271n2; reparative perception, 258, 287n8; shame and, 242

Reed, Trevor, 149

Index 317

refusal, strategies of, 21–24; structural vs. content, 23

Reid, Bill, 202, 219–22

Renihan, Colleen, 159

Repellent Fence (Postcommodity installation), 279n10

representational landscape music, 189–89

residential schools, 3, 6, 17, 40, 47, 56–58, 65, 104, 130, 132, 150, 151, 153, 156, 206, 282n5; government apology for, 17, 171, 215; performances about, 204, 282n5; TRC and, 38, 207, 223–24, 226–27, 261, 268n6, 277n11, 285n22

res nullius judgments, 212, 284n13

resonant theory, 15, 81

resurgence, 3, 11, 18, 21–23, 46, 103, 104, 189, 237, 254; resurgent listening, 62–65, 68, 72, 258

Rice, Tom, 286n4

Rickard, Jolene, 63

Riel, Louis, 159

Rogers, Shelagh, 206–7, 284n12

Roots (miniseries), 241

round dances, 242

Rowley, Sue, 69

Ruddell, Bruce, 202, 222. See also *Beyond Eden*

Sagard–Théodat, Gabriel, 118–19, 122

S7aplek. *See* Baker, Bob

Said, Edward, 144

salvage paradigm, 69, 151, 153, 202, 219, 223, 236; defined, 153, 285n18

Saul, John Ralston, 12, 118, 121–22, 128, 155

Schafer, R. Murray, 1, 5, 12, 155–56, 177, 205, 272n13; *Miniwanka,* 189;

Music for Wilderness Lake, 189; *North/White,* 182; *Snowforms,* 282n5

Sciarrino, Salvatore, 130

scopophilia, 236

"screen objects," 22

Sedgewick, Eve Kosofsky, 287n8

Səlilwət people, 166, 208

sensory-formalist analysis, 78, 93, 94–96, 273n1

"sensory veracity," 217–18

settler hunger and consumption, 23, 47–50, 53, 68–69, 73, 158, 236

"settler" term, 38–40, 269n9; Indigenous names for, 47–48; "settled" feeling, 40, 108, 109, 219, 230–32, 249, 250

Shadbolt, Jack, 49

Shankar, Ravi, 4

Shappa, June, 138–49

Simpson, Audra, 21, 23

Simpson, Leanne Betasamosake, 13–14, 21, 22, 23, 268n6, 275n11

Sinclair, Murray, 223

Singer, Beverly, 63

Situationism, 23, 255

Sivaurapik, Akinisie, 182, 186

sixties and seventies scoop, 3, 153, 278n15; defined, 278n3

Skwxwú7mesh Nation, 133–36, 166

sled dogs. *See* dogsled travel, representations of; qimmiijaqtauniq

Small, Christopher, 83, 205

Smith, Mark M., 57

So, Joseph K., 125

social art practice, 133, 172, 179–81

Solis, Gabriel, 18

Solnit, Rebecca, 255

Somers, Harry, 159–61

Sontag, Susan, 78–79, 273n1

sound territory, 53–54
sovereignty: artistic representations of, 63–64, 66–68, 143–44; Indigenous, 24, 25, 53–54, 63, 131, 134–36, 144, 239, 258; resurgent listening and, 62–68; "sensate," 24, 67–68; sovereign space, 235–36; visual, 64
space, 80, 123, 251; dancing and, 211–12; "irreconcilable spaces of Aboriginality," 24, 235–37, 239, 242; sovereign, 235–36, 239; subjectivity of, 96–100; visiting/gathering spaces, 170–73, 177
Spakwus Slolem, 4, 114, 123, 133–34
sqwálewel (thinking-feeling), 54, 170, 272n12
Stadler, Gustavus, 9, 251, 271n1
Stanyek, Jason, 5
Stoever, Jennifer, 271n1
Stó:lō term, 2, 47–48, 97, 224, 267n2, 272n9
Stories We Tell, The (opera), 4
subjectivation, 10, 37, 37
subjectivity: in musicology, 80–81; settler, 37, 244, 272n8; sound and, 15–16, 249; spatial, 96–100
Szekely, Michael, 78

Tafelmusik, 123, 140
Tagaq, Tanya, 4, **5**, 8, 128, 186, 281n3
Tait, Keane, 15, 151, 161–67, 170, 173, 236
Take the Dog Sled (chamber piece), 152, 181–82, 183–89, *187*, 254; event score for, 191–98; tour of, 280n15
Tan, Marcus, 5
Tate, Jerod Impichchaachaaha', 4
Taylor, Charles, 144

Taylor, Walt, 37, 45, 258
Teillet, Jean, 279n7
Teit, James, 152, 156, 168, 177
teleological structures in music, 203, 203, 217, 281n4; non-teleological music, 170, 282n4
"Thanksgiving Address," 52
Thrift, Nigel, 201
Thrush, Coll, 89
Thunderbird (Newman/Aradia collaboration), 276n6, 281n3
time, Western system of, 57–58, 119, 137, 141, 185
Todd, Loretta, 49
Todd, Zoe, 79
To Kill a Mocking Bird (novel), 241
totem poles, 169; of Haida Gwaii, 202, 219–23
translation, refusal of, 132
Trudeau, Pierre, 283n9
Truth and Reconciliation Commission (TRC), 6, 38, 241, 242, 277n11; contentious commencement of, 116–17, 276n2; regional events by, 117, 206–8, 223–26, 284n12
Tuck, Eve, 9, 17–18, 20, 39, 105, 152, 181
Turino, Thomas, 204–5
Turner, Victor, 204

utopianism, 113, 128, 213, 216–17, 230, 243, 252; "utopian performatives," 217, 230–31

Vancouver Cultural Olympiad, 17, 202, 209, 219, 221
Vancouver Winter Olympics, 207–16
Vanderhaeghe, Guy, 121
Vannini, Phillip, 79

Index

Videurunt Omnes (Hatzis), 113, 123–25, 128–33, 137
visiting, 170–79; methodology of, 172, 253
"visiting nations" concept, 134–36
Vivaldi, Antonio. See *Four Seasons, The*

Wahamaa, Kat, 209
Walde, Paul, 189
walking-based works, 254–57, 286n6
Wallaceton, William, 90
wampum, 64–65; wampum belt, 143
Warrior, Robert, 63
Waterman, Ellen, 239–53
Wee Lay Laq, Lumlamelut, 170–71
West-Eastern Divan Orchestra, 144
Western art music performance protocols, 7–8, 61, 88, 97, 100, 137, 177–78, 192
Western Front Artist-Run Theatre, 162, 166, 173
whiteness (and white supremacy), 3, 9–10, 18, 37, 81, 173, 251, 254–55, 269n13
"white settler innocence," mythology of, 129

Whitley-Bauguess, Paige, 134–35
Williams, Linda, 230
Wilson, Jordan, 69–71, 172, 177, 236
witnessing, 56, 70–71, 166, 179, 181, 224, 232, 261. *See also* xwélala:m
WochenKlauser, 180
Wolfe, Patrick, 10
Womack, Craig, 232, 275n11
Wong, Deborah, 239–53, 273n5
Wrightson, Kelsey, 162, 173

xwélala:m (listening/witnessing), 2–3, 52–53, 56, 58–59, 71–72, 224; in Chacon's *Report,* 108–9
xʷməθkʷəy̓əm people, 69, 135, 166, 208

Yang, Wayne, 39
Yeh, Clement, 171–72
Yoon, Jin-Me, 73, 254–58, *255–56,* 286n6
Young, La Monte, 255

Zhao, Wen, 4, 138
Ziegler, Jeffrey, 5
Zorn, John, 20

Dylan Robinson is a xwélmexw writer of Stó:lō descent and associate professor and Canada Research Chair in Indigenous Arts at Queen's University.